LANDSCAPE
AND
LIGHT

ESSAYS BY
NEIL M GUNN

AUP titles of related interest

POPULAR LITERATURE IN VICTORIAN SCOTLAND
Language, fiction and the press
William Donaldson

TEN MODERN SCOTTISH NOVELS
Isobel Murray and Bob Tait

A BLASPHEMER AND REFORMER
a study of James Leslie Mitchell/Lewis Grassic Gibbon
William Malcolm

LITERATURE OF THE NORTH
edited by David Hewitt and Michael Spiller

THE LAIRD OF DRAMMOCHDYLE
William Alexander
Introduction by William Donaldson

FROM THE CLYDE TO CALIFORNIA
Robert Louis Stevenson
edited and introduced by Andrew Noble

GRAMPIAN HAIRST
an anthology of Northeast prose
edited by William Donaldson and Douglas Young

A TWELVEMONTH AND A DAY
Christopher Rush

A BIBLIOGRAPHY OF THE WORKS OF NEIL M GUNN
C J L Stokoe

LANDSCAPE
AND
LIGHT

ESSAYS BY
NEIL M GUNN

EDITED BY ALISTAIR McCLEERY

ABERDEEN UNIVERSITY PRESS

First published 1987
Aberdeen University Press
A member of the Pergamon Group

© Introduction and selection Alistair McCleery 1987
Essays © Executors of the late Neil M Gunn 1987

The publisher acknowledges subsidy from the Scottish Arts Council towards the publication of this volume.

British Library Cataloguing in Publication Data

Gunn, Neil M
     Landscape and light: essays
     I. Title   II. McCleery, Alistair
     082   PR6013.U64

     ISBN 0-08-035060-7
     ISBN 0-08-035061-5 (Pbk)

PRINTED IN GREAT BRITAIN
THE UNIVERSITY PRESS
ABERDEEN

CONTENTS

Section III: Loyalties

Section IV: Light

ACKNOWLEDGEMENTS

I would like to thank Ian Campbell, Diarmid Gunn, Ian Gunn, and Andrew Noble for reading the Introduction to this collection in its draft form and for the helpful suggestions they offered for its improvement. On the other hand, any errors of fact or of judgement remain mine alone.

Alistair McCleery
Edinburgh

CHRONOLOGY

1891	Neil Gunn born in Dunbeath
1907–11	Working in London and Edinburgh
1911	Begins his career in the Customs and Excise Service
1921	Marries Daisy Frew
1923	Begins career as writer, publishing short stories and articles
1924	Meets C M Grieve, 'Hugh MacDiarmid'
1926	*The Grey Coast*
1927	J B Salmond becomes editor of the *Scots Magazine*
1929	*Hidden Doors* (short stories). Joins Nationalist Party
1931	*Morning Tide* is a Book Society choice. Involvement in General Election on behalf of John MacCormick, Nationalist candidate for Inverness-shire
1932	*The Lost Glen*. Beginnings of estrangement from Grieve
1933	*Sun Circle*
1934	*Butcher's Broom*
1935	*Whisky and Scotland*
1937	*Highland River* published and wins James Tait Black Memorial Prize Neil Gunn resigns from the Customs and Excise Service to become a full-time writer. He sets off on the cruise from Skye to Inverness, through the Caledonian Canal, described in *Off in a Boat* (1938)
1938	Visit to Munich
1939	*Wild Geese Overhead*, a Book Society Choice
1940	*Second Sight*
1941	*The Silver Darlings*
1942	*Young Art and Old Hector*
1943	*The Serpent*
1944	*The Green Isle of the Great Deep*
1946	*The Key of the Chest*
1947	*The Drinking Well*
1948	*The Shadow, The Silver Bough*
1949	*The Lost Chart, Highland Pack* (essays)
1950	*The White Hour* (short stories)
1951	*The Well at the World's End*. Appointed to Commission of Inquiry into Crofting Conditions (Taylor Commission)
1952	*Bloodhunt*
1954	*The Other Landscape*
1956	*The Atom of Delight*

1963   Death of Daisy
1973   Death of Neil Gunn

The authoritative biography of Neil Gunn is *Neil M Gunn: A Highland Life* by F R Hart and J B Pick (Murray, London: 1981).

A Bibliography of the Works of Neil M Gunn by C J L Stokoe will be published by Aberdeen University Press in 1987.

INTRODUCTION

Neil Gunn's place as the foremost Scottish novelist of this century seems assured. Most of his work is in print, or in the process of being republished; that work is the centre of much critical attention, both from within Scotland and without; the major novels are standard texts in many schools and centres of higher education. This collection of essays, brought together in accessible form for the first time, represents both the opportunity to compare the articulation of his major themes as non-fiction with their expressions in fiction, and an insight into the development of those themes over four decades of writing. The essays have been grouped accordingly under four major thematic headings and within each heading they appear by and large in chronological order. There is also a sense of movement, I hope, from the physical landscape to the 'other landscape', from the particular to the universal, which reflects Neil Gunn's own journey.

Neil Gunn is a regional novelist—in the sense that all of his work, with the exception of irregular excursions by some of the characters to Glasgow and Edinburgh, is set in the Scottish Highlands. However, that should not imply that he felt in any way inhibited by this restriction of locale. He wrote in retrospect:

> Though I spent most of my teenage years in London and Edinburgh there was never any doubt in my mind when I started writing that the Highlands and Islands comprised the basis of what mattered in depth and wonder for me. Not, of course, in any exclusive sense but simply that from this culture all other cultures could be looked at.[1]

Gunn exploited the strengths of writing about the landscape and community which he most intimately knew but he also recognised the narrowing of vision which could entrap regional writers. At a very early stage in his career, he acknowledged that: 'Our writers ... have a provincial flavour. They write more as emasculated Englishmen than as Scotsmen'.[2] In short, he sought a form of fiction that in its concerns would transcend the regional setting. While he may return again and again to the landscape and the culture of the Highlands, it is not with any parochial intent but to renew his creative ability to deal with these concerns. The landscapes of Sutherland

and Caithness provided him with two distinct types of scenery which, in turn, seem to typify two methods of writing about the Highlands. Sutherland is characterised by its wild grandeur; yet the emotions aroused by it, glory and pride, may be counterfeit or devalued in the viewer, 'a legacy of Sir Walter Scott and all the Highland romanticism to which that noble name must plead guilty'.[3] Caithness appears to the tourist to be dull and monotonous by comparison; yet Gunn found in Caithness a feeling deeper in its inspiration, 'a movement of the spirit that finds in the austerity, because strength is there also, a final serenity'. There might even be an allegory here of the development of Gunn's fiction, for, once he had eschewed the plangent but ready emotions that seemed the stock response to the Highlands of his day, he could look at his environment with a clear eye to find reflected in its strengths a sense of the spiritual, and physical, resilience and possibilities of man. He could, for example, in *Highland River* (1937) link the real environment, landscape and people, to the recurring patterns in our experience. A real river takes on a wider symbolic significance: which is not to say that the sense of actuality is ever lost; the quality and skill of Gunn's writing at this stage is such that the novel can function, without strain or loss of credibility, on more than one level. In conversations with Maurice Lindsay in 1959 and 1960, Gunn was asked whether the evocations of Highland landscape in his novels were products of observation or of imagination. His succinct reply stressed that they were 'actual landscapes, though sometimes their features re-arrange themselves into a new pattern'.[4] The supplementary question specified the river of *Highland River*: was it an actual river? 'Yes, but there again the dividing of the river into three parts, with the symbolism involved, grew into the writing quite naturally.' Realistic portrayal and symbolic meaning can not be divorced; 'I can't remember ... ever having described a Highland scene for the scene's sake,' wrote Gunn in 1959.[5] In the act of seeing, they are there; in the act of creation, the two come together 'naturally'; in the act of reading, the two interact and reinforce one another's authenticity.

The landscape, sea as well as land, is with figures—'a novelist cannot write about people in a vacuum'[6]—but not as an idealised form of pastoral, rather as the picture of a working community surviving in its environment. Gunn's various essays on the plight of the fishing industry reveal a concern for the threat to that survival that is one of the elements in his first novel *The Grey Coast* (1926). Ivor in that book faces the dilemma of remaining with the dying fishing industry in a community at best old and stagnant, or emigrating to Canada to start afresh in a new country full of activity and energy but, just as importantly, endowing men with freedom and independence.

> The fishings were dwindling, boat hulks lay rotting at their haulage. The day of the sail and small fishing creek was giving way before the ousting mastery of steam, the steam of the drifter and of the railway. The fishing industry was concentrating more and more in the big ports—Wick, Fraserburgh, Aberdeen— and the wealth of communal life that had enriched the bleak sea-board with a rare self-sufficiency was growing thin in the blood and cold, was dying without hope.[7]

The background of decline makes the situation of the characters more poignant but there is little that is positive asserted to counter it. It may be an antidote to escapism but it risks defeatism. Gunn's early novels with their descriptions of a depressed Highlands, of the dole and the sporting-estate, share Fiona Macleod's sense of a grandeur that had passed. But by 1937 Gunn is just as aware of the positive elements in Highland culture which can be drawn on to ensure its survival then as they had before, after the Clearances, in the 'Wonder Story' of the fishing boom. The Scottish system of family-owned boats embodies an individualism that 'always worked towards the family and communal good'.

> I suggest that the answer may be found in some system of co-operation similar to that which has proved successful in Scandinavian countries. Co-operation implies duties and restrictions, but such duties and restrictions would be imposed by the fishermen themselves for their own good and not in the interest either of shore capitalism or of state control.[8]

At the time of writing *The Grey Coast*, this answer was not so apparent and its appearance in fiction had to await Gunn's positive vision in *The Silver Darlings* (1941).

The essays present a parallel account of the development in fiction of Gunn's concerns. The novels turn from naturalistic pictures of decline, to possible sources of that decline in Highland history, to possible sources of renewal in the vision of childhood, to a positive assertion of the values of the community and the integrity of the individual, through to the later novels. There the need for a positive assertion that man is spiritual, not mechanical, and that spiritual fulfilment can be found in modern society, can overwhelm the fictional forms adopted so that they read like the essays or evolve into the final 'spiritual autobiography', *The Atom of Delight* (1956). Gunn was concerned in the early novels to capture and account for the sense of decline and decay he felt in the contemporary Highlands. This strand of fatalism found ready favour for a time with a public weaned on fictive Highlands created by the vague prose of William Black and William Sharp (Fiona Macleod), and living in an age when optimism seemed the preserve of fools. This pessimism, channeled by a growing Nationalism, could all too easily become a hatred of the scapegoat English. This happened in *The Lost Glen* (1932). Chambers rejected it because the novel contained too much politics and too little romance; Hodder and Stoughton did not like the bestial portrait of the English Colonel. The novel is a strong unrelenting picture of Highland decline and of a reluctant subservience to foreign usurpation of land and authority. Both *The Lost Glen* and *The Grey Coast* end on bleak notes: *The Lost Glen* closes on the murder of Colonel Hicks; there is little remission for the dying community. Despite the conventional close of *The Grey Coast* dictated perhaps, in this case, by commercial rather than artistic considerations, the lesson is taught that meaningful survival is only possible through migration. The individual must divorce himself from this dying community.

Yet in each book exists the germ of a more positive perception of the Highlands. The detailed description of a poaching expedition in *The Grey*

Coast anticipates Gunn's later and extensive use of poaching as representative of man at his most free from authority, the natural Anarchist, and at his most liberated from civilisation, man the Hunter. The very title of *The Lost Glen* marks a nostalgia for an anti-materialist idyll that may be lost in social and economic terms but which, in the novel, may be regained in spiritual terms through art, particularly music.

Both *Sun Circle* (1933) and *Butcher's Broom* (1934) could have become a similar retreat but into the Highland past. The temptation to follow the example of Neil Munro must have been acute. Where Munro sought in the fusion of childhood sentiment and the romantic past to present a historically-distorted picture which, like Scott, might divert anger into nostalgia and inculcate national unity (under the Campbell aegis), Gunn tried to find in Highland history the roots of contemporary malaise, the process which had led to the loss of communal identity and the imposition of the 'ghillie-role' or exile upon the individual Highlander. In both novels Gunn juxtaposes socio-economic decline and the possibility of spiritual fulfilment. Historical events, although not necessarily those of recorded history, are described in *Sun Circle* but what is more significant than these imaginative recon-structions of life in the ninth century is the persistence of the need for spiritual wholeness symbolised by the circle. The novel opens with the Celts dominated by an alien Christianity and recounts the further struggle between the Celts and the Norsemen. The love triangle of Aniel, Nessa, and Breeta is paralleled by the triangle of Celtic mysticism, Norse power, and Christian faith. Despite historical, physical defeat, the spirit of the people survives beyond history.

Butcher's Broom is more successful because Gunn is dealing with a period for which there is both much more evidence and also a felt experience mediated through the intervening generations. The figure of Mairi is also able to carry the representational burden which Breeta is not. *Butcher's Broom* anticipates Gunn's mature novels in two ways: the successful integration of form and content; the opposition of spiritual insight to dehumanising rationalisation. But it is also distinct from the mature novels in one important regard; it is a tragedy. It closes on the bleak note of exile and death that marked *The Grey Coast* and *The Lost Glen*. The fires in the glen, foreseen by the Master in *Sun Circle*, occur in *Butcher's Broom*. The community is evicted from its land by the one who has responsibility for maintaining the integrity of the clan, its chieftain, and the people are sentenced to exile. Mairi returns to the glen but is brutally killed by the sheepdogs. Because of the negative ending, the death of wisdom and insight, *Butcher's Broom*, in other ways a bridge to the later fiction, is more clearly seen as belonging to the first phase of Gunn's career.

The second phase opens hesitantly with *Morning Tide* (1931). It is the story of a boy's growth from boyhood to youth. Although the background to the community in which Hugh lives is that of *The Grey Coast* and *The Lost Glen*, Gunn has rediscovered a new wholeness through the child's vision. The reader gains his knowledge about the Highland community heuristically, through the eyes of Hugh as he grows in perceptiveness and awareness. There is no sentimentality, no gilding of the community's values as in Thrums.

Hugh's father barely survives a storm through his skill and courage; Hugh's brother Duncan has been drowned when his boat the *Fateful*, sank 'battened down and with sails set';[9] his brother Alan is almost killed in the storm more successfully weathered by his father; Alan emigrates to Australia, and finally Hugh's mother falls ill. This could have been the opportunity to prepare for a deathbed scene between mother and son to rival any kailyard sentimentality but Gunn draws the scene as the final stage in Hugh's rites of passage to maturity. The novel is realistic. Yet it also contains the portrayal of Hugh's initiation into full and individual membership of the community. Death, sex, exile, survival in nature, joy, art, communality—each is a lesson in Hugh's development—the community's norms and values are weighed against the vision of the growing boy. The material fate of the community is not disputed but a wholeness of vision and the cycle of Hugh's coming to manhood is set against it without anger or tragedy.

The advance between *Morning Tide* and *Highland River* (1937) is an ambitious extension in the breadth of significance. The locality in both books is similar. But, where *Morning Tide* recounted the boy's rites of passage, *Highland River* looks to the nature of a man's whole experience from boyhood to manhood. It is Gunn's *Prelude*. What happens to Kenn from the catching of the salmon to the discovery of the lochan has a universal and transcendent significance. At the source of the river, a feeling comes over Kenn, as it was to come to Finn in the heart of the circle, of direct access to what Gunn, coyly, calls 'the Ultimate', a 'timeless harmony'[10] echoing the phrase used of Caithness two years earlier, 'a final serenity'. In his later essays an analogue is found for this experience in Zen Buddhism. Satori comes after apprenticeship; 'the Ultimate' comes only at the end of the 'poaching expedition to the source of delight': the spiritual quest represented by the gradual gaining of knowledge about the river. 'Delight' is delight in the world, in the series of visionary moments of the world: moments marking the stages of Kenn's gradual development towards the final moment of harmony of self and 'Ultimate'. Thomas Mann wrote that 'in the life of the human race the mythical is an early and primitive stage, in the life of the individual it is a late and mature one'.[11] *Highland River* marks, without hesitation, the beginning of Gunn's mature fiction. It contains both story and myth. The shifts in narrative only serve to underline that the past lives in the memory of the individual; Gunn also draws attention to the survival of the past of the community, 'the folk, through immense eras of time', in the unconscious of the individual, from the well-pool to the lochan.

The same specificity and universality can be found in *The Serpent* (1943) and *The Drinking Well* (1946). Perhaps even more than *Highland River*, they are detailed re-creations of a Highland community, with episodes of the one set in Glasgow, and of the other in Edinburgh. And like *Highland River*, *The Serpent* uses memory to chart the movement towards redemption or wholeness. On his return to the croft, Tom the Atheist (the result of his experiences in Glasgow) becomes Tom the Serpent, possessed by an intellectual scepticism that is scathing and destructive. In rejecting the traditional ways of the community, he has also lost its traditional wisdom. The death of his father, in a paroxysm of anger caused by his son's apostasy, the tragedy of his love for Janet Morrison, and her death, switch Tom's thinking from the collective doctrines and mechanistic rationalism of his Glasgow apprenticeship as clock-repairer to a concern for the individual. Tom begins to show love for other people; he reads the correspondence of Hume and Rousseau and 'there gradually developed in him a profound sympathy for Rousseau';[12] he realises that his own life has been unbalanced, sacrificing the spiritual intuitions he identifies with the feminine in exclusive favour of the philosophical absolutes identified as the masculine rules of life; he reads the Bible to his mother, finding in it the 'cells that held the golden honey of wisdom'. He has become Tom the Philosopher. Again as in *Highland River*, Gunn has taken the particular—in place, in community, in time—and found in it this pattern of movement towards that state in which the individual 'remembers himself'.

Yet, by the close of this period of mature writing, in *The Drinking Well*, Gunn demonstrates a less assured skill in the integration of levels of narrative. The title refers to the symbolic place—found also in Celtic legend—where the central character of the novel, Iain Cattanach, finds, as Tom the Philosopher had done, redemption in love for the land and his fellow-beings. But the naturalness of the two elements, the link between object and symbol, is no longer present and there is a greater sense of a significance being forced upon the reader. What stand out in the novel are the descriptions of Edinburgh and of the bringing of the sheep from the bothy through the snow to the farm. The character of Mad Mairag has not, as George Bruce stresses,[13] the substance to bear the weight of symbolism she must take if the final reconciliation, of Iain to the land and to the girl Mary, is to be credible. The outlook is positive as Iain finds an active role within the community that promises eventual regeneration in material terms. Yet the reader remains unsatisfied. Unlike *The Silver Darlings*, the strong and gripping narrative does not fulfil all the expectations that it raises. When Gunn abandoned, in the later novels, this narrative strength to isolate and highlight their symbolic significance, he lost the reader's interest in them as works of fiction.

The Silver Darlings (1941) and *The Green Isle of the Great Deep* (1944) represent the peak of Gunn's fiction and are the outstanding achievements of the second, mature phase of his writing career: mature as artist and as man. Both are affirmative works of the triumph of man's spirit over hardship and the environment, in the one, and over Tom the Atheist's scientific, mechanistic rationalism, in the other. Both reveal Gunn's wish to convey 'the experience of being vividly alive' in the world. Both draw on 'objective correlatives' from the history and tradition of the Highlands. Most of the later novels, although retaining the Highland background, lack narrative strength and replace the essays that he had up to that point written in parallel with the novels. What he wished to express, he could no longer adequately convey using fiction and its conventions. There is too much static dialogue. Characterisation becomes lifeless. The fictive Highlands is divorced from the organic portrayal of individuals, the community, and the land which typifies the previous period, 1936 to 1944. To reiterate, the novels take over the function of essay-writing for Gunn and only really when he had abandoned novel-writing, after the poor reception of the central auto-biographical work, *The Atom of Delight* (1956), does he return to the essay form.

Most of the essays in this collection come from that period of maturity, 1936 to 1944. This was a prolific time for Gunn during which he carefully and clearly articulated his major themes and concerns. In terms of his fiction, as discussed above, he had moved away from the negative attitude of his earlier novels to the affirmative vision of *Highland River*, *The Silver Darlings*, and *The Green Isle of the Great Deep* but without the difficulties of combining positive assertion of spiritual fulfilment and fictional forms encountered in his later novels. In terms of his non-fiction, he found a ready outlet for his work in the *Scots Magazine* the editor of which J B Salmond, Gunn recalled, 'would print anything of mine and did'.[14] He also needed the money that this form of writing could bring in. He lost his salary and pension in 1937 when he resigned from the Custom and Excise service to become a full-time writer. Not only this but a drawing closer together with his wife from 1936 onwards after a period of estrangement mark a sense of a new beginning in his private life just as *Highland River* had been in his career as a novelist. As Hart and Pick stress, 'Nationalist politics had become an exhausting frustration'.[15] His active commitment to the SNP, evidenced by his work to form that party out of various nationalist groups and by his campaigning for John McCormick in Inverness-shire in 1931, diminished. It was not that he lost faith in the goals but he replaced the time and effort he had been devoting to party administration by the writing of essays in support of its ideas and ideals. There is in all these changes an element of escape, a turning away from community-orientated concerns—career, politics—to the individual's inner development and the close, 'intuitive' (Gunn's term) bond between husband and wife. The movement was checked by the outbreak of war when Gunn found it impossible to remain isolated from outside events. The introspective absorption in self and nature which might have been its outcome gave way instead to a deeper concern for humanity.

Nationalism in its broadest sense is simply a feeling of attachment to a particular territorial or cultural community. 'To love your own land, from which you draw your deepest inspiration, is as natural as to love the sunlight or a woman, is to understand what moves in the heart of a Pole or a Czech, is to salute Sibelius not in envy or hate, but in admiration and gratitude':[16] this, for Neil Gunn is the essence of nationalism. More often than not, however, nationalism implies an attitude to those who do not belong to that community. 'The English smile ... whenever the Scot objects to the use of "English" to include "Scottish".'[17] Indeed the nature of nationalism is frequently framed by response to those external to the community. It can be chauvinist, although attachment to one's own community does not in itself lead to a desire to deprive others of similar rights. The motif recurs throughout Neil Gunn's essays that nationalism, in this sense of a feeling for one place, does not create war. The Spanish Civil War or wars of religion could not be attributed to nationalism: 'the wise man does not become ashamed of the scriptures and throw them over because the devil quotes them'.[18] Moreover, and more importantly, nationalism is for Gunn a potent counter to uniformity.

> The small nation has always been humanity's last bulwark for the individual against that machine [of standardisation through centralised government], for personal expression against impersonal tyranny, for the quick freedom of the spirit against the flattening steam-roller of mass. It is concerned for the intangible things called its heritage, its beliefs and arts, its distinctive institutions, for everything, in fact, that expresses it. And expression finally implies spirit in an act of creation, which is to say, culture.[19]

Gunn, in fact, devoted his 1939 essay, 'Nationalism in Writing: Scottish Individualism', to this thesis that nationalism ensures individuality against the forces of conformity and uniformity.[20] In this anticipation of the theme of *The Green Isle of the Great Deep*, Gunn insists that maintenance of a separate Scottish identity is part and parcel of the retention of individual identity. Unpopular though this stance may have been during the war-years, Gunn did not cease from stressing the need for a separate Scottish identity— while acknowledging also the need in the war effort for the unity of all Britain.

This double allegiance masks a dilemma for the nationalist like Gunn, or more broadly, for anyone who, again like Gunn, underlines the importance of individual freedom so heavily. In a crisis such as a war, or in circumstances with which the resources of the individual cannot cope, some sort of collectivism seems inevitable. The problem is that collectivism makes the destruction of the individual's independence seem just as inevitable. Gunn solved this difficulty by highlighting the spirit of co-operation typical of the community of his childhood. Hardships beyond the capability of the individual to mitigate became the responsibility of the community at large. The community was self-sufficient; it owed much of this to its isolation but that isolation did not in turn lead to insularity. Through its emigrants, its sailors, and its soldiers, the community was aware of the 'outside world' and, accordingly, the strength of its own values. Gunn postulates, in *The Atom of Delight* that these values may have grown out of the clan system, 'with its devotion, mutual trust and social warmth'.[21] This was the real betrayal of the Clearances: that the man, regarded until then as chief but merely primus inter pares, should exert his legal but not moral right to evict his own clansmen, his family, from the clan lands. However, the existence of the clan system was not necessary for the survival of the spirit of co-operation among the people themselves. 'You cannot rub out the whole way of life of a people by manipulating the powers in a charter, not unless you rub out the people themselves.' That way of life, according to Gunn, was based on the interaction of individual independence and mutual co-operation; 'independence which being dependence on oneself was not directed against any other but, on the contrary, respected a similar independence in all others'; the spontaneity of co-operation that 'came from an absence of compulsion by one neighbour over another'. *The Atom of Delight* contains several instances of this. When a man is laid out with the rheumatics, the younger men of the community take over his work for him and are rewarded by the communal entertainment of a ceilidh. Peat-cutting is carried out by a band of neighbours, all working on one another's peat-bank. This is not a primitive form of communism; each man owns his own peat-bank and is independent of his neighbour but all share the duties in a task that takes two or three men to work a bank efficiently. 'People worked hard, for they liked to keep their heads up and preserve their independence.' It is a tragedy when an old woman of the community has to be taken away to the Poor House; it is a 'dark shadow implicating everyone, as if in some mysterious way they were all to blame'.

This could all too easily be summed up as the wistful idealisation by an old man of his childhood environment. That it was not, and that Gunn believed in this combination of individual freedom and mutual co-operation with some conviction, can be shown in two ways. Firstly the theme of co-operation recurs throughout Gunn's writing, both factual and fictional, and is not, therefore, the product of a nostalgic old age. Secondly, there is evidence from other than Gunn's writing that individual independence and community co-operation do lie at the heart of Gaelic social organisation. R J Storey, discussing, in 1982, the socio-economic factors in Highland development which led to the HIDB sponsoring a programme of community co-operatives, singles out as a striking characteristic 'the relative egalitarianism of Hebridean society'.[22] This comment echoes both the crofters' spokesman who in 1884 told *The Scotsman* 'we have no leaders; we are all leaders'[23] and the sociologist who in 1973 was surprised to find in Highlands and Islands communities an absence of the normal pyramidal social structure: 'the relatively egalitarian social system of the Highlands makes action possible only when it is generally desired and agreed'.[24] It is a question incapable of resolution whether economic necessity makes co-operation such a noteworthy feature of these communities or whether it simply reinforces an impulse to co-operation inherent in the people; either way it is clear that it has ensured the survival of the crofting system despite all the vicissitudes which assail it. A former chairman of the Crofters' Commission can conclude that values and practice in Highland communities serve to strengthen one another. 'It seems clear that the sense of belonging, of identity satisfies a fundamental human need. The communal element in common grazings is a cold, legal fact, the sociability of the fank has its rewards, greater than the economic return from the sheep handled.'[25] Neil Gunn himself served from 1951–54 on a Commission of Enquiry into Crofting Conditions under the Chairmanship of Principal T M Taylor of Aberdeen University. The Report of the Commission begins with a statement of the premise upon which it is based, that is, that crofting as a way of life should be maintained: 'we have thought it right ... to record our unanimous conviction, founded on personal knowledge and on the evidence we have received, that in the national interest the maintenance of these communities is desirable, because they embody a free and independent way of life which in a civilisation predominantly urban and industrial in character is worth preserving for its own intrinsic quality'.[26]

Throughout the Report, the preservation of the culture and tradition of the crofters is emphasised and this emphasis is usually accompanied by a corresponding stress upon co-operation and self-help. The Report describes the organisation of crofts: 'Most crofter holdings are congregated in townships. The typical croft is not a self-contained unit.'[27] Much of the township land is held in common by the crofters and its care depends upon the co-operation of the crofters. Often the attention of the Commission was drawn to the fact that drainage and fencing problems could not be solved by the individual crofter acting on his own but demanded communal action. The third and final conclusion of the whole report is to the point: 'the crofters themselves, or at least a majority of them, must be prepared to co-operate'.[28] The note of egalitarianism is also sounded strongly throughout the findings of the Commission: 'The crofter calls no man his master.'[29] Yet the problem of depopulation of the crofting communities is faced up to and its roots examined. Those communities which are dominated by the old stagnate and sink into a dullness which the young cannot tolerate. This is not an attempt to sweep the elderly away, perhaps to institutionalise them—the 'virtue of respect for old age' still retains its power in crofting communities, even if it has declined elsewhere—but it is an acknowledgement that there is a need for a 'certain reservoir of vitality in the community'.[30] Young people do not leave because the lure of better conditions elsewhere at less effort is necessarily overwhelming or, indeed, because they necessarily wish to: 'Highlanders as a rule are not anxious to leave their home communities. They leave home because they have to, and they would be glad to stay if that were possible.[31] The solution is more equitable distribution and tenure of the land (though not public ownership) with an administrative body created to safeguard the crofters' interests and encourage their co-operation. How far this would have been endorsed or qualified by Gunn is difficult to assess absolutely but the degree of his support can be gauged somewhat by his assent to the report and by his life-long championship of the values of the community described in *The Atom of Delight*. Principal Taylor could later write to Gunn thanking him for his 'sensitive and understanding approach to the whole problem' which 'has been reflected in the Report itself and is the main reason for its favourable reception'.[32]

While it might be objected that Gunn's work on the Commission of Enquiry was at a late stage of his career and that the conclusions of its Report represent a much diluted version of the picture contained in *The Atom of Delight*, there is evidence, from the earlier period, of Gunn's belief in the values of 'The Community' and of his enthusiasm when he found these values being translated into practical achievements. In 1945 Gunn published the essay, 'Belief in Ourselves', in which he looked to the post-war reconstruction of the Highlands.[33] He claims that the slump in the herring industry could be arrested if the individually-owned fishing boats could be organised into a larger co-operative. This had been successfully carried out.

in other countries and, within Scotland itself, Gunn quotes the example of effective co-operation in another field, sheepfarming clubs. In 1937 Gunn published the essay 'A Visitor from Denmark', in which he related the conclusions of a tour of Scotland by the Danish writer, Arne Ström.[34] Ström himself had been commissioned by a Copenhagen newspaper to write a series of articles on the economic condition of Scotland. Gunn passes on to his readers, by way of contrast, a picture of the economic condition of Denmark. It is a contrast favourable to the Danes. The lesson, Gunn continues by outlining, is that nationalists in Denmark, despite dominance by the Prussians, pioneered a system of co-operation that led both to independence and to viability as a small country. 'A Denmark defeated and in despair' turned to a nationalism based on an ideal, rather than simple desire for political autonomy: 'the ideal was strong, for it was not only based on faith but on knowledge; it was prepared not only with words but with deeds.' Where Denmark represents hope, the Highlands reveal 'tragedy succeeded by apathy'. The basis of the sort of nationalism Gunn was striving for becomes clearer in this essay. It was a nationalism which 'satisfied the aspirations of individualism while directing these aspirations towards the common good; and when personal needs were thus ordered, it continued organising these adult schools through which the mind may attempt to realise its spiritual potentialities'. Nationalism is the first step towards achievement of individual freedom within the context of a co-operative community; such a social organisation would lead to the second step, the opportunity for the individual to rediscover a sense of wholeness within himself. In the achievement of Denmark, Gunn saw the practical vindication of what others might dismiss in his own writings as impractical idealism. Indeed, rather than undermining his views, the War itself also seemed to substantiate them. For Gunn, as it seems for the Danes, nationalism, egalitarianism, and co-operation became real in the life of the community rather than remaining hollow watchwords for theorists. Gunn began with the example of the childhood community and from it gained the values which could hold true for the country as a whole.

Nationalism *per se* acquired a pejorative sense just before and during the Second World War; not only because of its appropriation as a label by the National Socialists in Germany but also because the war itself was presented in terms of an international ideological struggle—the enemies were not the Germans as a nation but those amongst them who had espoused the creed of Fascism. It was a creed, of course, that was not confined to Germany and the Nazis took a delight in discovering fellow travellers in the rest of (Aryan) Europe. Often they were literally travellers, given a free but guided holiday in Germany (or the Soviet Union) and ready on their return to proclaim to the British that they had seen the future and the trains worked on time. Gunn found little difference between the totalitarianism of Fascism and that of Marxism. He wrote in the 1940 essay, 'On Belief', that the Highland spirit 'still has an instinctive urge to dodge restrictive mechanism' and 'a system of ideology of the highest intention may in practice result in the most barbarous cruelty'.[35] But for others, it was somehow bliss in that dawn to participate in a world that renounced the intellect, demonstrated the healthy beauty of youth and gloried in what was natural and of the 'blood'.

There is superficial evidence that might seem to place Gunn among these fellow-travellers of the right. *Morning Tide* had been translated into German, by Fritz Wölcken, and published in Munich in 1938. (Gunn regarded Wölcken, who became a close friend in the pre-war years, as a 'good' German: one who had been caught up in an irretrievable momentum. Wölcken was held for a while in a British prisoner-of-war camp, which is where in fact he began the translation of *The Green Isle of the Great Deep*. Gunn continued to correspond with him then and after the war.) *Butcher's Broom*, however, had been published the previous year. *Morning Tide* predated *Butcher's Broom* by three years in its English publication but *Butcher's Broom* was preferred in Germany for its description of a traditional wisdom. Its German title was *Das verlorene Leben*. Gunn, in his writing, did use the frames of reference of the time, particularly the idea of race about which we are more coy today; for example, in 1929 he claimed, in a BBC broadcast, that 'Neil Munro stands for Gaelic spirit, that is for the essential spirit at the back of the Scottish race'.[36] Discreet approaches were made about the incorporation of Gunn within the ideological fold of Nazism. A friend received a letter from a German soliciting Gunn's attitude to the New Germany. There were hints, in the same letter, of the possible award of the Shakespeare prize from the University of Hamburg, given annually to those who had contributed in some significant way to the 'nordic ideal'. Gunn's contribution was *Butcher's Broom*. Finally, Gunn did travel to Germany on two occasions in the late 30s. He visited Munich in May 1938 and the mountains of Bavaria in February 1939. This was the birthplace of Nazism, yet, in the essay he published in *The Scots Magazine* in April 1939, Gunn seemed oblivious of anything except the joys of Fasching.[37]

> Fasching has its conventions, and one of them appears to be the natural irresponsibility of the healthily happy human being. Dancing was on at least three floors, with three bands, brilliant colour effects and decently subdued lighting. If a man felt like laughing in the middle of the floor, he laughed; and if he felt like saluting his partner, he saluted her; and if he encountered friends with whom he desired to join forces in a temporary jing-a-ring, he did that too.

Here are no goosesteps but dances, no raised right arms and clicked heels but the salute of a man to his dancing partner, no street brawls or beatings but the gaiety of a 'jing-a-ring'. It is surely not enough to excuse this blindness, as some of his friends do,[38] on the grounds of Gunn's naivety and unaware-ness; either it is acquiescence in the propaganda of the wholesome, healthy Germany or it has some other motive, but unawareness in 1939 will not do.

These 'proofs' of Gunn's sympathy with Nazi ideology can be refuted, each one in its turn. Gunn had little control over the question of foreign trans-lation rights to his novels. Nor, if he had, would he necessarily have put an embargo on the German translation of *Butcher's Broom*. In hindsight, it is all too easy to issue condemnations but, at that period, European events, and more importantly the patterns of thought underlying them, were not seen with the same clarity or knowledge. (*Morning Tide* had also been translated into Spanish in 1933.) Fritz Wölcken, as already noted, became a personal friend and was to translate *The Green Isle of the Great Deep* for its German publication in 1949. That novel is positive in its attitudes, positive against totalitarianism, but it is difficult to see, except at the most general level, anything so positive in *Butcher's Broom* that would give support to Nazism. The fault, if any, is not in the book or its author but in the climate of taste that seized upon everything and anything that seemed, however generally, to accord with it. That Gunn used the word 'race' freely is no ground for guilt; 'culture' can frequently be substituted for it. If we do condemn him over this, then we are guilty of a linguistic anachronism and ignorant of the change that took place, largely due to the War, in the acceptability of the term. We are judging from an inappropriate modern perspective. The award of the Shakespeare prize was never made to Gunn; we will never know whether he would have accepted it or not.

That leaves the question of the two visits. Firstly, Gunn enjoyed the fellowship of friends, particularly Wölcken, not the red carpet and champagne treatment meted out on official visits. His enjoyment of his time in Germany must be evaluated bearing that in mind. Secondly, by 1938 and 1939 attitudes were beginning to harden in Britain against Germany. Greater knowledge of the Nazis' climb to power, German involvement in the Spanish Civil War, Hitler's territorial ambitions: all had served to turn the tide of complacency. Although many wished to avoid conflict of any kind, there was no return to the *Punch* cartoon which showed Von Ribbentrop being cordially presented to John Bull by Eden. Gunn's essay must be viewed as written by a man who wanted to remind his viewers of the humanity of the German people. It is no attempt to gild Hitler, Goering or Goebbels. Within the confines of the type of article published by *The Scots Magazine*, it highlights the idea of the 'good German', that Germans are people sharing in a common humanity.

Such a stance runs the obvious risk of inculcating a false sense of brotherhood and of doing its job too well by leading its readers to forget the Weltanschauung of Hitler, Goering and Goebbels. Yet Gunn was no Candide wandering in a world of knaves. As early as 1934 Gunn and George Malcolm Thomson were exchanging correspondence warning of the growth of Mosley's Fascists. In his diary, written at the outbreak of war, Gunn expresses a deep sadness at the need for humanity to war with itself but he also notes: 'No special hatred against the German people. In fact no hatred at all—rather the knowledge, the belief, that the Nazi governing body must be destroyed.'[39] Such is Gunn's opinion about the evils of a Nazism which is exploiting the Germans as a people. Gunn's nationalism had as its object regeneration of individual and community.

To sum up, if Gunn worked actively, in this interwar period, for nationalism, then it was because he saw it fostering a spirit of individual freedom and ultimate fulfilment. This was no proto-fascism or crypto-Nazism, nor should it suggest that he took rather a lofty view of politics; his record of involvement in the 1931 election, as well as the testimony of such as John MacCormick, should undermine that assumption. Nor did Gunn feel that cultural nationalism should hold itself aloof from the struggles of politics: political nationalism and cultural nationalism could not be divorced. He wrote in the 1938 essay on the Theatre Society of Scotland: 'Associations or parties, aiming at the freedom of the body politic, have been more strongly at work, have received greater publicity and have been better organised than any associations working for a cultural expression. I do not say that they have been more important, for body and mind make a single working unit and neither can function without the other.'[40] Scotland needed cultural bodies, such as a national theatre, through which writers could express the nation's essential self. Writers needed the context of independence to provide them with the freedom for individual creation. There could be no vital culture, in Gunn's view, without a correspondingly strong sense of political identity.

It was to Ireland, rather than to the continent of Europe, that Gunn turned to find an example of what might happen in Scotland. Political independence would stimulate cultural flowering. In 1938 he published an essay (using the pseudonym of Dane McNeil) on Douglas Hyde's nomination as President of the new state of Eire.[41] The nationalism that produced the new state had also created the situation in which a Gaelic scholar, rather than a party hack, had been appointed as the country's leader. Here was proof that nationalism had resulted neither 'in war nor material aggrandizement' but in 'social and spiritual achievement'. Comparison is made with a Scotland that hitherto 'denying her own tradition, has looked to London for all things'. The comparison is obviously to Scotland's discredit. Upon the foundation of Hyde's nomination, Gunn again proposes the thesis that 'our inheritance of culture and high ideals of freedom' owe much 'to the small community or nation'. The only false point in Gunn's argument arrives when he quotes Joyce as an example of the product of this Irish environment. Joyce himself renounced the net of narrow-minded nationalism and chose exile rather than what he regarded as the constraints of a petty-minded, Catholic conception of Ireland. From exile, he described Ireland as he saw it, subject to moral paralysis but also suffused with a wistful Parnellism. He had little or no sympathy for the attempts of someone like Hyde to reintroduce Gaelic as the national language. Gunn names Joyce because he wishes to demonstrate the compatibility, if not the interdependence, of nationalism and membership of the Modernist avant-garde. To have named the more obvious figure of Yeats would have risked the taint of fascism and would have associated nationalism with the older Irish renaissance, passé as far as literary fashions went. Yet it was there that the parallel with Scotland really lay. Yeats tried to hold a position in the middle: nationalist yet supporting the independence of the artist. He defined national literature as 'the work of writers who are moulded by influences that are moulding their country, and who write out of so deep a life that they are accepted there in the end';[42] yet he also wrote: 'Literature is always personal, always one man's vision of the world, one man's experience, and it can only be popular when men are ready to accept the vision of others.'[43] Gunn, too, held a position in the middle; he advocated independence in a political sense because he saw that as a means of achieving independence for the individual, including artists. As political nationalism became less tenable in the post-war period, Gunn largely abandoned it in favour of the search for fulfilment within the individual.

The portrayal of the Highlands in decay that characterises the early novels demands a solution that goes beyond the social and economic; the origins of that decay, seen in *Butcher's Broom*, are not just in the betrayal by the chiefs who became landlords and drove their clansmen off the communal lands but also in the loss of a spiritual way of life, a loss that is symbolised in the death of Mairi. The novels of the middle period, particularly *The Silver Darlings*, demonstrate that the persistence of the spirit of the community can lead to economic regeneration. In a similar way, Gunn felt that nationalism and the spirit of the community he believed in were inseparable, despite the tensions which could exist between them. Political independence for the one would ensure the survival of the values of the other. These values entailed the marriage of individuality and co-operation which, if extended to the nation as a whole, as in Denmark, would create a regeneration in material terms and a renaissance in cultural terms. Gunn's constant sense of the independence and integrity of the individual militated against his ideas being swept up in the contemporary currents of Fascism or Marxism. When political nationalism seemed less worthy a goal—in the period of the Cold War—Gunn placed greater emphasis on the individual's achievement of the spiritual values of the community within himself as a prelude to any social change. In his most fruitful period, 1936–44, nation and community, the political and the spiritual, found a harmony together.

George Blake confirmed that 'a "consciousness of Scottishness" came to us all after the [First World] War'.[44] Nationalism provided an impetus to the Scottish Renaissance. This is true in the ideological sense which Gunn uses in his various essays on literature but it was also true in a social sense. Those figures who participated in the affairs of the National Party of Scotland, and later the SNP, to differing degrees of physical commitment, were often those, for example, who participated actively in the formation and organisation of the Scottish branch of PEN. It had been established by C M Grieve and William Power, then literary editor of the *Glasgow Herald*, and a focus for its activities was provided by Helen Cruickshank in her Edinburgh home. Beyond PEN, the complex social web connected the men and women of letters with musicians, artists and many others of various backgrounds. It is clear that there was in Scotland in the interwar period a vital and creative section of the population dedicated to the reawakening of Scottish national identity. The two exceptions to this picture must be Lewis Grassic Gibbon and Edwin Muir. The former rejected nationalism as a method of achieving a sense of community which would counteract the modern alienation of the cash-nexus and class-conflict and, faced with the alternative methods of a stone-like Communism or an impossible retreat into the past, closed *Grey Granite* (1934) on an anticlimax of resignation. Neil Gunn admired greatly the novels of Grassic Gibbon, despite the latter's derogatory comments in

Scottish Scene (1934). Gunn wrote that their qualities moved him to 'delight' in his 1938 essay on Grassic Gibbon.[45] This admiration stemmed, not from a sharing of the same Nationalist ideals, but from acknowledgement of a shared goal, a common quest. Edwin Muir was also reluctant to make a commitment to Nationalism (or nationalism) despite his ability to fulfil the Scottish Renaissance's need for an outstanding critic. As Neil Gunn wrote in his 1936 review of *Scott and Scotland*, 'literary criticism of the quality of Mr Muir's is rare in any country; in Scotland even its tradition seems to have got lost'.[46] Muir remained ambiguously in contact with yet detached from the particular set of political and cultural ideals which underpinned the Renaissance. In contrast to Gunn, he saw Scottish nationhood as no longer an important issue.

In the essay, 'Defensio Scotorum', written as early as 1928, Gunn demonstrates clearly his accepted link between politics and culture and expresses a desire for change and the rejection of past attitudes.[47] The economic and social condition of Scotland—'45 per cent of us live more than two in a room; we have the highest death-rate, unemployment rate, sick rate, infant mortality rate, emigration and immigration rate in the British Isles'—is inseparably linked to the parochialism of a cultural outlook that takes as its motto, 'Scotland: my auld, respected mither!'. Three consequences would follow from national independence: the process of social and economic decline would be arrested; Scotland could once again emerge as one of the major contributors to European culture; and Scottish individuality would be seen 'with such truth of vision, such certainty in delineation, excusing nothing, distorting nothing'. He concludes that 'in the last analysis the basic trouble is a politico-economic one, with Scotland thirled to England and her natural media for self-expression progressively inhibited'. Two years later, Gunn returned to the question of the Scottish Renaissance in one of a series of articles written for the *Daily Record*.[48] His initial concern is to redefine 'Renaissance' in the sense of a National Awakening, more than just a rebirth of the arts but perhaps possessed of fewer geniuses than the Italian Renaissance. It is, indeed, not primarily preoccupied with questions of genius but with 'the bringing to birth once more of ... a Scottish culture, on a national scale'. Past failures of Scots enterprise, in whatever field, have been due to the lack of a sustaining culture; too many individuals 'had no faith in, were not profoundly conscious of, their life-giving roots'. In a further article, three years on, on 'The Scottish Renascence' [*sic*], written for *The Scots Magazine*, Gunn reasserts the unrestricted nature of the movement: 'Altogether let it be emphasised that renascence does not necessarily imply or demand the emergence of one or more great figures ..., but rather a reawakening or rebirth of spirit amongst many people, ultimately discernible even in the minor social manifestations of a whole people.'[49] The spiritual conditions must first be created within a nation for individual genius to emerge and thrive.

As late as 1962, in fact, Gunn tried to counter the, by then, established view that Hugh MacDiarmid *was* the Scottish Literary Renaissance.[50] While he acknowledges that such a view is understandable bearing in mind the 'high

profile' of MacDiarmid, the simple equation of man and movement would
be an exaggeration and even a denial of the true situation as MacDiarmid
himself saw it then. 'Indeed his articles and editings would have been
pointless, unless there had been in Scotland sufficient activity and accomplishment in cultural affairs to warrant his use of a word like Renaissance.'
Even if great individuals like Grassic Gibbon or Muir chose to stand on the
outside, even if MacDiarmid's influence tended towards the divisiveness of
'megalomania', the movement itself, underpinned by its political ideals, held
its ground.

Communism must have seemed superficially appealing to many writers:
its identification with change, with youth, with a new and healthy society.
Gunn certainly admits such a sympathy in his diary for 1939, but James
Barke failed in his attempts to convert him to a marxist point of view. Roman
Catholicism was also an attractive option but a more difficult one for men
springing mostly from Presbyterian backgrounds. Yet, Compton Mackenzie
was a Roman Catholic, 'Fionn MacColla' became a convert, and many others
took the more passive step of condemning Calvinism for all that was wrong
with Scotland. The Established Church—in particular, its evangelical wing—
represented an identifiable target for literary attack. In many ways,
however, this attack was no more than a continuation of the struggle for
liberalism conducted by the Kailyard. A Nationalism, based on these
humanitarian values, the balance of individual and community, was stronger
in its appeal than either Communism or Roman Catholicism yet sprang from
the same impulse, the need for a spiritual cure for a sick society. And where
there was for many by the end of the 1930s, as Richard Johnston argues,
a 'general movement from idealism to pragmatism',[51] Gunn held both in
check until after the Second World War when his idealism (in the usual as
well as the strictly philosophical sense) dominated his later fiction. Gunn's
political commitment to nationalism was also founded on a belief in the
essential spirit of man. While his adherence to any particular denomination
is in doubt—his was a belief that permitted scepticism about many aspects
of institutionalised faith—Gunn's idealism survived beyond the thirties and
beyond his disengagement from politics.

Yet the point bears emphasis again that for Gunn in the interwar period
nationalism was the political expression of a deeper faith and that, in turn,
the most compelling literature was itself the expression of this nationalism.
Lennox Kerr wrote an article in 1936 (in *Outlook*, the successor to *The
Modern Scot*) attacking the policy of PEN that 'literature, national though it
may be in origin, knows no frontiers ...'[52] Kerr puts forward the conventional argument that literature originates in social class. All nations are
divided into classes and class-solidarity cuts across national boundaries. 'A
Glasgow stevedore has everything in common with a London Stevedore
except his choice of drinks and a trifling difference in language.' Internationalism—a euphemism for the uniformity of industrialism that Gunn
was reacting against—has caused, according to Kerr, the destruction of
national differences. Where the nationalists deliberately set out to accen-
tuate the regional variety of Scotland, Kerr welcomes the process that would

reduce the world to a monotone (a shade of red). The article contains few illustrations of his thesis. It is a sustained and impatient whimper bemoaning the lack of working class art. Literature, it implies, is dominated by the middle-classes who provide nationalism as a distracting escape from the class-struggle. Yet the article was sufficiently strident to draw a reply from Gunn in the following issue.[53] He defines the finest literature as 'the expression of a folk who together make a unique nation'. Within the terms of that definition, literature can deal with the problems of class-divisions in the nation. He quotes Lewis Grassic Gibbon as a writer whose imagination thrived when it came to deal with Scotland but remained creatively moribund in his non-Scottish work. 'Mitchell had to come back to his own country, his own people, before what moved him so deeply received its profoundest expression.' Yet that did not blind him to social inequalities and injustices within Scotland itself. Gunn himself was acutely conscious of the flaws and warts of Scottish society, and wanted to erase them, but he rejected Marxism as unlikely to lead to the imminent regeneration of Scotland. Gunn also looked forward to a vital working-class literature, one which, in terms reminiscent of Eliot on tradition, 'will not be divorced from past expressions of art, but, on the contrary, will be added to them, affecting them all by its presence, as it (and they) will be affected in turn by the art of a later age'.

Gunn's essay is also notable for his turning again to the example of Ireland: 'the magnificent outburst of literature in recent years in Ireland synchronised precisely with the national uprising of the people; and it is a fair assumption that had the national spirit not raised its head, the literature would not have appeared.' The names of Joyce, Yeats, O'Casey and the Abbey Theatre are invoked as examples of the achievement that the 'national spirit' has created. This is contrasted with Scotland whose relationship with England produces both subservient attitudes in the Scots at home and a desire in the brightest and best to become Scots abroad. 'The relationship is essentially parasitic, working at second-hand, and provides the mechanism of escape for those who have not the courage to assume direct responsibility.'

Towards the close of this article, Gunn takes up the cudgels in defence of Calvinism. He wishes to argue that those who claim Scotland's failure in the arts to be due to a surfeit of Presbyterianism, rather than, as was his own view, to the surrender of nationhood, are misguided. Again Ireland provides an illustration. Despite remaining true to Roman Catholicism, Ireland, until the regaining of nationhood, 'remained deep in superstition and despair'. By contrast, the Scandinavian countries, bastions of Protestantism, display a 'brilliant progress' in literature, sculpture and architecture. Three years later, at the close of the decade, Gunn discovered an ideal in the Presbyterian community of Iona; it combined the three elements of his own 'faith'—nationalism, community, and spirit.[54] The aim of George MacLeod seemed to Gunn to be 'to revive in a small way the old Columban idea of fellowship, communal labour and ministry, together with a realisation of what we call "modern conditions", and of the urgent need within the Church of Scotland itself for a revivifying impulse'. The grounds of the appeal to

Gunn are here made manifest: in this aim, there is an awareness of a national tradition, the reference to Columba, but also a determination to bring the values in this tradition to bear on contemporary problems; these values are, in turn, those of the co-operative community, fellowship, and an awareness of life lived beyond the material. Gunn used the essay in *The Scots Magazine* to defend this aim against its three principal types of opponent. There are those who call any interference with the Abbey ruin itself a form of sacrilege. The stones must be left in their present state so that subsequent visitors can find a sense of history and a sense of awe there. For Gunn, this antiquarianism is a non-creative defeatism, clinging on to the past, in the grip of nostalgia, to avoid consciousness of a creative present. The reconstruction of the Abbey would help it realise its original purpose; what is important is not the condition of the fabric but its role as symbol of the nation's spiritual heritage.

> The spiritual heritage of a people is the most real thing about them, and all the institutions they have formed have been instruments for its expression, in church or law or social custom. It is their tradition. It is that which distinguishes them from another people. Through it and it only can they express themselves to the full; can they draw from life its profoundest savour, its deepest meanings. To interfere with this heritage in a harmful or destructive way is to limit the full expression of each individual. Whereupon the whole people suffer, and that which they created of spiritual value tends to decay, and the common stock of humanity—its civilisation, its culture, call it what you will—is diminished at least to the degree in which the contribution of that people was unique.

There are, secondly, those detractors of the scheme who claim that a Christian brotherhood on Iona in the twentieth century is simply another example of futile escape from the problems of the world outside the cloister. Gunn stresses that community co-operation is no retreat from these problems.

> Young men will meet here in brotherhood, will toil with their hands and have the communion of fellowship before setting out to bring what understanding and selfless devotion they may have learned to their brothers in the derelict areas of our civilisation. There is nothing unreal or heretical about this. Even in the matter of secular education the Danes have a parallel in their folk schools, where men and women over eighteen meet and learn, and wash up their dishes and make their beds. It is the very ancient ideal of brotherhood and service, and the world would be none the worse of a lesson in its potency from whatever source, religious, educational, or political.

Finally, there are those opponents of the Iona community who claim that the world of the individual spirit has been superseded and disproven by the world of technology and economics. Gunn underlines the necessity of the individual spirit in such a world.

The increasing mechanisation of life, the loss of individual freedom under political tyrannies, the suppression of original thought and the manufacture by the Press of a public opinion—everywhere massed force, under a lust of power or a psychosis of fear, is robbing man of his dignity and life of its ecstasy, its profoundest delight. It is not inconceivable to forecast a rigid condition of affairs when little colonies of persons, secretly, will once more, in the old phrase, go out into the desert, to save man's spiritual life from extinction. And by spiritual life I mean the striving towards the achievement of harmony in the mind, that condition of synthesis, of fulfilment, which all the religious leaders and mystics and poets have striven for throughout the human history of our planet; which the scientist searches for in the consitution of matter; and which Columba knew so profoundly as a state of light.

Iona is the island of light.

Neil Gunn, in drawing on his own inheritance of egalitarianism and co-operation, using the Nationalism of interwar politics as the social vehicle for change, and believing profoundly in the spirituality of man, transcends other contemporary novelists in his concerns and in his writings. His novels and his essays express the light he found in Iona.

From Iona this light, this vision without which the people perish, might in some measure be made manifest again. That Scotsmen should attempt the effort is logically sound, for they will start with a tradition and environment that is their heritage, physical and spiritual.

NOTES

1 Gunn to Ian MacArthur, 8 July, 1969. Gunn Papers, Deposit 209, National Library of Scotland.
2 'The Furthest North Nationalist, Mr Neil Gunn', interview in the *Daily Record*, 11 January, 1929.
3 Essay No 1 'Caithness and Sutherland'.
4 Maurice Lindsay and Neil Gunn, 'Conversations with a Novelist', *Scottish Field*, May 1961, p 39.
5 Essay No 11, 'Landscape Inside'.
6 Ibid.
7 *The Grey Coast* (London, 1926), p 38–9.
8 Essay No 6, 'The Family Boat'.
9 *Morning Tide* (Edinburgh, 1931), p 152.
10 *Highland River* (Edinburgh, 1937), p 254.
11 Thomas Mann, *Essays of Three Decades* (London, 1947), p 22.
12 *The Serpent* (London, 1943), p 7.
13 George Bruce, 'Handling the Unbearable: *The Serpent* and *The Drinking Well*', in A Scott and D Gifford (eds), *Neil Gunn: The Man and the Writer* (Edinburgh, 1973), p 221.
14 Gunn to Francis R Hart, 29 March, 1966. Gunn Papers, Deposit 209, NLS.
15 F R Hart and J B Pick, *Neil M Gunn: A Highland Life* (London, 1981), p 125.
16 Essay No 25, 'The Essence of Nationalism'.
17 Neil Gunn, 'This "English" Business', *Scots Magazine* 37 (July, 1942), p 295.
18 Essay No 25, 'The Essence of Nationalism'.

19 Essay No 33, 'Nationalism and Internationalism'.

20 Essay No 19, 'Nationalism in Writing III: Is Scottish Individualism to be Deplored?'

21 *The Atom of Delight* (London, 1956), p 119–21. Gunn was also aware of Prince Kropotkin's theories of 'mutual aid' and the ideas of anarchism. He wrote to Naomi Mitchison in 1944: 'And when you accuse me of anarchism, do you mean the anarchism of Kropotkin or individual chaos? There's a mighty difference.' Hart and Pick (1981), p 180. He wrote also to Margaret McEwan: 'I was always an anarchist.' Ibid. After escaping from Russia, Kropotkin in fact came to Edinburgh to visit Patrick Geddes.

22 R J Storey, 'Community Co-operatives—A Highlands and Islands Experiment', in J Sewel and D O'Carroll (eds), *Co-operation and Community Development* (Galway, 1982), p 72.

23 *The Scotsman*, 19 November, 1884.

24 Adrian Varwell, 'Highlands and Islands Communities' in M Broady (ed), *Marginal Regions* (London, 1973), p 73.

25 J S Grant, 'The Importance of the Part-Time Holding', in P G Sadler and G A Mackay (eds), *The Changing Fortunes of Marginal Regions* (Aberdeen, 1977), p 154.

26 Report of the Commission of Enquiry into Crofting Conditions, 1954 (Cmd 9091, p 9.

27 Report, p 26.

28 Report, p 88.

29 Report, p 33.

30 Report, p 34.

31 Report, p 34.

32 Sir Thomas Taylor to Neil Gunn (nd), quoted in Hart and Pick (1981), p 325.

33 Essay No 28.

34 Essay No 31.

35 Essay No 40.

36 BBC Talk, Scotland Today Series, 'Scottish Letters', February, 1929.

37 Essay No 36, 'As Drunk as a Bavarian'.

38 Hart and Pick (1981), p 163.

39 Gunn Papers, Deposit 209, NLS.

40 Essay No 18, 'Nationalism in Writing II: The Theatre Society of Scotland'.

41 Essay No 35, 'President of Eire: The True Value of Tradition'.

42 Quoted in David Craig, *Scottish Literature and the Scottish People* (London, 1961), p 5.

43 Quoted in F S L Lyons, *Ireland Since the Famine* (London, 1973), p 243.

44 George Blake, untitled essay, in David Cleghorn Thomson (ed) *Scotland in Quest of Her Youth* (Edinburgh, 1932), p 158.

45 Essay No 17, 'Nationalism in Writing I: Tradition and Magic in the Work of Lewis Grassic Gibbon'.

46 Essay No 21, 'Muir's *Scott and Scotland*'.

47 Essay No 26.

48 Essay No 13, 'New Golden Age for Scottish Letters'.

49 Essay No 15.

50 Essay No 16, 'Scottish Renaissance'.

51 Richard Johnstone, *The Will to Believe: Novelists of the Nineteen-thirties* (Oxford, 1982), p 9.

52 Lennox Kerr, 'Literature: Class or National', *Outlook* (June, 1932), p 74–5.

53 Essay No 20, 'Literature: Class or National'.

54 Essay No 44, 'The New Community of Iona'.

SECTION I

LANDSCAPES

CAITHNESS AND SUTHERLAND

Scottish Country, 1935

IN NEARLY ALL the popular guides to Scotland, Caithness is ignored or referred to as a place of little or no interest. I have beside me one of the best of them, *Scotland for Everyman*, where the author in his otherwise excellent and exact survey proceeds to warn the reader, as follows:

> East of Tongue the scenery rapidly decreases in grandeur as one gradually returns to civilization and tarred roads. Caithness is really rather a dull county, not Highland at all but rather Norse, at least near the coast—as the place-names show. Consequently the traveller will not be ill-advised if he decides to cut short this tour by making Lairg direct. If he does so, he will miss the kudos of having reached John o' Groats, but not very much else.

This 'return to civilization' (after wandering in Sutherland) may have its points for a Caithness man, as there has always existed a certain rivalry—and raillery—between the two remotest counties of our mainland. But plainly he is not to be comforted by very much else. And as civilisation is a vague word and quite different in its implications from that other overworked word, culture, it might be said that the Sutherland man scores—particularly as some of his roads (including the famous old rocky highway to the Ord) have recently been tarred to perfection.

But the inwardness of this matter really centres in the use of that word grandeur. It is a legacy of Sir Walter Scott and all the Highland romanticism to which that noble name must plead guilty. Byron caught the note and sang it 'wild and majestic'.

> Oh, for the crags that are wild and majestic!
> The steep-frowning glories of dark Loch na Garr.

To see patriotic Scots roused by this gorgeous stuff is to realise in some measure the religious intensity of the old wife who would not believe that Jerusalem is on this earth. There is a magniloquence about it all, a lack of reality, of exact description, that flatters our vague emotions at the expense of our sight and insight. It is admirably reflected in those pictures for sale in stationers' shops where gigantic crags, their tops swathed in Celtic mist, form a background to smooth purple slopes and the wan water of a loch on whose near shores long-haired Highland cattle for ever stand and dream.

From all this, the curious reader may conclude that I am a Caithness man—preparing the way. He is right. The mind must be prepared for the reception of beauty in its more exquisite forms. The old man of the ceilidh-house realised this, and, before beginning one of the ancient classic poems of the Gael, he tuned the listening minds by telling of the poem itself and of its heroes. But he always followed with the poem. And now I am prepared to follow with two.

But as the Eastern sage has it, 'Haste is an attribute of devils'. Let us see one thing well; let us, then, as we turn east from Tongue, keep our eyes on Sutherland's own mountain—Ben Laoghal. Ben Hope comes before for contrast. And moors and sea-inlets and skylines keep us company. Around is all the grandeur of all the fabled West—with Ben Laoghal added. Watch Ben Laoghal play with its four granite peaks on the legendary stuff of history, or is it of the mind? Sometimes they are the battlemented towers of a distant Mediaeval Age; in the smoke-blue drift of the half-light they are the ramparts to the high hills of faery; a turn in the road or in the mood, and they have become perfectly normal again, unobtrusive and strong as the native character. Let me add that once going down towards bleak Kildonan, I unthinkingly glanced over my shoulder and saw them crowned with snow. I have never forgotten the unearthly fright I got then.

From that background, or as it were from that door, you walk out upon Caithness, and at once experience an austerity in the flat clean wind-swept lands that affects the mind almost with a sense of shock. There is something more in it than contrast. It is a movement of the spirit that finds in the austerity, because strength is there also, a final serenity. I know of no other landscape in Scotland that achieves this harmony, that, in the very moment of purging the mind of its dramatic grandeur, leaves it free and ennobled. The Pentland Firth, outreaching on the left, is of a blueness that I, at least, failed to find in the Mediterranean; a living blueness, cold-glittering in the sun and smashed to gleaming snowdrift on the bows of the great rock-battleships of the Orkneys, bare and austere also. The wind of time has searched out even the flaws here and cleansed them.

That is the first picture. Before we come to the second we follow the road' by stone-flagged fences and broad fields to Thurso, a charming old town with a fishing-quarter of rather intricate design and a piling of roofs that, seen from the beach, has a certain attraction. From Thurso, like all good tourists we proceeded to John o' Groats, so that we may sing about the end of the road. Picture postcards are here, and an hotel, and the legend of the house with the eight walls, the eight doors, and the eight-sided table, so that the eight men might enter and be seated without raising questions of precedence or prestige. But while listening to this local lore and, with luck, sampling the country's whisky—and old Pulteney, well matured, does no dishonour to its birthplace—we find our eyes attracted by that long lovely beach of white sand.

Not the poet's 'dove-grey sand', but the crushed shells of whiteness from which all the sticky humours have been withdrawn. It is in its way as typical of this clean-swept county as that first picture I have tried to describe. Hours may be spent on this strand looking for those lovely little shells, the John o' Groat buckies. In the process, too, the native spirit enters and quietens the soul.

But the leisureliness of an older age is gone. A look and a rush and we say we have seen it! The evening is upon us. Yet we have hardly got under way when from the low ridge of the Warth Hill, Caithness suddenly spreads her whole body before us to the blue distant ridges of Morven and the Scarabens.

This, my second picture, is impossible even to suggest, for the effect is entirely one of light. It is not that the quality of this light is magical or glamorous, tenuous or thin. There are few places in Scotland where level light from the sinking sun can come across such a great area; but it is not altogether that. Robert Louis Stevenson, who knew Wick well, may here have first found his 'wine-red moor', but I have seen it of a paler gold than amontillado. The mind does not debate: it gets caught up into that timelessness where beauty is no longer majestic or grand but something more intimate than life or death. Across the moor, the sun gone, the colour darkening, the far blue turning to deep purple, shadow and more shadow, until the peewits cry in the dark of night.

There is a third picture of Caithness but it is a composite one: the sea-cliffs that form its coast. In a sense, these cliffs are more typical of Caithness than all else for they have entered so much—and so violently—into the life of its people. As sheer rock-scenery, too, they are often magnificent, while the flatness of the coastlands permits of tremendous perspectives.

On entering the county from the Ord one may from almost anywhere near the cliffs get a view of the rock-wall all the way to Clyth Head. There are 'flaws' in this structure—fortunately, because they mean so much to the inhabitants, for here they have their harbours or creeks from which they fish with such skill and daring, or, should I say, have fished, for the decline in the sea industry has left an air of sadness and decay along the whole Caithness coast. In small places like Dunbeath or Lybster, where today only four or five motor-boats pursue the old calling, little more than a generation ago anything up to two hundred boats fished in the season from each harbour. What activity was there then! Every creek round the coast swarmed with life, while Wick, now going derelict, was a fishing-centre of European importance. Folk worked hard in those days, played hard, and drank hard, too. To live and prosper on such a coast required unusual intrepidity and endurance in the seamen. Few of the mean 'safe' qualities found time to sprout, and as the money came so did it go, with that element of careless generosity that is ever present in the greater games of chance. And sea-fishing is the master game of chance, for not only does a man risk all he possesses, with every grain of skill and strength added, but also he stakes down the hazard with his life. The fish-curers' stations employed as gutters nearly all the available women of the surrounding districts, whose gay tongues were as nimble as their fingers. Shopkeepers prospered. The produce of the land was needed. If there was never great wealth, there was all the living warmth of a healthy communal life.

When we look at the boarded windows of the ruinous curing buildings, we may naturally wonder what cataclysm or what blight descended here. The use of steam, the big drifter, the concentration of the industry in great ports like Wick, were the reasons given. But what of these reasons now? The drifter is in debt to more than a critical extent, and Wick is proportionately as derelict as Lybster.

Politics entered into it, and in a sense with far more drama than is usually found in the interactions of any 'economic law'. The export of cured herrings to the Baltic was lost when Russia began her social experiment. Not that Russia no longer required herrings, but that the British Government kept changing its mind about dealing with her. The herring is immensely more important to Scotland than to England. But Scotland could not deal separately in this matter. Norway, however, could and did. The Norwegian Government guaranteed Russian payments to the Norwegian fishermen to the extent of many millions of pounds. The Norwegian Government never lost a penny and the Norwegian fishermen got the market. It is interesting to reflect how the attitude of some politician seven hundred miles away may affect a seaboard and its people. Mr Winston Churchill, let us say, decides on a little affair in Russia, and our northern coasts come under the grip of a grisly hand that slowly closes. They were such a fine breed of men, too, these Caithness fishermen, daring, self-reliant, rarely hypocritical or sanctimonious, game for whatever life offered in the sea-storm or in the public-house, and God-fearing over all.

Their qualities have been inherited, normal qualities of a healthy stock against an environment demanding courage and faith. Hospitality was the social gift, and the old need for quickness of wits may perhaps today find more or less a natural outlet in education. But whether the change from being skipper of a sailing vessel to being a school teacher, minister of the Gospel, clerk, professor, Civil Servant, or what-not, is a change for the better in the human story, may hardly be debated here. Personally, I am inclined to do more than doubt it.

All the coast is studded with castles mostly now in ruins and indicating an older age of tribal rule and self-sufficiency. Sinclairs, Keiths, Gunns; with Mackays, Sutherlands, and the ever land-hungry Campbells, impinging upon them from the outside. The tale of their deeds and depredations is as stormy and bloody and treacherous and heroic as tales from anywhere else in the Highlands. As a good-going example, may I be forgiven for recalling the ancient feud between the Keiths and the Gunns. The chiefs of these two clans agreed to settle their differences by a fight to the death of twelve men against twelve. The Gunn, with his chosen dozen, several of whom were his sons, was first at the lonely moorland rendezvous, and had barely ceased asking the Creator for His blessing, when the horses of the Keiths were seen to be approaching. Twelve horses behind the Keith, yes—but what is this? ... Each horse carries two riders! ... The Gunn puts it to his men. There is plenty of time to fly. But the Keith strategy, for some obscure reason, merely fires them to encounter any odds, and the battle is joined. It was a long and bloody affair, in which the Keiths claimed victory, but in the end three of the Gunns, albeit sorely wounded, were able to leave the field on their own feet.

A certain delicacy of feeling might well make a Gunn hesitate to tell the traditional story, were he not sadly aware that the clan did not know then—and certainly none of them has ever learned since—the technique of acquiring land or indeed notable material wealth of any kind. Nor from this story is any particular moral intended for our age, though I cannot help being conscious of a certain diffused light! We are landless! cried the Macgregors. And not only in the small clan of the Gunns, but in the large clan of the common people of Scotland, the cry has an intimate ring to this day.

These counties of Caithness and Sutherland may be said to have a prehistory of enthralling conjecture. Those interested in the archaeological aspect of things may here dream and dispute to their heart's content. Who built the brochs?—those round dwellings whose walls may still be seen from twelve to fifteen feet thick and whose original height must have been anything from fifty to sixty feet. They are structures of unique interest, crammed with novel features. The ruins of a great many of them are to be found in Caithness; rather less in Sutherland; and they diminish in number as we go south, until they become rare in the Lowlands. And perhaps the most remarkable fact about them is that they are to be found only in Scotland. Not a single example in Scandinavia, or Ireland, or England—those countries from which at one time or other Scotland is supposed to have got all she may be said to have! What race built them then? Was the seat of their power actually in the extreme north? Long ago Columba had to travel to Inverness to meet the high king of our country. Had the governing centre shifted south to Inverness by Columba's time, much as it later shifted to Edinburgh; and still later to London?

It is all a game of questions. But clearly in the courses of time these northern counties have had their day.

No writer can now refer to Caithness without using the word Norse. 'Not Highland at all but rather Norse'. A hundred odd years ago a traveller from the south would have had to penetrate into the county as far as Clyth before he could hear a word of English, no other tongue than Gaelic being spoken. True, you will find Norse coastal names; but you will also find them in the Outer Isles, where the Norse held sway just as long as they held it in Caithness. But they were conquerors, with the conqueror's technique of spoil-getting and land-grabbing. Their exploits are fabulous, and the only adventurers who can be compared with them are the Spanish Conquistadores. They were, however, few in numbers, were not of the soil they held, and in time the native folk of Caithness's hinterland, through their women, largely bred them out. That is not to say that Caithness folk are mostly Gaelic, any more than are other parts of the Highlands. There is an older more predominant strain in the Highlands than either Gaelic or Norse. What folk composed this strain I do not know, just as I do not know who built the brochs; but I have the uneasy idea that they rode one man to a horse.

All of which has brought us a little distance from the rock scenery. Not that the rock scenery is to blame, for it has beauty quite apart from its human associations. The geos and stacks and contorted strata, the colouring of caves and seaweed, the bird life, are elements of ever-varying allure. Memorable days may be passed haunting this world that swings between life and death. Great care should be taken, too, for on a windless sea where no waves are breaking there is always some degree of a swell that may all in a moment lift a small boat on to a sloping ledge and, receding, leave her to turn turtle.

For the rest, Caithness is said to be a flat treeless plain, and perhaps that impression may have been confirmed here; yet like so many general impressions it is only partially true. For Caithness has many shallow straths of delicate beauty, that penetrate inland from the coast and fade into the moor with an air of still, listening surprise. The Strath of Dunbeath is considered to be about the finest example, though I have found Berriedale and Langwell of inexhaustible attraction. There are others, many of them not at all impressive to the casual eye, that yet achieve for the lover an intimacy and charm that may be comparable only to the fragrance of the finer wines.

Possibly I am prejudiced in favour of Caithness, knowing, as I do, that it possesses qualities which, like the qualities of its people, are not readily paraded. Yet let me say immediately that had Caithness denied me, I should have desired, over any other place on the earth's surface (including the vineyard countries), to have been born in Sutherland!

Caithness and Sutherland are, in a way not easily made plain, a mating of the two great elements of sea and land. You can get lost in Sutherland, in its mountain masses, its great glens, its hidden lochs, its peat hags, its woods, its barren moors. It is shaggy and tough and often terrifying. The eye reaches over great vistas where no human being lives or moves. And on the west the traveller finds himself for ever playing a game of hide and seek with the sea. Narrow inlets meet him round corners, sudden flashes of colour drawing his eyes away. The memory of a trip from Scourie northward is curiously jewelled. The greenness of mountains where one had expected to find heather, the land between mountain and sea assuming every shape, fantastic, ancient, grey, brooding in peat black, glistening in loch blue, unexpected in goblin green, dreaming in brown, the wind touching it, passing over it, carrying away its loneliness to some place still more deeply withdrawn. To think of the Caithness coast now is to think of something simple, elemental, masculine. Here is the beauty of ceaseless change, full of a wild charm, alluring, beckoning, heedless, feminine.

Sutherland has always been a pastoral crofting county and the tragedy it suffered in the beginning of last century may best be realised if from Caithness we go 'over the Ord' by the south coast road and come down upon the fishing town of Helmsdale.

Helmsdale, like the Caithness creeks, has fallen on evil times these latter years. But its story is interesting in that it was a direct creation of what is known to history as the 'Sutherland Clearances'. These clearances consisted in the evictions of thousands of crofters from their homes in the glens by a landlord who desired, for his greater profit, to rent his land to sheep farmers. It was the era throughout the whole Highlands of the creation of the large sheep farm, and of the dispossession of the people, frequently by means so ruthless and brutal that they may not bear retelling easily, and always with a sorrow and hopelessness that finally broke the Gaelic spirit. What the disaster of 1745 and the penal enactments of 1747 began, the clearances finished.

We know rather exactly and vividly what happened in the glens of Sutherland because of the accounts of eye-witnesses and the explanations of contemporaries. Donald Macleod, whose wife and family were evicted into a night of storm when he himself was absent, with no neighbour they dare go to without bringing immediate doom to that neighbour's house, described the lurid scenes of burning and destruction in a series of letters to an Edinburgh newspaper, afterwards printed in book form under the title *The Gloomy Memories*. These letters make terrible reading. The Rev Donald Sage, in his *Memorabilia Domestica*, tells of the hundreds of homes that were burned around him and of how, when he came to preach his last sermon, he broke down and all his people wept with him. For untold generations they and their forebears had inhabited these glens, a courteous people, hospitable, full of the ancient lore and music and ways of life of the Gael and the pre-Gael. No army of invading barbarians ever left behind it desolation so complete as did that ruthless handful of the chief's servants. And Sutherland to this day is haunted by that 'gloomy memory'.

The folk gathered on the seashores, eating shellfish or whatever they could find, while they dug small plots of coastal land and tackled the sea. Helmsdale gradually became a fishing port of consequence. Then Helmsdale declined, as the sheep farms declined, and the great experiment in Progress had its mask torn from it.

From Helmsdale the traveller should take the road that goes up Kildonan strath, over the Heights, and down Strath Halladale to Melvich on the north coast, both for the scenery and to experience, as I think he may, a still lingering intimation of that gloom. For this is the area that, with Strath Naver farther west, suffered most cruelly.

And the first reaction may well be one of surprise that a land so barren and wild could ever have harboured townships of people. How did they manage to live? ... Until finally he may wonder if the 'clearances' would not have happened sometime anyway.

The further north he goes the bleaker it gets until crossing the high lands he observes little but endless desolation. Then all at once he comes on Dalhalvaig.

In Dalhalvaig there is a public school, a post office, substantial houses on the surrounding crofts, white-washed walls, an air of comfort, of material well-being, of everything, in fact, except that which suggests poverty and misery. Yet half-close the eyes, let the houses disappear, let the heather creep up to the hearth-stones, let all sign of human habitation vanish, and the present Dalhalvaig becomes a place more desolate than any to be found in Kildonan.

How do we account, then, for the Dalhalvaig of today? On no other grounds that I can think of than that Strath Halladale was not 'cleared'. It escaped the horrors of 1813–19 because the greater part of it was at that time under the Mackays, and when it did fall into other hands (in 1829, by purchase) public feeling against the evictions had got so inflamed that the new owners found it more advantageous to pursue the intriguing ways of Parliamentary influence than to continue making deserts.

Down the Strath from Forsinard to the sea the descendants of the old crofters remained. Many of them caught the emigration fever as the nineteenth century advanced and went abroad meaning to return, but few of them ever returned to settle, though they sent home money regularly and in other ways exhibited the passion of the Gael for his homeland and his kindred.

In talk and correspondence with the present scholarly parish minister of Kildonan I have been given a glimpse of the kind of men and women Dalhalvaig has produced not only in the past but in living memory. 'Some of the finest types of Northern Highlander, physically and mentally, have come out of this area from Kirkton to Forsinain on both sides of the Halladale river', Dr Scott maintains, And he proves his case with fascinating instances of versatility, strong personality, and occasional genius.

I was interested in this contrast between Kildonan and Halladale, and pursued my inquiries quite dispassionately. I think there is here an underlying significance of real importance. A great human stock cannot be planted in a day. What was uprooted so swiftly may not all at once be given root and permanence by a decision of any individual or any Board. But the glens are there. And the final—and representative—opinion was given me in these words: 'All the northern glens might have been like Halladale, if the people had been treated as human beings.'

But this is a depressing subject and for all that may have been written to the contrary, the Highlander loves news and gaiety. As Kenneth Macleod reports of the island schoolmaster, 'My curse on gloom!' Only it is necessary to get some understanding of the forces, human and economic, that have been doing him down in the past in order to appreciate even the scenery amid which he lives now. For not only does environment affect human development, but human development in its turn affects environment. In a happy thriving community the very land, to our senses, takes on a certain pleasant friendliness. Children feel this particularly, and in after life have an enhanced memory of sunlight and of flowering growths. On the other hand, in Kildonan there is today a shadow, a chill, of which any sensitive mind would, I am convinced, be vaguely aware, though possessing no knowledge of the clearances. We are affected strangely by any place from which the tide of life has ebbed.

And Sutherland, as I have suggested, is a land of endless variety. There are no big towns, nothing at all like Wick, which in the height of the herring season in the old days used to double its population and present a scene of human interest continuously dramatic. The county town of Dornoch is best known for its golf course. Golspie and Brora also have good golf courses.

Here a tourist industry is developing. And as this part of the county is also the seat of landlord power, there is a certain residential feeling in the atmosphere. Surrounding the castle are fields with trees like English parks, while on a high hill dominating all this part of the coast is a tall monument to that Duke of Sutherland under whose reign the clearances took place.

Let us go inland to Lairg, which is the proper centre for the exploration of the real Sutherland. Anything in the nature of motor-car or bus service may be had at the Sutherland Transport garage, where a genial manager, in Gaelic or English, will tell you what you want to know and what you had not thought of. Three main roads radiate from Lairg to the west. The first up the quietly beautiful strath of the Oykel to Lochinver; the second by the long barren stretches of Loch Shin to Scourie; and the third northward across the moors, passing the Clibric Hills on the right, to Tongue. All three roads run into the road of the west which winds from Lochinver to Tongue, and is, to me at least, literally the most surprising and magical road in Britain. Not that speedmen would call it a road at all, unless indeed certain parts might be selected for 'observing'.

Through Strath Oykell, by Altnagealgach, and on towards Loch Assynt, where great mountains all at once crowd around: Ben More Assynt (3,273) on our right; Canisp and the remarkable Suilven on our left; Glasven and the Quinag in front. This is the happy hunting-ground of geologists, archaeologists, and botanists. Historians, too, will look at the ruins of Ardvreck Castle on the edge of Loch Assynt and think of Montrose and what happened there of 'deathless shame'.

From Lochinver, a pleasant place, there is a coast road by Clashnessie and Drumbeg to Kylescue Ferry (for Scourie) that no summer traveller should miss. It is not much frequented, but I have always found a great fascination in the wooded inlets that give on Eddrachillis Bay, with its many islands.

Islands, indeed, accompany one along this western seaboard, and exercise their power on the romantic imagination in diverse ways. Some look upon them quiescently, others dreamily with vague thoughts of Tir nan Og, while not a few feel an impulse to own one doubtless out of some innate urge for security and over-lordship. All hopes—or illusions—may be indulged on this road. Life is short, but eternity may be dreamed in a minute.

From Scourie to Laxford Bridge, where the Loch Shin road ends or begins. All this is sporting country. The Laxford River has patrol paths on both sides, and I have heard of young men who strike a match in the dark of night by this lonely water and then wait to see how long it will take keepers to come out of the void upon them! A remarkably short time, I am told. Whether or not it has its point as a game, it certainly illustrates with some irony the whole subject of sporting rights on which I have not touched here. It is really difficult to write of the Highlands without appearing to deal in that accursed gloom. When the sheep did not pay, the deer took their place. I may leave it at that. As for getting a rod on the Laxford, you would first have to buy out the wealthiest duke in England. So you may leave it at that also!

The hotels have, of course, some loch-fishing attached to them. It is the custom, I know, to deplore the heavy charges—six to eight guineas a week—

of most of them. But their season is short, their rent and expenses heavy, and they desire profit as naturally as a duke or a grocer. For the rest, they know their business. The Highlands, of course, may yet become a popular tourist playground dependent on tourists and nothing else. After sheep, deer; and after deer, tourists. It is the ascending order of our age of progress. For those who know the deep humanism of a past age, there will be regret at the gradual passing of the human stock that was bred of it.

But by the time a man has footed the track to Cape Wrath, where there is no habitation other than the lighthouse, and looked down upon the rocks that take the Arctic on their bows, he may feel that men's faiths or creeds, economic or religious, change with the centuries, that his wants and desires change with the days, but that certain deep racial forces persist with extraordinary strength, and that the end of this great country is not yet.

EAST TO BUCHAN

Scots Magazine [SM] 1939

'We are coming up to Inverness for a day or two. Can you recommend some outings that would give us an idea of the far north of which we have heard so much?'

That is a typical inquiry, and the easy answer takes the roads to the west, by Garve and Achnasheen to Loch Maree and Gairloch, or right through to Lairg and then by Loch Shin to Scourie, Cape Wrath, Durness and the north road to Caithness. You never make a mistake if you send a traveller into those regions, for the appeal of the scenery is immediate; and indeed it is very beautiful.

But there is another road that I am sometimes tempted to send a discerning friend, though I try to make sure first of all that he cares for two things: the sea itself and the way of life of those who draw their livelihood exclusively from the sea. Once assured on these points, I suggest the coast road along the southern shores of the Moray Firth 'east to Buchan'.

For the normal traveller in our country, this remains an unknown region, because it is so rarely written or spoken about. Yet what a fascination it can have for landsmen who care to linger about the fishing villages and see and attempt to understand the strange ways of life that are here so quietly followed!

The other night I spent with a friend who has entered into possession of a fisherman's cottage that overlooks one of the harbour basins of Macduff. He is an artist and writer, of a distinguished sea ancestry, who knows the seamen of Brittany or Italy as well as he knows those of the English Channel, but who has come to live here from choice. And after spending a couple of days with him, I may put it mildly by saying that I see his point! For no one can 'retire' to a small fishing-port, in the sense that he may sit down and fold his hands and let the days go by. There is always too much going on, or about to go on, or held up—according to the weather or the season of the year. For this traffic with the sea is essentially in the nature of a continuous gamble, a gamble in material results, but also a gamble not infrequently with life or death where the winning counters are knowledge and endurance and courage—and these counters do not always win.

The distinguishing feature of the fishing villages along this coast is the cleanliness of the houses, not merely inside but also outside. You can see they are seamen's houses, for they are all shipshape and bright with paint. Macduff is no exception, and when you turn and look at it from the harbour wall, it stands against its uprising green brae like a little town that one might come upon in a southern land—at some distance, let us say, for Macduff's appearance of solidity and brightness stands the closest inspection.

They are very go-ahead in Macduff: at a short distance they have constructed a spendid bathing-pool, and on the hillside above it there is a golf-course. It is not unknown for a woman to be seen baiting her husband's sea-lines in the morning and to be golfing in the afternoon. Which is surely one of the first and best of any reasons for the existence of a golf-course. Macduff is not—as yet, anyway—a fashionable resort. For the most part, the visitors who come here are workers who have earned their short holiday and live in the houses of the people, with whom they make friends. The real old Scots democratic feeling and no nonsense.

At six o'clock in the morning we were on the quay seeing the handful of drifters coming in with, as it happened, their very small shots of herring, which were auctioned on the spot. Here are one or two women with their barrows, trundling away baskets of herring to be used as bait for the small lines, which later in the day will be taken to sea by the smaller boats engaged in the white fishing. My friend is given a fry of herring—and presents them to me. To get the real flavour of almost any sea fish, you must eat it the day it is caught. A lemon sole fresh from the sea has a salty tang that I have never got in any city hotel.

The town of Banff lies across the bay, but no fishing is carried on there now. At one time Banff was a very important seaport, as well as a social centre for the country, but the high stores by the harbour are derelict and the slipway is empty. The ruins of crofting houses in the glens can be a sad enough sight, but they do not convey to me so immediate a feeling of desolation as do the boarded-up windows of cooperages, the grass-grown yards and crumbling stores of these fishing villages all along the Moray Firth that once knew so busy, so thrilling a life.

Beyond Banff, we dropped down into the fishing village of Whitehills that still lives on the sea. The fishermen were putting their small lines aboard. Some ten lines to each boat, and each line with five hundred hooks, baited with herring. It's a saying that there mustn't be a lazy inch in a fisherman—or in his wife. Whitehills is in many respects typical of the small sea villages along this coast. Usually the road, from the wide plain above, drops very steeply, and the village is come upon suddenly and conveys the air of being shut away from the world. In such a place, the houses have generally their gables to the sea, and group together as if for comfort and warmth. Which is understandable and wise enough, when one reflects that it might be unskilled advice to suggest to these seamen and often anxious women that they should build to have a 'good view' of the sea! The sea is always with them, and when a storm is blowing up it's not a bad thing to be shut away from it, even if the 'view' is then no more than the back wall of a neighbour's house. At least that wall is stable—even though it doesn't shut out the unending roar.

To paint a solid stone cottage all blue may seem as absurd as to paint it all pink. But when you see the blue cottage and the pink cottage there is no absurdity, but on the contrary a pleasant surprise that they should look so well. They paint their houses as they paint their boats. This indeed is the most striking characteristic of all the dwellings along this coast. The cottage may be painted blue, but each stone is picked out in straight white lines. Though there again it is a matter of shade or tone. And this contrasting of colours on the one house, they have brought to a careful art. Yellows, blues, greys, dark reds passing into maroon. Mostly, of course, the whole wall is not painted, though there is a soft dark-blue stone that loses nothing by being enclosed within narrow white lines. And some of the red fluted tiles are tarred black and look ancient and very well. The tar preserves the tile. The individualism of the Scot comes out, too, in the case say, of two dwellings in the one building·(semi-detached), where each has its own colour scheme, as if the houses want to show that they need not necessarily be on speaking terms.

It was raining heavily when we crossed the Bridge of Banff, heading for Buchan along the coast road. This road is as surprising as the villages, for surely along the flat plain of Buchan the road should be fairly level and for the most part straight. Actually the road turns and twists as continuously as it goes up and down. One expects—and finds—the usual dangerously steep gradient going down into the very attractive fishing village of Pennan, but once more up on the plain one may be forgiven for almost stalling when, a short distance further on, one encounters a sudden incline which at the turn to the top must be pretty nearly 1-in-4. These twists and declivities are caused by the little green valleys that are always finding their way to the sea. Intimate valleys, with the wind whitening the bracken on their green braes.

The sun came out through the watery skies and opened up and brightened the mist-shrouded land, and in that fresh, warm light Buchan was anything but the cold, bleak region that a traveller may expect. Large bien farms here, and comfortable steadings, and inland the slow austere sweep of the land. A good, sound, strong country. Up over the rise of a field in the lifting brilliant mist came a ploughman behind his horse, a great beast stepping quickly and proudly against the gradient and the pull of the scuffler behind. And there the picture was complete: the sea and the land. The man who harvests the sea and the man who harvests the land. In a last resort we can do without all others: kings, emperors, political leaders, financiers, merchant princes, moderators, artists, writers and all. For in any age the folk of the land and sea have never failed to produce their own writers or ballad-makers, their own poets, just as they have never failed to produce their own artists in paint and stone. But for those others—in the final count they can be forgotten and perhaps even forgiven.

The advent of steam, of the steam drifter, drained the living power from innumerable fishing villages on the Moray Firth into the big ports of Wick,

Fraserburgh and Peterhead, and as we now approached Fraserburgh this became increasingly evident. but before we entered Fraserburgh we came upon an extraordinary sight, that was surely a portent and a sign: a cemetery of drifters. It was as if a fleet of them, like a school of enormous whales, had run themselves aground, become permanently stranded, and rotted. From some the planking was entirely gone, leaving the gaunt ribs for wind and salt spray to whistle through. They had all taken the ground head-on, some had slewed round, at least one had broken its back. It seemed a tragic end to a story that in every case had been charged with danger and courage, hope and despair, continuous vigilance, ceaseless adventure, in summer seas, in winter's smashing storms. If each skeleton could tell its true story, and tell the stories, too, of those who had walked its decks and of those who waited on shore for a return that brought the welcome news of safety first and of plenty or poverty next, this bay, this cemetery, would be the birth-place of an imperishable epic. Each boat had been deliberately stranded. When a skipper-owner walks away for the last time from a vessel that he has sailed on the right side of death for thirty years, a vessel that he and his crew and their families have depended on, through good fortune and bad, what a parting must be there! Perhaps only those who deal with the sea can understand.

Fraserburgh was in the thick of the summer herring fishing, and drifters were continuously arriving as we walked about the quays. But herring were scarce. A few crans were the order of the day—and a few crans are not enough to earn the £60 a week that one skipper told me were needed to keep things going. These drifters are in a bad way, and the banks know it. A skipper-owner, pointing to his drifter, said he had offered her in full commission to his banker as security for a loan of £50, and his banker had refused the loan. Another suggested that the days of the drifter are num-bered. He cast his eyes over the scores of vessels about him, as they crowded in, nose to the quay, and remarked: 'Not one of them is under twenty years old'. One could feel the air of gloom all along the quays. Most of these quiet, hardy men had known the port in the old sailing days. One intelligent skipper's verdict: 'Things in the port are better organised now, but times are not so good.' Which was rather a terrible comment on what we call progress.

Peterhead, swarming with drifters from ports as far apart as Buckie and Lowestoft, presented the same state of affairs. Old drifters and remorseless debt—making one think back to that portentous sea-cemetery. Yet the tenacious seamen fight on. One or two good shots, and their spirits rise again and hope is renewed. They are a great race.

I got the impression, too, of a spirit abroad in Peterhead that is not going to take defeat easily. Some of the keenest minds have begun to understand that the final value of a sea's harvesting may rest not entirely in the realm of economics but more and more in the realm of politics. They see what foreign governments have been able to do for their fisheries. They are asking shrewd questions—and are likely to go on asking them. One wise old worker on the quays began to explain how and why the industry had never gone ahead in organising new selling methods, as all other great industries had done. For fifteen years, he said, he had been advocating such a simple thing as the packing of cured herrings in small, round tin boxes, but no one would take the matter up. Who wants to buy half a barrel at a time? And I must say I think he is quite right. If one cannot get a few cured herrings at a time—one buys none at all.

But this is not an economic essay. It is no more than a suggestion that there are many ways of spending a touring holiday and that there are more things to look at than mountains in this old heroic northern land of ours.

AUTUMN IN THE CUILLIN

SM, 1931

SOME YEARS AGO, in a little hotel on the west coast of Skye, I put it to a celebrated member of the Alpine Club: 'But *why* do you climb mountains?' Our nightly talks had gone far enough to make the question less naive than it seems, and, as though about to say something revealing, he paused a moment ... then, with the reticence of a faint shrug, suggested: 'But why do you play golf?'

The counter was the more amusingly effective in that no disparaging comparison was really intended. Before, however, I had imaginatively accompanied him for a few days and nights on the Himalayas, the amusement passed into something more resembling that shiver in the spine, that cold thrill of fascination, which only boyhood is supposed to experience to the full ... and possibly for much the same reason, the difference being one of degree; for rock-climbing in its great aspect is to the, say, reputed Red Indian adventures of Buffalo Bill what the religion of the higher mathematics of Bertrand Russell is to the emotions that govern the accountancy of a boy's penny bank. The serenity, the austerity, of the peak ... that is also a peak of personal conquest. In that high, rarefied air, with the world in its dizzying danger conquered and underfoot, there must come to the true climber a satisfaction so profound that aspiration itself is drained for the moment, and all the earth in its hills and valleys and seas unrolls itself like a mighty map which one looks abroad upon—and slightly down.

'But why the Cuillin rather than other Scottish rocks?'

'Because,' I was informed, 'the rock is reliable and the surface of just the right texture for a hold.'

The time was autumn, and in autumn this world of the Cuillin is a lovely world. Nowadays the rush to Scotland (apart, of course, from the normal shooting influx) is associated with long daylight and summer at its height. One can understand it—and yet sympathise, for a perfect early autumn day has a glory in its light and colour and strength that July has never dreamed of. This must inevitably come to be generally known, as will also the early summer period of fairy greens and invigorating tangs, and the Highland holiday season will stretch its two months into five. Meantime, for the discerning, there is the approach to Coire na Creiche from Carbost, when not so much the heather is in bloom as the ling is in gold.

Ford Madox Hueffer tells of an English day spent with Conrad trying to get the right term to describe the blue-purple colour of a field of cabbage. Every likely sound in English and French was called up, listened to, and dismissed. Against that cabbage plot—this honey-golden moor, and one is provoked, to a smile that, let it quickly be said, is perfectly wrong, but that may be pardonable because of the humour that inhabits all perfect understanding.

Yet there is no surer way of proving one's impotence in anything like precise expression than by an effort at getting the right epithet. If not at the actual moment of experience—then afterwards. 'Now, how would you describe it?' meaning: 'How can we fix it for ever?' And one man would run through all the sherries from Amontillado to East India, and another would wonder about the ever-changing lights in some women's (meaning, no doubt, some woman's) hair, and a third would be dead certain that, anyhow, 'wine-red moor' didn't come within a mile of it.

And beneath these stumbling, half-articulate efforts would be the glory that was the moor and the grandeur that was the Cuillin; and of these two the glory would linger the more disturbingly because of that in it which had been intimate in a nameless way and yet impossible to hold, leaving the mind in the dead days craving for it once more, for that essence of perishable beauty which it has secretly discriminated but for which it can find no word.

And so dipping down from the Glen Brittle road, you wander across the fringe of this moor towards Coire na Creiche—to come upon a stream ... whose rock-basins instantly take your breath away, as though your hot body had physically met their cool shock. The rounded boulders are an indescribable shade of blue—or is it green?—no, blue; and the water that covers them is almost invisible, so crystal pure it is. The colours of moor and hill had a depth which only a Gaelic adjective can make an effort at conveying, but the colour of these rock-basins held a surface quality and purity altogether classic. Perhaps we are too readily at the mercy of our Greek mythology, of a dipping foot, of a slim white body; after all, quite an airy imagining, for is not the water blue and cool and passionless, with all of life in its exquisite moment of contact, of recoil?

And half-way up the two thousand feet, taking the easy climb by the scree, we pause for breath and a look around—and are suddenly held by the sight of a woman, across the gully from us, poised on the cliff-edge, a loop of rope in her hand. The moment has its thrill. True, her male rig-out denies her the identity of a Greek goddess, denies her almost any identity, but her position there on the sheer rock-edge, so that one could imagine a breath blowing her over, holds the fascination of the peril that is separated from destruction by no more than a matter of faultless balance.

And then the top of the Cuillin and the roof of this western world. Loch Coruisk, dark and still, lies below us, but so far below us that it might well be below the surface of life altogether—at any rate, of our life, if not of the Shades. Gaunt mountain walls shut it in, except at its far end, where it issues to the sea ... the sea, the ocean, which man so readily makes his symbol for eternity, or Nirvana, with the individual life no more than a bubble on its surface.

So long we rested on the top that a touch of chill came like a living fore-breath, and presently white cloud was not so much descending upon us as enveloping us and passing us by, torn into ragged, fantastic masses by the dark rock-peaks about us. To see a cloud being wracked and torn before your eyes, yet never pausing in its eerie, hurrying silence, yet never departing, to feel its ghostly fingers on your face, its chill touch on your body, is an experience that will also crave to be relived ... and that will succeed, whether one wishes it or not—in sleep!

But the keyword that opens all this western world of the Gael is—leisure. Not to do a lot in a short time, but rather to do a very little in a long time. Perhaps, after all, East and West do meet—in the ancient saying of the Orient: 'Haste is an attribute of devils.'

DOOM IN THE MORAY FIRTH

SM, 1935

ON A RECENT fine morning, the quays of Wick were enlivened by as ardent a piece of discussion as has been heard there for many a day. Indeed 'discussion' is a polite term for the epithets that flew about with the vehemence incidental to an older and happier age. There in the selling mart it was almost as if Wick had come alive again, as if the independent spirit of the daring seamen of past generations was once more raising its face, bloody perhaps, but still unbowed!

The storm arose through an action taken by the recently constituted Herring Industry Board, an action that might have had its ironic humour were it not fraught with such misfortune for so many fishermen on the Moray Firth coast. And here let it be said at once that every consideration is extended to the Board in their admittedly difficult task of regulating a national industry fallen on evil times. It is only too easy to crab the efforts of a constructive body. In any form of reorganisation or rationalisation, someone it seems is bound to suffer. No one realises this better than your clear-headed northern fisherman. But any sort of reorganisation or national control that inflicts needless hardship on the very people whom it is presumably designed to relieve or assist must expect an outcry and damaging criticism. And this is precisely what happened.

First let it be explained that in the old days the summer herring fishing, from such ports or creeks as Wick, Lybster, Dunbeath, and Helmsdale, ran from about the last week in July to the end of October. It was from the inshore herring caught and locally cured in September and October that the surrounding countryside procured its full barrels and half barrels for winter use—'the tattie herring'. They did not wish herring caught and cured earlier in the season. A herring, like any other fish, does not improve the longer it is kept in brine. Anyway, such has been the traditional practice. Again, as September approaches, the herring come inshore and may be caught in the drift nets of the new type of motor boat (just under forty feet) which these last few years has been making a valiant effort to bring the decayed northern harbours to life again. This lively sea-boat, with its equipment of seine net, cod net, and herring net, is of an ideal size for Moray Firth fishing, because it can cover the local fishing grounds adequately and because its overhead or running expenses are negligible compared with those of the large drifter. But when it comes to competition in deep sea fishing with the large drifter, which carries a crew of ten men and a fleet of a hundred and twenty nets, the local motor boat is at a grave disadvantage. This was completely exemplified during the herring fishing season in Wick this summer. The large drifters went fifty to sixty miles to sea to meet the herring shoals, returning to port with their catches for immediate sale and cure. The motor boats of Helmsdale, Dunbeath, and Lybster, could not follow them there and accordingly had a very thin time. They did not complain about that. The battle is still to the swift and the money to the rich. And in this case let it be clear that the majority of the drifters engaged were from the south, owned to a considerable extent by large English syndicates—a factory system that runs completely counter to the old Scottish ideal of the skipper-owner. In Wick, once the greatest fishing port of the north, counting its boats by hundreds, there are now six drifters and less than six motor boats. But, as I say, there was no complaint on the score of an English invasion, no outcry against big financial interests raiding the home fishing banks. The drifters scooped such pool as there was, and then duly prepared to depart to other waters where shoals were forming. By the first week in September they were gone, the herring had come inshore, and the motor boats from the creeks were getting good catches of excellent quality. Their season had at last arrived and haste must be made if outstanding debts were to be met and the winter was to be looked forward to with anything but dark misgivings.

With shots varying up to thirty crans, local boats arrived at Wick—*to find that no curer could legally buy their fish.* The Herring Board had caused to be published a day or so before a Notice prohibiting the cure of herring on the East Coast of Scotland 'between the 2nd day of September and the 31st day of October, 1935'. The Board was wired to the London address given on the Notice. Could not the herring be cured locally for local consumption? No. The herring could not be cured by anyone for any purpose whatsoever!

But this seemed absurd. Had not each boat its new licence from that very Board permitting the catching of herring up until the end of September? True. They were not debarred from *catching* them during September; they could even sell them for freshing or kippering; but—they *must not have them cured.*

After the consternation, the discussion, as has been said, became more forceful than polite. The tragedy of the fishing decline on this coast ensured that only a few boats were actually concerned, which made the principle at stake all the more important, for there is wrapped up in it the question of profit which alone makes general revival possible. What could be sold was sold in small quantities to local carts for cadging about the countryside, and a few crans were sent to Aberdeen as samples, it was understood, for tinning purposes. But the biggest catch of all had to be held by the skipper, who would have accepted an offer of roughly half of what had been the ruling price a few days before. He decided to defy the new powers and to cure the herring whatever came of it. To do that, it was pointed out, would possibly call down upon him severe measures, including even the suspension by the Board of his fishing licence. The retort came to the effect that nothing could be severer or more desperate than the position in which the honourable craft of deep-sea fishing had already landed him! Whereupon he procured barrels and salt and set about curing his catch on the quay-wall in front of his own boat.

And there, at the moment of writing, the position rests. Strong representations have been made from the fishing ports named above, but so far the Board have declined to move. In Helmsdale the writer found that two crews of women had actually been engaged (on the strength of the licence to fish during September) to deal with the September catch for cure and subsequent local sale. And now not only will loss be entailed by the fishing community there, but the surrounding country of crofters and others will be done out of their winter herrings—or, at least, they will be compelled to buy herring cured earlier (which they don't want) at the big ports at a bigger price.

Again with every desire on our part to be fair and to appreciate the difficulties involved in reorganising a national industry, yet this Order of the Herring Board does seem hasty and ill-considered. To permit during September–October curing of herring caught by local boats along these coasts could not interfere with whatever major designs the Board may have, because the large southern drifters would not want to take part in it. It is essentially an inshore fishing, of anchor nets and small fleets of drift nets, peculiarly suited to the new motor boat. The objection, mostly hinted, that the herring is not of good quality for curing was completely disproved on the quays of Wick. The herring is of a smallish size and of excellent quality— and certainly superior to much that was landed, and cured for export, in mid-summer on these same quays.

But the real tragedy of this business lies in the blow struck at the strong local endeavour of recent years to revive the fishing creeks of the coast. Let one instance be given. In Dunbeath, the fishermen organised themselves and through an energetic local secretary managed one way or another to raise the very considerable sum of £500 for extension and repairs to the local harbour. In face of this earnest effort, the Government stood in handsomely and the work of extending the pier was started and duly completed. Further work of dredging and embanking has still to be done—and will be done by local effort, if the future shows any hope at all. And now it would appear that what the Government gave with one hand they are prepared to take away with the other. For this order restricting curing amounts to this: a discrimination in favour of the large southern drifter against the local boats. This policy, proceeded with logically, will inevitably mean the extermination of the fishing communities along our northern coasts. The big fish curers, the wealthy English syndicates, may not object. They can control the finances of any port. But surely the fishermen and crofters bred out of that northern land are still citizens of our country and their need desperate enough to entitle them to consideration and fairness. Yet fishing creeks like those named were not even consulted about this new measure, though they have a sea tradition behind them that is as splendid as any in these Islands.

The problem of the Moray Firth, with its seine-netting (which everywhere carries its own self-destruction) and trawling, is of major importance, for there are no finer breeding banks in our seas. If this recent Order is typical of what may follow, then our coastal fishermen may be justified in their growing belief that it would have been better for them if the Herring Industry Board, complete with London address, had never been spawned.

ONE FISHER WENT SAILING

The Plight of the West Coast Herring Ports

SM, 1937

FOR WEEKS WE have been cruising down the West Coast of Scotland in our small boat, and if our personal adventures have been many and exciting, there has been one constant factor in our experience, and that is the poverty of the sea-fishing. We had anticipated no difficulty in catching white fish of all kinds: we found that apart from being unable to catch fish ourselves, though we had most of the usual lures, and used all sorts of bait from mussels to crushed partan, we were unable to buy fresh fish, except in the towns of Tobermory and Oban—and there the fish was not locally caught but came from distant cities.

I am aware that this, to dwellers on the East Coast, may seem an exaggeration, for where are there finer fishing banks in the world, both for quality and quantity, than on the West Coast of Scotland, with its innumerable inlets and bays, its sands for flat fish, its rocks—a glance at an Admiralty chart should be enough to frighten any but the most foolhardy amateur navigator—for lobsters, and its endless variety of bottom-feeding for the usual marketable white fish? Yet I am stating no more than a fact from personal experience, and when I cast back carefully through that experience, I find myself hesitating over only one modifying instance, and that occurred in Iona, where we got kippers from Stornoway, and, being McIver's kippers, they were first-class.

We did come on one small kippering station on the mainland, where the herring were gutted and cleaned by a rather marvellous machine, but after that they were not smoked but dyed in vats, and we were sufficiently prejudiced in favour of the smoked kipper, with its crisp flavour, not to care for this dyed article of commerce, however brown and pretty it might look. It was shortly afterwards that we saw something of the controversy in the press on this subject, arising out of statements made in the House of Commons by the Member for Argyll, and though our sympathies are flagrantly in favour of any system of herring cure that will ensure a popular sale and thereby assist the fishermen, yet after taking every factor into consideration we were inclined to support the Member for Argyll, and for this overriding reason, that in the long run it is the best type of article that pays, and by that we mean the most palatable and wholesome. The trouble so often with the smoked kipper as exposed for sale in our shops is that it was not a herring in really prime condition to begin with. A housewife can tell this at once by its thin, watery taste. After having had bad luck once or twice in her purchases, she simply stops buying. It is possible that the dyeing process may conceal lack of quality to some extent by keeping the flesh apparently more moist and full of oil, thereby ensuring readier sale to the poor or the indiscriminating: but at the back of this there is the undoubted fact—as in the case of these Stornoway kippers we got in Iona—that a sound herring, properly cured by smoke, is the most palatable form of the kipper, and therefore the most likely in the long run to win a steady and increasing market. Those we got were so delicious that we boiled some of them, and the flesh came away from the bone as it does from the bone of a prime finnan haddie.

But we got them only once, and we were never lucky enough to find any fresh herring at all. The West Coast season has so far (I write in the first days of August) been a complete failure. At Mallaig we saw a couple of drifters when we should have seen fifty. In Oban we were saddened by the spectacle of herring curing stations overgrown with grass and cooperages dilapidated, a scene all too familiar to us in so many of the Moray Firth fishing creeks. A fish salesman gave it to me as his opinion that Oban as a herring port is finished.

'But what if a late herring season comes along on the West?' I asked.

'Make no difference', he answered. 'Mallaig and Castlebay will handle it easy—particularly so far as the Scottish boats are concerned.' I asked him what he meant by that. 'The Scottish boats are so much in debt that they can't fit out for a late fishing—very few of them, anyway.'

It was the answer I had expected. I asked him if the Herring Industry Board's report was out. In the same laconic voice he said it was. Later, in the press, I read extracts from it and recognised it as the most desperate document yet issued on the subject, amounting in pith to little more than a statement endeavouring, by the aid of analytical reason, to show the inevitability of the early death of the whole Scottish herring fishing industry based on the system of the family boat. As far as I could see, there was not one constructive suggestion in it, and what I wrote two months ago in these columns was being borne out exactly. (See following essay, 'The Family Boat')

Meantime, standing on the quay at Oban, where two trawlers were unloading and a third manoeuvring for a berth, I asked the fish salesman how it was that we could not catch fish on the West. As he looked at the trawlers, a dry expression came into his face. I could not help smiling at this silent comment, for the depredations of these trawlers on the inshore banks had been mentioned to me by fishermen everywhere. Now, though I knew the trawlers could clean up a fishing bank pretty thoroughly if they got half a chance, yet I was not disposed to blame them altogether. Let me put it mildly by saying that the West Coast does tend to breed a natural inertia. If one has food today, tomorrow is soon enough to try to get some more: and if one has cash to buy fish from Glasgow, why worry at all about catching them? Moreover, I had got a pretty thorough insight into the operation of unemployment benefit or the dole on the West, and more particularly in the Islands, where occasional instances of what is termed 'faked employment' have attained the perfection of an art. But I cannot begin to go into this here without appearing to misrepresent those who draw benefit—and to do as much would not only be unjust but stupid, for we are now discussing an Act framed for industrial areas and completely inapplicable to the conditions of life and work in the Highlands and Islands. I can sympathise with the Scottish Office in the task it has in front of it—and even more with the man who can achieve the certainty of the dole over against the tempestuous uncertainty of catching fish that no longer appear to exist!

What the outcome of all this is going to be is another matter. From my own investigations, I can see no outcome, if the present conditions continue, but the end of the old Highland life and polity as we have known it, and in its place a sporting landlordism and tourism all complete. I do not write this lightly. But neither may I avoid the facts, encountered everywhere, of depopulation, of disappearing crofts, of half ruinous fishing villages, of young men refusing to go to sea—except as deck hands on summer yachts or trading vessels. I know of places where the young men not only do not know how to handle boats and to fish, but—more deadly even—do not know where the fishing banks are, a knowledge dying with the old.

So I come back to these trawlers at Oban and wonder if they have helped this decline in some measure.

'How much fish have they landed today?' I asked.

'I don't know today's figures but on Monday they landed 2,600 boxes. Some days it's less.'

For one small quay it seemed an astonishing quantity of fish, and no day passed without hundreds of boxes being landed. I remembered a solitary fisherman on the Ross of Mull who used slug worm for fishing flounder in the Sound of Iona. He told me he had been getting good catches of small haddock in a bay on the north of the Ross. A trawler came in one night. 'After that I didn't see a tail.' He was not the sort of man who would exaggerate. He had no particular animus against the trawlers. He accepted them as he accepted bad weather. And he would have worked his fingers off rather than try for the dole.

A man in Tobermory visited forty creels one morning without getting a single lobster. He was very despondent and felt like throwing the whole business up. From Skye, round Ardnamurchan Point, and down the Sound of Mull, there was the same tale from the men with whom I talked. Somewhere thereabouts, I ran into the theory that trawling affected the lobster spawn. The trawlers can get blamed for too much—like giving a dog a bad name—and this theory sounded pretty far-fetched! Yet in the long run there is a balance in nature, so that, for example, one would not expect to find peregrine falcons where there was no other bird life. That trawlers poach inshore banks there can be no doubt. That the official effort to detect them is ludicrously inadequate there is likewise no doubt. One cannot blame the fishery cruiser, any more than one would blame a single gamekeeper for failing to keep down poaching in the whole of Argyll.

To blame the trawlers is to ask too much of human nature. Indeed, as I looked at these iron vessels, their rust whitened by salt water and gulls, I knew I was looking at the most daring vessels afloat, manned by the finest and most intrepid seamen to be found on any of the oceans of the world. They have the air of buccaneers. No slacking or grousing against the Government here. They take their living out of the teeth of danger, in the worst seas fought by man, and a slowly meandering fishery cruiser's gun or the wailing of a pack of crofters is not going to trouble them much. You won't stop trawling by appealing to something called a moral sense, certainly not in a world dominated by Stock Exchanges and by shore syndicates, which inform a skipper that his existence depends on getting boxes of fish. Besides, the power of these shore syndicates is felt in official places, in a way that the lack of power of the crofter-fisher is not.

The whole existing process is cumulative, and its end certain, so far as our old Highland life is concerned. That does not mean, of course, that the process could not be stopped or at least very tangibly affected. It could. Trawling could be stopped on the inshore banks tomorrow, for example, if the Government really wished to stop it; just as the Scottish herring fleet could be revitalised, if certain things happened to its organisation and the Government decided, for purposes of food and defence, that its seamen were too invaluable to lose. But we have discussed that before. Meantime, the one certain thing I have encountered in my cruise is the common decline of the West.

'But at least these trawlers bring a lot of business to Oban?'

He shook his head. 'They have the fish all ready in iced boxes, and load them direct on to the train for the south. That's all.'

We watched this neat dispatch of business. The train shunted on to the quay.

'Are there no local boats fishing from Oban?'

'There is supposed to be one,' he said.

And there we were back at a sore point. For there is something in the reputed lack of initative of the West Coast man. How this has come about, by what discouragements and official repressions or neglect, by what succumbing to a feeling of hopelessness in the fight, it may not be easy to determine.

Then suddenly our thoughts got a queer twist. When the East Coast herring fishers—whose history proves them men of initiative, fearlessness, and a tremendous capacity for the most gruelling toil—are at last down and out, their boats derelict, under age and debt, will some chance visitor, eating trawl-caught fish from Hull in the hotels of Wick or Buckie, wonder at the supine local concerned no longer with catching fish but with wangling money out of the Buroo? Is that an impossible situation? In some degree, is it not happening already?

We could not find the solitary boat that was supposed to fish out of Oban, so we bought white fish in a shop and were assured that it was fresh and very good, as it had come direct from Aberdeen.

THE FAMILY BOAT

Its Future in Scottish Fishing

SM, 1937

NO MORE CERTAIN indication of the desperate condition of the herring-fishing industry could be found than in the recent insidious press campaign against the Scottish system of family-owned boats and in favour of the English system of company-owned boats. Responsible fishing opinion in Scotland is satisfied that the campaign was officially inspired, though direct evidence is naturally difficult to obtain. This may be a political point and therefore not to be pursued here, though there are so many parallels to precisely this sort of attack in Scotland's economic history that at least Northern opinion may be forgiven its apparent assumption of official inspiration. The truly insidious nature of the attack lies in this: it is known that the Scottish boats are heavily in debt; if to this fact could be added the idea that the Scottish system is uneconomic compared with the English, then not only a Government department, but banks, ships' chandlers, and private individuals would hesitate to finance such a system and its ruin would be inevitable. Discredit a man or a system in so subtle a way and his or its doom is written, economic collapse being hastened by the very despair that overtakes the human factors involved. Evidence of this truth may all too readily be found in practically every port on the east coast of Scotland at the present moment.

The Scottish Herring Producers' Association resisted this attack strongly in letters to the Ministry of Fisheries, the Secretary for Scotland, and the Fishery Board for Scotland, and produced facts and figures designed to show that the Scottish system of individual ownership compared favourably with the English company system. If the Scottish boats made a smaller number of landings per boat during the English fishing season, it was because, unlike the English boats, they did not go to sea on Sundays. And if the average shot was smaller, this again had to be offset against the fact that in the given period (6 October–28 November 1936) the English boats had fished on Sundays during October and on Saturday and Sunday nights during November, and accordingly must have landed considerable quantities of overday's and salted herrings. 'The present system of individual ownership in Scotland is not doomed to extinction,' declares the Association, 'and will never be replaced by company ownership.'

It is a valiant declaration, but even in the moment of making it the Association is aware that 'the English boats are backed by capitalists, who may keep on making losses, hoping to recoup themselves later on by the extinction of some of the individual Scottish owners, whose capital is tied up in his boat and gear.'

And therein lies the real danger. 'The cold truth is that from 1931 to 1934 herring boat-owners, both Scottish and English, made considerable losses. There was an improvement in 1935, and again in 1936, but the English-owned boats have no more surmounted their difficulties than have the Scottish.' True; but being 'backed by capitalists', they are more likely to surmount them, because they are better able to last the desperate pace.

The large company can always smash the small individual in any sphere of industrial effort from the local multiple shop to the foreign market. Moreover, when it comes to any such test of endurance, many factors other than the purely financial automatically align themselves in favour of 'big business'. Let me illustrate with a simple instance. There is more than one fishing port on the Moray Firth where fishermen's houses were condemned because they did not comply with local bye-laws regarding sanitation and cubic airspace. The humane local authority accordingly proceeds to build 'council houses' for those affected. The fishermen move in, but find that now they have no lofts and outside sheds for storing gear, painting buoys, or mending nets, as they had in the old homes. Result—they have to pay for storing their gear and for having it mended or repaired.

It may be protested that surely such a position could have been foreseen. I suggest that it might be an interesting exercise among the factors that manipulate our local authorities to discover why it never is.

Or take the case of the men who have cut their losses and gone in for the motor-engined boat and seine-netting for whitefish—an individual enterprise. I have talked to the best of them on both sides of the Firth and already they foresee the end. The slaughter of immature fish has been enormous. The grounds are getting less and less fruitful. Drag after drag often produces nothing of value. They are naturally tempted to poach within the three-mile limit. Many of them are already prepared for any workable system of restriction or regulation that would ensure a reasonable future for the catching of 'flats' and other white fish. But all they actually see in front of them are foreign trawlers in the Firth (where British trawlers are prohibited) swinging round on a three-mile radius and systematically cleaning the grounds. They have no feeling of security; no conviction that the Government will ever interfere to protect their interests against state-subsidised foreign boats or attempt in any way to assist them with grants or wise organisation. When the Government votes 1,500 million pounds for the defence programme it forgets about the drifters and trawlers, though the Admiralty used over 2,100 of them in the War. All that colossal sum for destruction, yet not one penny for the solitary part of the defence arm that in peace time is productive! It is reckoned that the Buckie fleet in the last fifteen years has lost over a million sterling. And to-day Buckie fishermen, the majority of whom are unemployed from November to June, have the pleasure of watching Danes landing fish at their home port.

Perhaps the basic trouble is that in Britain the fishing industry is not sufficiently organised—in England of not sufficient value—to be of importance in the political game. If Scotland had to deal with her own affairs, her fishing industry would at once be of major importance in her economy, and she would very soon be compelled to give it the attention that the Germans, Danes, Swedes and Norwegians give to theirs. Consider how energetically the Scandinavian countries, for instance, deal with the foreign trawler! But as things are, trouble on the London buses takes precedence in the minds of our Westminster legislators. Though that is less than the truth, for I have been unable to trace any Parliamentary discussion of the fishing industry throughout the life of the present Government. And as for the Herring Industry Board's plans for the reconstruction of the herring fleet, these 'moneylender's terms', as they have been aptly called, it is difficult not to agree with the fish-curer who suggested that their terms were meant not for restriction but for destruction.

Now in the absence of the staying power of shore capitalism, in the neglect of the Government, in the competition from outside by the state-subsidised foreigner, in the impossible nature of the Herring Board's financial offers, and finally in view of the crippling burden of debt already piled upon the Scottish drifter, it is difficult to feel as sure as the Herring Producers' Association apparently do that the Scottish system of individual ownership is going to stand the pace against the English combines or capitalism. For even at the worst, it is not a straight fight. Whenever the individual gets into debt he enters a region where the manipulator of finance begins to make his power felt. If you buy up my IOU's, you can smash me. The case may not be so direct and simple as all that, perhaps, but the principle is the same, at however many removes it may now be operating. The directing power of the English combine in Scottish fisheries is steadily growing. And there is a suggestion of over-strong protest in the statement by the Herring Producers' Association that is at least indicative of the trend. Not panic yet—but the trace of fear.

That is roughly the position, and for the Scottish herring fishing—and white fishing, too—it may well be a tragic one, and not only in the smashing economic loss to those concerned, but in the loss to our country of a system of work and craft requiring the finest human qualities. For though the Scottish system was built on the national love of individualism (stigmatised by some of our country's critics as her fatal bane in these days of capitalism or totalitarianism), yet this individualism always worked towards the family and communal good. This is a fact that cannot be too clearly emphasised. Within it, indeed, lies the suggestion of any contribution Scotland might make to world affairs to-day, for all her ancient institutions do show this concern for the rights and initiative of the individual coincident with the larger concern for the community. The skipper of the typical Scottish fishing boat has always been not only owner of his vessel but one of the crew, who called him naturally by his Christian name. He is one of themselves, one of a small company working for their common good, with powers of leadership and decision vested in him by necessity of their calling. Because of their common religious beliefs, for example, it would not occur to him to go to sea on Sunday—nor would any outside power compel him to go, whatever the material loss involved. To the dangerous business of the sea, he and his crew bring not only the anxious desire for gain, but also their beliefs and decencies, all the human factors that give to man his integrity and dignity. History shows that there have been no harder or more fearless workers in the world, but they have always carried their individual judgments of right and wrong with them. And this, I suggest, is of some significance in the world at the moment. For the problem as I see it is this: how to manage efficiently the economic machine and at the same time retain the maximum amount of individual freedom. The Scottish system of family-owned boats represents perhaps the only great industry left in the world to-day where some attempt at solving the problem continues to be made.

To contrast the English capitalist system of boat ownership, where skipper and men are like so many factory hands under orders from shore, would take too long here, though some day, by way of sidelight, the whole story of the Hull trawlers, directed by wireless under the ruthless demands of 'the market', may be told in all its dreadful detail. I know about it only at second-hand, but if half of what I have heard is true, then the stories of sociological novelists about the more infernal aspects of our city life would make, by comparison, merely pleasant Sunday afternoon reading.

In their fight against the English capitalist system, the Scottish Herring Producers' Association should be supported by every Scot who still has any care for individual liberty and decency. The Association itself should muster all its strength, organise it, approach Scottish MPs, compel their active assistance, and hammer at Westminster. I fear they might not get much out of Westminster. Nothing, if we may judge from the past. But in the process they might get a lot out of themselves, and in particular a clearer vision of where Scotland stands *vis-á-vis* Westminster. This is no veiled Nationalist suggestion. The matter is far too vital for it to get lost in political moves or prejudices. Though I am prepared to offer the Association this tip—if they come out with a strong demand for Scottish self-government, even threaten to join the National Party, they would get more attention from Westminster in ten days than they have got in ten years!

Assuming, however, that it was possible to get from any Government two immediate vital needs: (1) cancellation of existing boat debts and reasonable provision for new boats, and (2) proper protection of home fisheries together with active concern for foreign markets, would the individually owned Scottish fishing-boats be then in a position to face up to English capitalism or Continental subsidies?

They might for a time, but again, as I have suggested above, they would in the long run be on the losing side, simply because they would not have the backing and resources to tide them over difficult times. What further step, then, in organisation could they take so that, while retaining the principle, with all it implies, of 'family boats', they could at the same time be in a position to meet English capitalism or foreign subsidy with a combine of their own.

I suggest that the answer may be found in some system of co-operation similar to that which has proved so successful in Scandinavian countries. Co-operation implies duties and restrictions, but such duties and restrictions would be imposed by the fishermen themselves for their own good and not in the interests either of shore capitalism or of state control. If this were done on an inclusive scale, then they would find themselves in a superior position to the English combines for two reasons: (1) they would not have to provide profits for a capitalist organisation ashore, and (2) they would continue in their own interests to look after their own gear in a way that no driven wage-hand ever does.

With regard to (2), let me quote again from the Scottish Herring Producers' Association's letter: 'It is a well-known fact that the figure for upkeep of nets and management expenses for an English boat is on an average about £350 to £400 in excess of that for a Scottish boat. The Scottish fishermen have no management expense for their boat, no cost for storage of gear, and no shore staff to look after their gear. The fact that the nets are owned by them makes them more careful than the English fisherman in the handling of gear at sea.'

There is truth there, though it must not be forgotten that the English shore organisation does at least keep the boats going, while often relieving the fishermen themselves of many hampering tasks. With fish on the grounds in a short season, it would help the Scottish fisherman to know, for example, that, should he be unfortunate enough to lose his drift of nets, there was an organisation ashore that would rig him out again under conditions that his brother fishermen and himself had co-operatively agreed upon.

Co-operation in this way would be merely an enlargement, to meet modern conditions, of the old communal way of running affairs that is at the root of Scottish institutional life. Once they got their system properly organised and functioning, it would be extremely formidable. If Orkney can make three times her agricultural rental out of her own co-operative way of selling eggs, is it beyond hope that the Scottish fishermen with their great traditions and renowned fishing grounds could make shift to get out of debt? Co-operatively organised, Scottish fisheries would overcome English capitalism, and with a Government prepared to fair play on the international market, they would not need to fear even the state-subsidies of foreign countries.

THE WONDER STORY OF THE MORAY FIRTH

Anarchy, 1968

THERE WAS ONCE A TIME—and old folk still alive can remember the tail-end of it—when the seaboard round the Moray Firth went up in a human blaze—as hectic a blaze as ever was seen in any gold rush to the Klondyke. In the whole history of the Highlands, I know nothing like it. And the story has always fascinated me because here, for once, Highlanders were suddenly given the chance to get gold, for themselves—and how they set about it! The Klondykers certainly had nothing on them. It threw—and, I maintain, still throws—a light on all those notions about Highlanders being indifferent or lazy. Give them the proper chance ... however, let me stick to the story of what did happen when they got the chance.

The beginnings of the story coincide with the peak of the Clearances in these northern parts. From whole straths, up Kildonan way, the people were evicted and their homes destroyed. We all know something about that tragic business, and happily I am not concerned with it here. How reluctant we are even to remember it—and how pleasant to tell a story of another kind! If I mention it, then, it is because, though great numbers of the evicted were shipped to Canada, many of them built shacks by the seashore and managed to keep alive long enough to take part in the new great adventure—the adventure with the sea.

Behind them was the land—and they knew what had happened to them there. In front of them—the sea; and the wonderful thing about the sea was that it was free to them all. They could sink or swim in it. Haddock and cod and flukes and herring were not game within the meaning of any Act. What they could catch they could eat. Only, to begin with, they were not very good at the catching. Probably many of them, from far inland glens, had never even seen the sea, for pony tracks or drove roads were the means of communication then. However, they learned, and always there had been those, living near the coast, who had ventured out in a small boat from a wild creek or narrow beach. So knowledge spread and help was given in the way help always was given to neighbours in distress in any Highland community. To transgress the ancient law of hospitality brought deep shame.

Well, that was roughly the position along great stretches of the Moray Firth in the opening years of last century, and if, in what I am going to say, I stick in particular to the northern coast—from well south of Helmsdale right along to Wick—it is because here the difficulties were concentrated. In the first place, it had no hinterland with economic resources, no towns, no industries, no sources of capital for boats and gear; and, in the second place, from Helmsdale to Wick the coastline was—it still is—one menacing wall of cliff, with little more than stormy breaks in it, and few enough of them. To triumph, to make a Klondyke of the sea, *here*, must have seemed utterly unthinkable.

The position was even worse than that, for such historic efforts as had been made, by royal or parliamentary action, to encourage Scottish fisheries, had always, in the main, proved ineffective. Over a long period of time the Dutch had been the real sea-fishing masters, with their well-equipped fleets of boats and their accompanying large vessels or busses for curing herring at sea. The success of the Dutch is summed up in the old saying: 'Amsterdan was built on herring bones'.

Then someone had a thought, and the thought was a stroke of genius. More wonderful still, it was translated into an Act of Parliament, in the year 1809. And the stroke was this: that for every barrel of sound herring cured *on shore* a bounty would be paid of two shillings. Now there had long been a small bounty payment for fish *exported*. But here the bounty of two shillings was to be paid whether the barrel of herring was exported or not. No need now to emulate the Dutch way of catching and curing at sea. To the curer of one barrel of good herring *on shore*, a bounty of two shillings—or subsidy, as we would say.

That two shillings then were worth many times more than two shillings today does not give the whole picture, not for those folk whom I have mentioned, too many of them with miserable strips of land that in the best of seasons could hardly keep body and soul together. In the absence of written records, we have to use a little imagination, if we are going to get an echo of the kind of conversation that must have passed between them. And even then we would have to translate it from Gaelic, for Gaelic was the mother tongue from far south of Helmsdale to within a few miles of Wick *then*—and, indeed, for another two generations. However, they came at the English in time and I can hear them sizing up the situation in 1809 like this: 'Boys, if we can get something that will float, and a herring net or two nets, and bring four or three creels of herring to the curer, we can be sure of two shillings in our hand, we can be sure of that whateverway—not to speak of what the curer will add to the two shillings, which should be another two shillings for us at the least, if there's competition among the curers at all. Four or maybe five shillings for a cran of herring—in our hand!' It was a big thought. And a thought they were free to multiply. The Highlander has never been deficient in imagination and he was a born hunter. The whole thing was right into his creel. It went to his head. And so he started.

Even the Government must have cheered, for in 1815 they lifted the two-shilling subsidy to four shillings. That did it! If the doing was necessary—but then the Government must have begun to realise that not only were these Highlanders hauling gold from the sea, but helping to sweep the Dutch off it. It had become a national affair in wealth—and international in trade and policy.

What extraordinary scenes must have been enacted then, scenes of contrivance and ingenuity, bargaining, a promise to pay the rare one who could lend a pound or two, a promise not in writing but, more solemnly, by a spit in the palm and a handshake!

By the courtesy of the Fishery Board—I suppose I should call it the Department of Agriculture and Fisheries now—I was given permission many years ago, when I was researching into this whole matter, to inspect official records where I could find them, and I can remember calling on the Fishery officer in Helmsdale and discovering a ledger of official transactions for that very year of 1815. At the moment I cannot recollect the exact number of curers already operating in Helmsdale in 1815, but if I say a round dozen I am near enough. There were entries also regarding fishing creeks from south of Helmsdale and north to Lybster, for Helmsdale then was the official headquarters of all that stretch of coast and its business centre. In this way I got a grasp of the earlier stages of this extraordinary story.

However, as we know only too well—stroke of genius or no stroke of genius—what the Government gives with one hand it has the other and stronger hand ever ready to take back. So in the 1820s the Government decreed that the subsidy would be withdrawn, not in one fell swoop, but shilling by shilling, until by 1830 the lot would be gone. You can imagine the outcry. Ruination! What happened was that the industry took the loss in its stride and swept on to greater triumphs. By the 1840s there were up to 250 boats fishing out of Helmsdale in the summer season. But the total of all the crews of the boats is only one item, for behind them were curers, coopers, women gutters and packers, makers of herring nets and creels, shopkeepers, carriers, seamen engaged in the export trade—a whole complex living swarm of human life. Then, remember that Helmsdale only started herring fishing less than 30 years before, in those years when the terrible Clearances were at their height.

I look at the map in my mind, with *some* of the fishing place-names south and north of Helmsdale: Embo, Golspie, Brora, Portgower, Helmsdale, Berriedale, Dunbeath. Latheronwheel, Forse, Swiney, Lybster. After that, Clyth and the high cliffs, with the remarkable Whaligoe, on the way to the great fishing port of Wick. Of course, Wick had long had commerce with the sea, but as late as 1767 its fishermen still regarded herring as bait for white fish. But by 1840 Wick had 428 native boats and 337 strange boats at the herring fishing. But again, by official record, *total* personnel engaged at the peak of the summer fishing was no less than 7,882. May I say, in passing, that anyone interested in such statistics, and in the kinds of boats and gear used, will find it all in that fascinating and authoritative book by Peter F Anson, called *Fishing Boats and Fisher Folk of the East Coast of Scotland*.

Meanwhile, let me glance at a more directly human aspect of the story and in a somewhat different light. In that same year, 1840, was published a

Statistical Account of Scotland, written mostly by ministers of the Gospel about their various parishes. Here is the Reverend Charles Thomson counting the number of—no, not boats, but public houses in Wick and reaching a grand total of 45. Says he: 'The herring fishing has increased wealth, but also wickedness. No care is taken of the 10,000 young strangers of both sexes, crowded together with the inhabitants during the six weeks of the fishery and exposed to drink and every other temptation.' So he called the pubs, 'Seminaries of Satan and Belial'. Apparently on occasion up to 500 gallons of whisky were disposed of in a day in Wick. A fair dram, I admit! And how interesting it would be to find out just how and where and with what results that dram got drunk! But I have only time to balance this by another picture of life, from which Satan and Belial were certainly absent, and which continued to within living memory: that of the crews of hundreds upon hundreds of boats at sea on a quiet evening, after their nets had been shot, taking up, one after another, one of the Psalms of David, until it seemed the sea itself sang and the cliffs and the cottages were held in wonder.

A tireless, tough, and God-fearing people, taking their lives in their hands, on these treacherous coasts, in their small open boats—and sending their tens of thousands of barrels of herring deep into Germany, into the Baltic Sea, and far into Russia.

I cannot pursue the story here and tell how boats got bigger, got decked, until finally the steam drifter took over and concentrated the herring fishing in a few large ports. Many of the smaller creeks, which once knew such a surge of warm life, are now quite derelict. But the men and women of that time—for nearly a whole century—did something more remarkable, with more wonder of achievement in it, than any story of mine could ever adequately   tell.

THE FRENCH SMACK

SM, 1940

LESS THAN TWO MONTHS before the outbreak of war I was on an island in the Outer Hebrides, the guest of a seaman who had a thirty-five-foot fishing boat driven by an old Kelvin engine. I have described elsewhere how we loaded her with young sheep and set out for certain distant rock-islands in the Atlantic, whose green tops were used as grazing grounds. I did little more than mention a French smack encountered in that wild remote region, because our real interest centred in the exciting business of pushing the sheep we had taken with us up the cliffs and, even more difficult, driving those on top down and into the heaving boat. Many an actor has gained distinction on the films for less hazardous work than that accomplished by two or three young members of our crew on these rock-faces.

Events have happened since then, however, to bring the French smack into memory's picture with particular vividness. She was first sighted when the skipper and I were down below, and by the time we got on deck, she was disappearing round one of the high islands. I gathered from the remarks that were passed that she was a Frenchman and that she was poaching. Poaching what? Lobsters. And at that I was assailed by a shock of wonder and admiration. I knew of the grumblings and lassitude of some of our native lobster-fishers—and on that heaving sea it seemed a far cry to France!

However, when we had finished with two of the islets, and were rounding some rocks to deal with two more, we came upon the Frenchman innocently at anchor, and I thought to myself that the skipper had been mistaken. How could they be sure that this vessel was engaged on such an enterprise so far from her own shores? The answer came with dramatic swiftness. There was a yell from the look-out, the wheel was spun, and I just had time to see some cork floats being sucked under before the engine gave a mighty thump—and then silence. The engineer's astonished head appeared. The gear lever had all but hit him. For one moment he had thought the whole engine was being torn out of the boat. We had fouled the rope of presumably one of the Frenchman's lobster pots in the open seaway!

It was surely a moment that warranted on the part of our quiet-mannered skipper a slight exclamation of annoyance, to put it mildly. There was none.

It was now after ten o'clock at night and the overcast sky, if not immediately threatening, did not herald serene weather. There was no harbour here, no place where a boat could be beached; nothing but rock walls and, in one or two spots, the most fugitive of anchorages. I remembered the trouble my wife and I had had when the painter of our dinghy had been sucked down by the shaft and wound round it so tightly that after we had cut the rope we could not disengage the coils from the shaft, and could not shove the gear-lever forward or astern.

When at last the rope had been cut on both sides of the shaft, I saw the skipper quietly taking the severed floats on board. After one of the lads had worked for a time at the coils round the shaft with the boathook, it was decided to try the engine. She started; she took the gear lever; she went forward. At twenty-five years a Kelvin can be moody, as I knew; but— 'Mohooker, she's tough!'

We slid on, heading for our landing, and passed close by the Frenchman. 'Has anyone a pencil?' There was a hunt, and finally her name and registry number were duly noted.

But meantime not a sign from the Frenchman. Not a light. It might have been a ship of the dead. A deserted pirate ship. Her mainsail, all set, clacked loudly as it swung from side to side in the wind, while she rolled in the swell. Green-painted, with square stern, she was not a big vessel. I doubted if she was more than forty-five feet. She was beamy certainly, but when I was told that in addition to all her gear of ropes and lobster pots, she carried a great internal tank in which she stored alive a vast catch of lobsters, I was inclined to be sceptical. But I was wrong. Why? Because a vessel like her had been caught by the Fishery Cruiser and all her gear and lobsters confiscated and duly sold at public auction. Where? In Stornoway. There had been well over a thousand fathom of new rope; and who should know better than our skipper who had bought a large part of it? Which was that!

And the lobsters?

No one wanted to buy them, until one man thought he would have a long shot, if he got them cheap. One of the crew alleged that the purchaser netted about a thousand pounds for the lot. But that seemed fantastic, for a simple sum in arithmetic made the total of lobsters too colossal surely for so small a vessel to carry.

'I'm not so sure,' said our master. 'What the skipper himself said was that if he had got off with it it would have been worth to him a small fortune.'

'Would he have made direct for a port in France and sold them there?'

'I don't think so, I believe they sail up the Mediterranean and sell them at a good price from place to place.'

I looked at the Frenchman again and, inwardly, saluted him. I thought of the Frenchmen from the little ports of Brittany who engage in the Iceland fishings. Great seamen!

'Whenever we get back, we'll let the Fishery Cruiser know.' There is a duty one owes to the fishing interests of one's own people.

I asked what evidence had we, after all, that the Frenchman had set the pots? It couldn't be said that he was sheltering here from bad weather, perhaps, but still if, on a voyage, he found himself running out of fresh meat and supposing—supposing he alleged that he had come in to make the hunt on certain wild goat-like sheep that inhabited these rocks?

The skipper smiled. The evidence would be all right.

If she comes in time I thought to myself; for I had a notion that though there were no visible heads on the *Marie Louise*, there were many invisible eyes.

The Frenchman was forgotten in the incidents of the hours that followed, and one that gave me a real fright is still clearly etched. I was going down some steps in the rock, shepherding the rear, when directly beneath I suddenly saw a figure between me and the sea. I knew at once what had happened. A sheep had left the lighthouse steps where, between them and the brink of the cliff, was a yard or so of irregular rock. One of our lads had followed and, as I looked, I saw his body stand out from the rock clearly defined against the white surf far below. As his body swayed, wrestling with the sheep, I thought he was gone. It was not a pleasant moment.

But we got our job finished, and about one o'clock in the morning, in that dim half-light of the summer night that never grows dark in these regions, we cried farewell to the men of the lighthouse and turned to the sea—and proved there was life in the pirate ship after all, for now at her masthead, like a large French glow worm, shone her riding-light! She had seen us all right—if she had never let on! There was a smile all round at that. The yard-arm still clacked as she heaved at anchor. We nosed past her with a wary eye for lobster entanglements.

There was an incident on that homeward trip that may be worth noting, before I mention how I ran into Kenneth on the quays of Stornoway some days later and got my last news of the Frenchman.

When we had left the heavy roll of the Western Ocean behind and come into sheltered waterways between small islands, the morning was well advanced, but there was still no human life about the cottages seen here and there beyond sandy shores or in little bights of the land. They have their own conception of time in the West and early-rising is not greatly favoured. The cottages were still asleep and there was peace everywhere. Though in truth it did not seem sleep so much as an arrestment of time in a clear enchanted air. As we had now been on our feet and tossing about or climbing for some twenty-four hours, I had a rather pleasant bodiless feeling myself. It is a feeling that one may have to go through considerable stress to attain, but it does bring with it a certain serentiy, a smoothing away of all ill-humours, a sense of companionship, a clear apprehension of the friendliness of peace and of the idiocy of strife. Indeed in such a moment the conception of brutal strife belongs to another order of existence; it does not seem evil so much as remote and senseless and idiotic. In that moment, too, is born the positive conception that, quite simply, life is good, that it is a rare and lovely thing in its own right, like the blooming of a wild rose. And also in that moment sleep, death itself, is apprehended in the clear air of the mind as a 'translation'; translation into what, one does not know, except that it holds in these fleeting instants a mystery one no longer fears.

But mechanism put an end to all speculation when the engine suddenly conked out. The paraffin tanks were dry!

What should we do? We had a long way to go yet. Try to sail her in the slight wind? Or use our only remaining fuel, the tin of petrol, required for starting her? Many factors were involved. The second and last trip was to take place immediately, while the weather held. The skipper had a good stock of paraffin at home, but no petrol, which had to be brought from Stornoway. If he used all his supply of petrol now? And, in any case, there was hardly enough to take us to the ferry, and we had a long way to go beyond that before we could land our sheep. There was a thought—the ferry! Who knew but that petrol and paraffin, belonging to some one or other, might not be sitting in large tins on the jetty? To me it seemed fabulously unlikely, but still it could not be ruled out categorically as impossible! And, anyway, why meet trouble until it met us?

'I think you may as well put the petrol in her.'

'Very good,' and in a short time we were under way. We pressed up the sound, and on the last little wash of petrol in the tank, we drew alongside the small and utterly deserted jetty.

Obviously no life had stirred there this morning. But our eyes were arrested by two interesting looking drums. We landed and tapped them. They were full. We unscrewed the bungs. There was petrol in one drum and paraffin in the other! And they were completely innocent of any label of ownership.

'Isn't that luck?' said Kenneth calmly, going down for empty petrol tins.

I looked at the skipper in, I suppose, a wordless way.

'The owner will know,' he said, 'that the one who took it needed it. That's the way we work here. Besides, I'm fairly sure I know whose it is.' He noted the quantities withdrawn from the drums, so that they could be made good in due course.

It was not the sort of happening designed to lessen an early-morning faith in either the goodness of life or its magic! I could not take part in the second trip into the Atlantic but, as I said, I ran into Kenneth on the quays of Stornoway some days later and would have passed him by had he not hailed me, for he was all dressed up in his naval suiting.

'Where away?' I asked in astonishment.

As a Naval Reserve he had been suddenly called up and was on his way south to join the fleet. 'For a couple of months,' he added. 'I don't think there will be any trouble.'

'I don't think so,' I agreed.

War seemed too impossible a madness on that July morning.

Off and on, the Frenchman had been in my mind, and now I asked for the latest news of him. Kenneth smiled. The Fishery Cruiser, it appeared, had gone out that way—to find the Frenchman gone. 'Not a sign of him!' We laughed.

'Ah, well,' said Kenneth, 'I would have been sorry if anything had happened. It was plucky of them coming all that way.'

We agreed heartily, and when we shook hands I promised to come out to see them all soon again.

It may not be soon now, but I hope that it will be again, and that I shall see them all. One conviction remains, that there is nothing above the sea or on the sea or under the sea can stop, in their natural alliance, those lads I knew and the daring seamen of the *Marie Louise*.

THE FIRST SALMON

SM, 1938

UP IN THE DARK of a February morning, with a good three hours' motoring in front of us before we reach the river. No salmon has yet been grassed, although the opening day is already a fortnight old. Perhaps we shall be lucky enough to land the first for the season! Worth a smile; but then I have heard many an owner of a half-ticket in the Irish Sweep (before the legal ban, of course) confidently dispose of a fortune before the drum had spoken.

It was a good morning to jet about it anyway, and when we came to the top of the southern escarpment that overlooks the Dornoch Firth and beheld the panorama in front of us—surely the most magnificent on the whole East Coast—our hopes were even heightened, despite the long white streamers on the water that told so frankly the strength of the wind. There and then we modestly decided that we should get only one fish, and as my friend, though a sound angler, had never previously thrown a salmon fly, we agreed that he was bound to be the lucky' one. I always think it is wise to be clear on these matters beforehand. A certain small amount of excitement, of course, would come my way, but it would take the shape of kelt.

'Will you know it's a kelt whenever you hook it?' asked my friend.

'At once,' I replied, almost sadly, visualising the lazy turn-over of the body under the water, the wallop on the surface, the eel-like wriggle, the sluggishness, the lack of power and fire.

But on a morning like this, driving along that ever-varying north-east coast, with its mountain curves and pines, its bronze bracken and brown birch woods, its ravines and bridges over little streams, what would it matter whether one had luck or not? (Which merely made the luck seem all the more certain!) The engine of the car sang away to itself. And even the miles of 'Road under Repair' (why should this form of desolation always stretch for about ten miles?) merely made us change the nature of our language, not its positive tone.

There may be better places to arrive at than the cosy private parlour or office of an hotel, but if so I have been unlucky. And while we were having what we had, the talk got going and a gillie was persuaded to tell his famous story of the man who went to bury his third wife. By the time we got to the river we were in good trim.

And the river was in good trim, too—except for the wind, which blew so strongly upstream that my fourteen-foot rod was voted too light and our host presented me with his own, which was sixteen feet (if it wasn't eighteen) and carried a fly fully as long as a man's middle finger. 'It is guaranteed,' he said in his pleasant way, 'to break your back inside two hours. After that you will be sore for three days.' Which would have been all that one might desire— were it not for the contrary wind that required at least a double expenditure of force.

Down through some bushes and over grey grass and yellow moss, and there was the first pool, dark moving water with white flecks and ripples. How lovely a thing a fishing pool is! It has intimacy and ancestry in it. Old as the blood-stream itself, and as full of intimations and hopes and queer elusive memories. There is an urgency to be at it, and a contrary impulse to take one's time, to do things leisurely and rightly, with a glance up the glen and a glance down, smiling at the flow of the hills or at oneself. The world can get on with its rearmament now, or with any other perverse or bloody madness! All through the dark winter months, the universal cry has been: 'The world needs peace.' Standing by the river's brim, one wonders if it is merely the soul of a man, this man and that man, that needs peace. Peace like this, immemorial and good, lapping against the flesh, soaking into the bone and to the marrow of the bone. Peace not as an absence of war, but peace as a living reality, a positive thing like the scent of the bushes and the ling, or the first notes of a young chaffinch, or the cry of a newly arrived peewit—or the song of the reel.

How carefully one fishes the first pool! And reflects at the end of it that it would be wrong to get anything in the first pool.Nothing worth doing should be easy. One salmon a day should satisfy any man. And it should be caught at some moment when he would almost have been justified in being careless—but wasn't. Yet truth compels me to say that I once caught an eighteen-pounder in my second full cast, that I have never forgotten it, and that I am dogged by an unworthy desire to find out again precisely how it felt.

There was to be no eighteen-pounder this day. And by the time I had finished the pool, the vertebral bones were creaking, certain muscles were tremulous, and the wind performed its only useful service by drying a bared forehead. Hitherto I had thought the wind rather cold, but now as I sat down to change my fly, I realised that it was a spring wind full of promise of long days to come. The year was opening its slow door to summer pastures. There is an emotion of gratitude to this old scarred earth that runs very deep. Or is it very high, like blown thistledown in a sunny wind? About as light as that, anyhow, and with an echo of laughter blown with it.

And so to the next pool. And to the next. With never a tug or a swirl or a rise anywhere. No, the salmon cannot have started running yet. In the last few years, I was told, the salmon in this river have decidedly been running later—to the extent even of affecting the letting. No reason could be given for this. And the whim might pass.

'Have you no special theory?' I asked my host, making my last cast at the tail of the pool and half turning my head. But I never got the answer, for in the same instant I was 'in him'.

A kelt? No, said my host. No, said the gillie. Decidedly no, thought I, as he took the current with a strong head. There had been no turn-over, with the silver gleaming ruddy through the brown water—a thing one should not see until the fight is ending. After five minutes I would have offered fantastic odds that I was in a clean fish, had there been anyone to take me. Indeed I had landed many clean fish that had behaved with even slower stubbornness. I could not get him to show himself. And when at last he was tiring, I began to grow anxious. My host was ready with the gaff. The gillie was all eyes. I brought him in. He showed himself. It was a kelt—foul-hooked!

The gillie tailed him, undid the hook, and he sailed away into deep water, none the worse.

The first part of my prophecy had come true.

And the second part followed in due course, for my friend got into a salmon. Again speculation was favourable—but this time with the mighty difference that it was correct. A clean-run hen fish of seven pounds, exquisite in line as anything that was ever created. The first fish of the season, of the year. The river was at last open.

It was an occasion to be toasted properly, with bonnets off. Even to be toasted twice. Nature was fulfilling her ancient contract to man. The local reporter could put his paragraph in the press.

We got no more fish that day. Which was right and proper. We had started in the half-light of the morning, full of hope. We left in the half-light of the evening, full of blessed tiredness and hospitality, convinced that fine men lived in a fine world—whose life-streams are its rivers.

BLACK CATTLE IN LOCHABER

SM, 1942

WHAT SORT OF BEASTS were the 'black Cattle' of the Highlands? In many places and of old men I had asked the question but never could get a definite answer. Yet obviously if I was to draw a clear picture of the old Highland economy, of which black cattle and sheep were the mainstay, the inner eye must first be able to see the real animals roaming over outfield and hill-pasture. There would be a difference, for example, in the human reaction to a douce black polled cow as compared with that to a dun-haired, long-horned Highland cow, and if the reaction was not visible but of the stuff of the imagination or the unconscious it might be none the less important on that account. In truth, it was just as necessary for me to know the kind of cow as the kind of scenery. Smooth lowland country has a quite different effect on the mind from that of mountains and glens.

But how difficult, often, to get exact information about what were the affairs or objects of everyday! Except for two or three travellers' books, what would we know about the past domestic and cultural life of the Highlands? I got my description of the black cattle in the notes to a poem, called 'The Grampians Desolate', by Alexander Campbell, published in 1804. Here it is: 'A cow, of the Sky or Kintail breed, is a remarkably handsome animal; it carries its head erect, which gives it a deer-like air, peculiar to the cattle of those districts. Besides a straight, thick back, deep in the rib, elevated head and neck; small blue or clear yellow horns, tipt with black, and sharp-pointed; the hide of a dark brown colour, short legs, and large bushy tail—are marks truly characteristic of a cow, ox, or bull, of the real highland breed of black-cattle.'

The other month I saw a beast approximating very closely to this description, and what specially caught my eye was the strength and fulness of the shoulders and neck. The head was up like a stag's and the brute looked as if it could charge. It was well knit, full of vitality, and native to its rough heathery background. It seemed much hardier than those very picturesque 'Highland cattle' we see now and then at cattle sales or on picture postcards, though clearly of the same breed.

The notes to the poem fill half the book and they are often fascinating. The verses themselves 'are professedly', says the author, 'of a political cast;

but, disclaiming all connection with the politics of the day, they aim at something very different—and that is, to call the attention of good men, wherever dispersed throughout our island, to the manifold and great evils arising from the introduction of that system which has within these last forty years spread among the Grampians and Western Isles, and is the leading cause of a Depopulation that threatens to extirpate the ancient race of inhabitants of those districts'. The system, of course, was that of sheep farms—or sheep-stores, as they were called.

The author gives details of the earliest beginnings of the system, and what he has to say on the old economy which sheep-farming supplanted is of particular interest to those of us who to-day would like to see the Highlands coming into their human own once more.

As for the black cattle, so he has a good word for the native sheep, which Donald Monro mentions to have seen 'feeding masterless, partayning peculiarly to no man', about the end of the fifteenth century.

Of the Linton or black-faced sheep which were introduced to the Highlands, he writes: 'Without doubt, the Linton sheep are hardy, and easily reared in mountainous districts; but then they are very subject to a loathsome and fatal distemper called *braxy*, which carries off prodigious numbers. ... But the native breed seem not liable to that disease, as, previous to the introduction of the Linton breed, I am credibly informed no such disorder as *braxy* was ever heard of in the Grampians or Western Isles.' He then contrasts the 'shaggy coarse' wool of the black-face with the native fleeces 'of a texture remarkable for fineness, closeness, and softness to the sense of touch; and when sent to the market fetch double, nay, treble the sum the merchant allows for the coarse wool'. And the flesh of the black-face, however preferable to that of the Leicester, is still 'infinitely inferior to the small, delicious mutton of the real native breed'.

And the author knows at first hand what he is talking about, for he took in hand the management of the family affairs in Lochaber when his son-in-law, Captain Alexander McDonell, was serving abroad with his regiment (1791 to 1799); 'a pretty considerable live-stock concern, consisting mostly of sheep and black cattle, which were kept on the upland pastures on the side of Lochtraig, a part of the extensive Highland property of his grace the Duke of Gordon in the district of the Grampians'. On the low ground were various farms carrying a considerable number of sub-tenants. These were what we would call crofting areas, and the author says that the mode of their farming 'was wretched in the extreme'. Clearly, though his sympathies were with them as children of the Gael, he considered them a somewhat thriftless and lazy lot. They built their houses of turf, 'usually cut from the best sward of the whole farm, being the firmest, consequently the best, for that purpose'. They did not trouble to collect manure, and when any was needed for potatoes or barley, down they hauled the end of the house which had been well smoked, 'and being ready to crumble to pieces, it was most excellent manure'. Then they cut more sward and re-built!

When the author took charge in 1794 he decided to put an end to this. Besides, to see the women working hard while their men idled about was a bit too much. Not, as he points out, that the women objected. They worked 'cheerfully, for they always alleged that too severe labour did much harm to the make, vigour and constitution of their lords and masters, and consequently spoiled the breed'. Moreover, when they did work, the men kept their plaids on. Clearly a difficult matter for the author to regard with equanimity.

But what to do about it? Now the author had a manager, a wily and able man named Macnab, and his solution was simple. Put up the rents, said Macnab, and that will quicken 'the exertions of individuals who otherwise were rather less inclined to industry, when they found both ends meet (as the saying is) and slip easily through life'.

'What sir!' exclaimed our author, 'ruin our tenants by a *rack-rent!*—are you in your sober senses?'

'Perfectly so,' replied Macnab.

And the scheme was put 'to the test of experiment in the year 1796. And in 1797 a farther rise was exacted, at which they murmured much, and threatened to leave their possessions in disgust.' But the author was the less alarmed because the price of cattle was on the rise as a result of war, and he had already found that the use of the word *ejection* would achieve almost anything, including the removal of the plaids during toil.

But our author was not satisfied. He was a man of considerable foresight and decided that what was really needed in these crofting areas was joint-stock farming, a co-operative combine. This, he was satisfied, would at one and the same time increase the size of the rent-roll and better the conditions of the tenants. So he set about it in one area, and in the end 'prodigious opposition and cabal were at length subdued'.

The experiment proved financially successful for all concerned. 'Still, however, they did not relish the change of system; and the rest of their neighbours, who had not yet submitted to this mode of uniformity of goods and gear, agreeable to rural economy, sneered at their simplicity—they also were invited in turn to unite in the community of the *joint-stock* system, but they flew one and all in the face of it, and gave it a most firm and decided opposition.'

And now for the first time the magic word *ejection* refused to work. The author was 'inwardly troubled'. But by this time he had not only tasted the dictator's power, but realised what is the mainspring of the dictator's philosophy. Though inwardly troubled, he decided that 'what is once begun, when substantially *good*, ought steadily to be persisted in; and I had resolved—it must, and shall be done—and it was done'.

At the end of all protestations the threat of *ejection* worked.

And the new system also worked apparently, for the author 'cannot help recommending it to the consideration of reputable tacksmen, thoughtful landholders, and patriotic members of the British Senate, as it appears to me, from the trial made previous to the year 1799, and since that period, under circumstances, too, verging toward the oppressive system of *rack-rent*—that the *population* and *means* of subsistence in the very wilderness of Lochaber, do actually exist, and may still be preserved by wise, and prudent management.'

This was an extremely interesting conclusion to have been reached through the joint-stock experiment. And indeed in recent years we have seen something of the kind work satisfactorily in our club sheep-farms in the Highlands, particularly when they were set up under favourable financial conditions (which was not always the case). Also there is raised the important consideration of sheep *and* native cattle. Anyway, here was an enlightened landlord, quite aware of the evils of rack-rents, turning the wilderness of Lochaber into a going concern for the human inhabitants, the black cattle, and the native sheep. That he was humane and scholarly, with a true aptitude for the customs and culture of the folk, is abundantly clear.

But now his drama takes a new and revealing turn. His son-in-law obtained leave of absence from his regiment, then in Portugal, and our author placed before him, on his return home, the joint-stock scheme which he had brought into being.

Captain McDonell was perfectly satisfied. It happened, however, that his lease from the Duke of Gordon was about to expire, so 'he wrote to his Grace, reminding him of old times; (for the Keappoch family were vassals of the family of Gordon for many centuries), and requesting a renewal of his lease, but without putting Keappoch on the same footing as the general run of tacksmen in that part of the country. His Grace was pleased to answer Captain McDonell's letter in the handsomest manner; and in one paragraph expresses himself thus: "I continue disposed to mark my regard for your family, by a degree of favour which no common tenant could expect."'

Meantime the prosperous conditions of the joint-stock lands had been 'marked by the neighbouring tacksmen and shepherds with an evil eye'. There was a boom in the new sheep-farms that swept the tenants off the land. The clearances were coming into full swing. And then follows this delicate exercise in irony by our author: '*Secret* offers were given in, amounting to *four times* the former rent of my friend's possessions; but the noble proprietor, true to his promise, with a princely munificence, says in his second letter, dated London, May 15th, 1799, which now lies before me, that he might let the possessions for *four times* the former rent, but that he did not mean to put him on the footing of ordinary tenants; and therefore he was willing to let him continue to hold the possessions for *one-fourth* less than what was actually offered'.

In short, Keappoch's rent was trebled at one stroke by his gracious overlord!

Keappoch, we are informed, was 'amazed at the prodigious rise', and did not know what to do, for he had merely been defending his country abroad for seven years 'during the hottest of the war'.

As things were, he could not pay the rent demanded. Clear the folk off the land? Turn the whole into a sheep-run? But his family interest was at stake. What to do?

And our author comes to his aid thus: 'Apprize the tenants ... you are their chieftain; some of them fought by the side of your grandfather Keappoch who fell on Culloden-moor; and several of them fought with your father on that day when our immortal Wolfe fell on the plains of Quebec—try what they will do of their own accord ... leave the affair to their own management, and wait patiently the event.'

So Captain McDonell laid the matter before them, and the third turn to the drama came in their unanimous resolve 'That they would support their chieftain to the last shilling.'

And this they did, paying 'punctually their proportion of rent, notwithstanding its absolutely verging on that hateful and alarming evil, *rack-rent*'.

All of which was perhaps hardly a drama, little more than a curtain-raiser, a prelude, to the ferocity with which the magic word ejection then set about clearing the glens and the straths of the Highlands. But it has its moments of illumination in matters, both empirical and imperial.

LANDSCAPE INSIDE

Saltire Review (SR) 1959

A NOVELLIST CANNOT write about people in a vacuum. They must have a background, and the background becomes part of them, conditioning to some extent almost everything they do. When this works at a fairly deep level, it can be quite unconscious. I can't remember (though I may be wrong) ever having described a Highland scene for the scene's sake. Always the scene had something to do with the mind of the character who found himself there. The difference here is like the difference between a colour photograph of a landscape and an artist's painting of it. In the painting, the artist, with his kind of mind, is present. In the colour photograph no mind is present. Perhaps this explains why so many set descriptions of scenes, like sunsets, can be boring or why lovely Highland glens, shot in colour film, have sometimes been dubbed picture-postcardy by critics. However, let me stick for a moment to the novelist, who does in fact often describe the mood of a character by describing the background, the physical scene. Or vice versa. There is a sort of oblique traffic between the two, and this can thicken the texture of both. When the character, for example, is on top of the world, the world becomes a wonderful place. When he is feeling depressed or nihilistic then the world around him becomes detached and uncaring. When one hears a critic describing the background as the principal character in a novel, it means that the background is actively directing the character. This can often happen in the Highlands.

Possibly it happens because of the powerful nature of the Highland scene: the mountains, the glens and straths, the moors, the features that never change? Yes—and no. For there is really a continuous change going on in these physical features—or, at least, in the way they appear to the eye. This, of course, is due to the light which can change from minute to minute. It sometimes produces fantastic dramatic effects, not merely in colour but in bulk, in mass. On a hot summer day, for instance, the mountains lose height; they seem to flatten, to squat down, as Highland cattle do, or deer, or other brute beasts. Then the sky hazes over, the evening comes, and wisps of mist form here and there. If one of these wisps begins to tie itself round a mountain, the mountain slowly rears up and sticks its head in the sky. I remember once, in Glen Affric, we had been out on the hill all day, and when we got back I found myself standing at a front window of the lodge, looking down the loch. To the right, rising sheer from the loch, there is a row of mountains over three thousand feet. They were covered with snow, with black ridges or stripes here and there; in the fading light they now looked gigantic, fearsome, and I realised, as never before, how small would be the chances of survival of anyone caught there with the long night coming down. Even as I watched, outlines were being smothered.

Perhaps I may seem too concerned with the effect of background on the individual. But finally that is the only thing one can be sure about—the effect on oneself. Too much is generalised about the Highlands, so vague romantic notions are born, often sentimental, nostalgic. However, one knows what happens to oneself, and then one meets others and gets their experiences, and so one may with reasonable confidence go on to talk in a general way about the effect of the Highland background on the Highland people. Yet I must confess that I always feel happier when dealing with something specific. So let us take music—say, some of these haunting old Gaelic songs or melodies, the sort that can change a Highlander's mood in a moment in spite of him. In how many of them, especially from the Outer Isles, is the rhythm of the sea. How often through the centuries his folk listened to the wind on stormy nights, heard the tumult of the sea, the mounting tumult, the thunderous smash, the recession. Or had long thoughts on a summer's day as they looked down on cockle strands. Something of this comes into the music, so that a snatch of it, at any time, anywhere, will have its profound effect. It will bring him to himself, the essence of himself, however buried under social or other accretions. 'When I am with myself' is a literal translation of the title of one of these old songs. Yet from this individual experience to the general experience may be but a step—say, across a threshold into a genuine ceilidh. In this particular region of the mind, place and people meet. The outer and the inner landscapes merge.

Yet there is a difficulty here, for the general experience or ordinary ceilidh can on occasion, as I have hinted, generate the vague emotionalism that so readily spills over into sentimentality. This is the point where one could wish to be as precise as a mathematician. But one cannot have both the emotion and the mathematics? I wonder.

Some time ago I was invited to a dinner on top of the Outlook Tower in Edinburgh by a group, a club, of distinguished Edinburgh and Glasgow men, trying to prove that though East is East and West is West the twain can meet on occasion. By a happy chance, a regimental pipe band was heard on the Castle esplanade, so we all quite naturally trooped out from the claret to a high grandstand view of the pipe band going through its paces, beating retreat. A vague mist hung around the capital city, and the sun, low down, was a rich red, doing its best to look as if it had been painted by William McTaggart. And there, down there, were the pipes, with their music from the islands and the glens, from far off things long ago, from the Celtic mist or twilight. But when we really listened and looked what we actually saw were pipers and drummers going through their evolutions with absolute

precision, like geometrical designs in fluid motion, as if the whole performance had been laid on by some ultimate mathematician. Yet the emotion was
of the pride and the power and the glory.

From music to colour. And there is no need to despair at the mention of
colour in the Highlands. Of course an ordinary writer can do nothing about
it, except set down the simpler facts which he may have observed, as, for
example, that the best time for colour is spring and autumn. In the height
of summer the glens, the straths, are too uniformly green. And then a Czech
film director and refugee, sweeping my seasons aside, said to me, 'No, no,
no: if only we had a colour process for that.' Spring had not yet wakened,
the mountain sides were withered, and a shafting sunlight played on the
blaeberry bloom of the bare birches. The moment so seen by a stranger
warms the inner landscape and is never forgotten.

Or, again, in Skye. Many years ago, I was staying in a small hotel at Carbost.
The only other guest was Professor Collie of London University, the distinguished mountaineer, who charmed more than one evening with descriptions of climbs in the Himalayas, the Rockies, and elsewhere. His quiet
precise manner gave an extraordinarily vivid verisimilitude to the solution
of sudden rock-face problems of great difficulty and danger; in particular
a certain feat of endurance can still haunt me. Once, when the talk must
have veered to the local scene, he told me that the most memorable stretch
of colour he had ever seen anywhere was on the moor in front of the
Cuillin—on the Glenbrittle side, as you come up from Talisker. I had seen
it the day before. Its tone was somewhere between amontillado and a
medium or richer sherry, but it looked like an immense living golden hide.
The wind rippled and played on it in a light-hearted frolic. The glow of life
was there, as if the earth were a beast. Perhaps the earth has a life of its own.
Every new physical fact discovered by the scientists is more astonishing than
the last.

To see the Hebrides along the horizon on an opalescent evening; to look
at your chart, at the small cross marking an unknown anchorage; to head
towards an island that keeps its distance in the silence beyond the beat of
the engines as the opalescence deepens.

But landscape is more than a matter of stringing beads. There is a way of
looking at the simplest scene if it is to remain. An artist once told me that
you must consider a bit of landscape three separate times before it really
sticks in your memory. The first time you look at it very carefully, going from
detail to detail, all round. Then you come back and take it in all over again.
Then a third time. After that it remains with you. For in the ordinary course
scenery is the vague sort of thing we rush through—like a conducted tour
on television. Nothing much remains beyond a glorified blur. One has got
to stop and look, be quite precise, factual. You can't stop the tele, of course,
but you can draw up if you are in a motor car or on a motor bike or, better,
on your own two feet. So when a scene surprises, stop and look at it with
the artist's eye by way of experiment. After that you go on and, in the
ordinary manner, forget all about it. But later—years afterwards perhaps—
that scene will come back with an extraordinary clarity. Like a tune you had

completely forgotten. But no tune will come back to you unless, when you first heard it, you made some *effort* to remember it.

I know that raises difficulties; for example, the value of a *first* impression; or, for that matter, impressionism in painting generally. But I think that we may take it that Cézanne looked at many apples, even more than three times, before he painted them in a memorable way.

However, there is something further here that I hesitate to mention because it is so elusive, so difficult to convey.

Have you ever, as a small boy, wandered farther from home than you meant to or were aware of—say, up a strath or valley—until you found yourself in a place where you had never been before? All at once you realise that *you* are in this strange place. Stock still, not breathing so that you can listen, you stare at grey rocks with whorls of lichen on them like faces, tree-roots like snakes, the trees themselves heavy with leaves and silent. Your heart comes into your throat. Quietly, very quietly, you get back onto the path, then take to your toes for all you are worth. This may have been the first experience of panic fear—the first meeting with the old Greek god. But you also met someone else there, much nearer to you than Pan: you met yourself.

There is no esoteric or hidden meaning here. I am trying to be quite factual; simply saying that unless you come upon yourself in some such way, as an element present in the scene or landscape, the chances are that you will forget it, however long you look at it. And I suspect that the artist's exercise of looking three separate times was not only to observe the detail, which is essential, but to give this special kind of awareness a chance to happen. It can be magical and memorable when it does, and only when it does.

HIGHLAND SPACE

SR, 1961

THERE IS THE STORY of the man who after the last war (he had done most of his fighting in the desert) came back to his home, a croft between mountains, and stood the austere scenery for three days and nights, and then beat it. The mountains had got on top of him, the silence, the loneliness. I was told the story at the point where he was passing through Inverness on his way south. Apparently he had no definite destination. He was a piper, too.

Experience on that level, at that pitch of intensity, can be understood only by those who have had something like it. There are lower levels, as in the case of the two ladies to whom I had suggested a three-day motoring tour of the Western Highlands by way of brief introduction to that inexhaustible variety of land and sea. They cut the tour short, one saying to the other, 'When you have seen one glen you have seen the lot,' and returned to their native city.

Not to mention those who exclaim, 'Ah, how lucky you are, living in the remote and beautiful Highlands!' when you know that after one tough-weathered week there, with 'nowhere to go', they might have their first dim notion of what troubled the piper. In comparison, there is innocence in the face with the considering eyes and the mouth that asks on its own, 'Do you mean to say you stay here all the year round?'

But however the instances be added, what is fundamental in the lot is the fear of empty space; at first, fear of the 'vacant' places, brooding mountains, sterile distances; and then of the appalling outward swoop into space itself, into infinite emptiness, into Pascal's horror of it, the *horror vacui*. So fundamental does this seem that one takes it as a permanent, if submerged, element in our mental make-up, in what we call human nature. Certainly some of the first English poets to visit the Highlands were afflicted in this way.

But is this experience in fact universal; is it really an invariable psychological ingredient, a constant, in the nature of the human animal? Or are we up to the old game of equating human nature with our particular culture pattern? This is the kind of question that sent Jung, I understand, to foreign places and other culture patterns, so that he might look back at the one he had left. When this is done, astonishing things can happen.

My own particular astonishment came from looking at some Oriental pictures, and, in particular, reproductions of the works of Sesshu recently published in Japan. It is one of those luxurious editions of the works of an old master, but as I turned over the pages I became disturbed by an element other than the novelty or strangeness of what was portrayed, by an element that wasn't as it were in the picture at all but yet was there—if only I could uncover it. To take a simple example, with the translated title, 'Plumtree'. It is a vertical picture or hanging scroll, painted in ink on paper. The limb of an old plum tree comes out from the right of the picture about halfway up and disposes a broken, mis-shapen branch and a couple of long slender stems on the air. This, of course, is exquisitely done; but, still this was not all— and then suddenly I realised that what 'made' the picture was the unpainted surface, the empty air. At such a moment both the picture and the mind are lit up; all is included and questioning vanishes.

To take a more complex example of natural scenery, described simply as 'splashed-ink landscape', and completed by Sesshu in 1495 at the age of seventy-six. I feel sure a lot has been written about this picture, and indeed the considerable amount of pictographic writing at the top of the scroll was added, I gather, by other hands. However, the only point in my writing here is to try to show the effect of the picture on one completely ignorant of pictographs and informed native criticism, if not without some response to the natural scene. My concern is with space.

The eye, then, is caught immediately by a tree in the foreground, and behind it—or, more exactly, above it—the looming shapes of two mountain peaks. These three objects are discontinuous; they are not linked together in the perspective with which the Western eye is familiar, so familiar that its absence instantly conveys a sense of bewilderment. ... Then within the bewilderment came the uncanny feeling that these vague peaks were not simply apart in space but were being actively created by space. They were being born out of it. Space was the creative source.

But there was more than that—though now I hesitate, for, when the eye looks steadily, an odd, perhaps entirely personal, illusion can arise; in this case it was the illusion of movement, of, as I have suggested, active creation. To compare broadly: whereas in a Western painting the moment is arrested, static, here the moment is caught from what has been described as the eternal flux of becoming and unbecoming. I know this has inexhaustible philosophic implications, but I am not concerned with these at this point, only with seeing and experiencing. Just as I once saw the dawn coming out of space on the mountains above Lochbroom. The curve of the mountains took the light in a way which made me realise that the earth was a great ball turning in space. Dawn was not entirely the rosy-fingered affair of our traditional poetry. Nor, for that matter, did the rosy fingers thereafter lose their appeal or our human condition its interest; quite the contrary: because of that which had been added.

As for the third—or at least now the fourth—element in the picture, the splashed-in tree, it was no longer 'the tree' so much as 'tree'. Nor was this quite the platonic notion of the ideal tree. Somewhere I have read that Sesshu got the splashed effect of the foliage by taking a little bunch of straw, dipping it in the ink, and then dabbing it on the paper. Which may permit the reflection that American action painting is neither so new nor so revolutionary as has been bruited; and the further reflection that in Sesshu's case this irruption of the irrational is not the whole picture. These old masters had a way of putting things in their place.

One more picture by Sesshu I should like to mention, though it is not included in the de luxe volume. It is called 'Seven Sages in a Bamboo Grove'. Why such a title should warm the human breast I hardly know. Perhaps it is not so much what they might say or do as that they should be there saying and doing it. Anyway, tradition has it that the seven met in the bamboo grove and gave themselves to painting pictures, making poems and playing music—having, of course, already attained freedom from the clogging absurdities of all negative and destructive emotions. But what particularly struck me was a final remark by the Japanese critic to the effect that such a picture could be painted only by one who had himself attained the mind which would adorn the bamboo grove.

And that is the mind that brings us back to space. Many of those old master painters in Japan were, like Sesshu, Zen priests. Zen is a sect of Buddhism and enough is being written about it in the world today to make it unnecessary for me to say how little I know about it. Not that knowing, I find, or learning or even deep study helps much, for the central experience of enlightenment (revelation is, perhaps, our word) can come only when thinking or the logical processes stop. That is not to decry thought, of course; merely to make it clear that enlightenment is not an end product of thought. However, the one thing I wish to avoid is verbal entanglement, so let me say briefly, then, that apparently our fear of space, the *horror vacui*, is not a fear or horror for all mortals. Certainly it is not a fear in Zen, which uses words like Emptiness, Nothing, the Void, quite commonly, but always in the paradoxical sense that Emptiness is not emptiness, space is not Void, yet, again, that they are these in the moment before they are not. To take the further step and hold these ultimate opposites in unity may be a true experience, but if so its expression—the communication of such a state of being—can never be more than a hint by the use of paradox. At this point the interesting thing about Sesshu's landscape is that in it you see him resolving the paradox. He paints his picture (in the bamboo grove, I hope) and the eye sees *his* space or Void, the plenitude of his Nothing.

But let me quote a verse from a living Scottish poet to help me out. It might have been written on a famous Zen anecdote concerning the master who referred to a flock of wild geese. 'But, Master,' replied his pupil, 'they have already flown away.' The master administered a physical shock (sure way of stopping logical processes) and the pupil, instantly experiencing the enlightenment he had so long and painfully sought, saw that though the geese had flown away, they had not flown away. Here is the verse from the poem 'Advices of Time' in Norman MacCaig's recently published book, *A Common Grace*:

The bird flies in the mind, and more than bird:
Times dies somewhere between it and its flight.
The bird flies in the mind, and more than mind:
Sunsets and winds and roofs enrich the light
That makes it bird and more than bird, till they
   Can never fly away.

I am not suggesting that this is a description of the enlightenment (*satori*) that comes through Zen. But clearly it is 'on the way'—the opposite way to what the piper took, when he beat it from the looming mountains, or from some childhood fear of vacant places, loneliness, the dark.

SECTION II

LITERATURE

NEW GOLDEN AGE FOR SCOTS LETTERS

Daily Record, 1930

WOULD I CALL IT a Renaissance? Either that, or an Awakening. The Scottish Awakening would be rather an amusing description, and even an arresting one to those countries that have come to think that the Scotsman never sleeps.

To suggest that a Prime Minister is likely to awake, or an Archbishop to yawn at the devotions, or a Mr Maxton to turn in his sleep (other than uneasily) might make the world wonder.

But as it is the obvious desire of the new writers (despite their critics) not to covet publicity wantonly, I certainly would be inclined to vote for 'Renaissance'. To most of us it happily means nothing. But to the rest it raises the classic challenge.

Let the word connote a rebirth of letters, of the arts. But really it stands for much more than that to us.

We at once think of something like the Italian Renaissance, that is a period where we now are not only in at the birth but also, as it were, at the death.

In this way the Scottish effort invites amusing but irrelevant ridicule. We expect it to take off its heady dram without a cough, when in the normal way it should be gurgling over its mother's milk. A child is never ridiculous. But its grown-up critics nearly always are—even when they're friendly.

Though that doesn't mean that the critic in your columns recently who suggested that this hailing of every new Scottish writer as a genius, is bad for him and worse for Scottish letters, is in any better case. He is taking his own wisdom altogether too seriously.

And it is not much in the way of satire to imply that a 'genius' is not a genius. To flatter a writer unduly always adds to our gaiety, even when, if the writer is sensitive, it is in bad taste.

There is always some excitement in a true enthusiasm. But not every writer who is called a genius tries to dress accordingly. So the critic may calm himself.

In fact one or two of our finest young writers have told me that they dislike the label intensely!

It is possibly a handicap in the sense that it may make them blush and gnash their teeth. But we need not agree with them, for in the process of gnashing their teeth there is always the sporting chance of cutting one or two new ones.

And, anyway, it is a desperately beguiling handicap. It worries and annoys—and drives. It may help those who have it in them to out with it. Birth is a notoriously painful process. And not every critic is a twilight sleep.

But apart from that, wherefore the label Renaissance? Firstly, because of the distinctive work done these last few years, and, secondly (and more importantly), because of the existence of an immense national reserve awaiting the act of creation. As to the writers who have so far distinguished themselves, I say nothing here.

If they aren't all geniuses, neither are the writers of any country at any time, barring the odd one. Nor is a renaissance exclusively concerned with genius in any case. Not that I subscribe to the idea that genius will out willy nilly.

There's quite a lot in the 'mute inglorious Milton'—particularly when he has not merely been forcibly inhibited but at the same time directed to an outlet that can never let him out. Renaissance is really concerned with the bringing to birth once more of a culture, in this particular case a Scottish culture, on a national scale.

If, however, we had not this immense reserve, which cannot be properly worked by anyone but a Scot, the whole idea would be absurd. As it happens, we have. And on a truly magnificent scale.

Whether we like it or not, our ancestors spoke Gaelic for many more centuries than they spoke English. How they came by it we may not know, even if there are those who are prepared to plump for the Garden of Eden.

But we do know how they came by English; they acquired it. That doesn't mean that we must all start writing in Gaelic at once.

Even our critics' logic can be occasionally amusing in this respect. But it does mean that we should gain some knowledge of a culture which was in its most perfect flower centuries before even the beginnings of English Literature.

Why? Simply because we derive from it, and all art starts from self-knowledge in its profounder aspects. In a more restricted way we derive also from that powerful variant of the English tongue called Scots, the ballads and the Makars.

We need not consider here how it came about that we grew rather self-conscious of both. All that need concern us is that we did, but that we are now better able to assess not merely the value of what we discarded, but also the value of what we tried to put in its place.

And once the Scot has got his sense of proportion again, his reborn pride in his heritage will be a driving force that will know no early or timid or baffled exhaustion. Why is it that since Scott there have been so many Scotsmen of promise, men who have started off brilliantly but who have weakly and unaccountably petered out?

I believe it is simply because they had no faith in, were not profoundly conscious of, their life-giving roots.

But the world knows the Scot for a fighter. And once this fight is properly joined I can hardly think of his giving in easily.

In a word, I cannot see how we are to avoid, even if we would, a new age, possibly a golden age, in Scottish letters.

But though an individual genius may emerge in a day, a culture is not born in one. This means a horrid process of 'gradualism'? Not at all.

In the historic sweep, for a big movement to be born and flower in half a century is near enough the instantaneous not to matter.

THE SCOTTISH LITERARY RENAISSANCE MOVEMENT

This essay first appeared in what may have been the only issue of the Wick
Mercantile Debating Society Magazine *in April 1929. It was rediscovered by
Daniel Hay and W R Aitken and reprinted in the* Scottish Literary Journal
in December 1977.

THERE CAN BE NO SPACE here in which to trace the course of this new movement in Scottish Letters and to assess the achievement of its leading writers.
What I should like to do is to get at the spirit informing it, to see more or
less distinctly what it is aiming at, and whether accordingly it can be justified
in terms of reality and significance. And even that is practically impossible
for it implies finding the spirit's background—that is, the historic causes
which leave it dissatisfied with its recent written expression (dubbed the
'Kailyaird') and striving towards something ampler and finer. It further
implies at least a slight knowledge of what other nations have made of
literature in recent years. If, for example, in drama, in poetry, in all forms
of prose from the novel to the essay, critical testimony of the highest kind
can be brought to show that Scotland for some generations has made no
contribution of first-class importance to world literature then our enquiry
has got to be both searching and sincere.

Yet even now I have not touched my real subject, for I must admit that
what is at the back of my mind as I write these words is not the casual reader,
not even that skilled hunter for weak links in a logical chain, the 'Mercantile'
debater, but that possibly rather lonely figure who walks along the cliff-
heads, and looking at the sea, wonders. Not an unusual figure on the
'braeheads' of Caithness, and from amongst his numbers we can be sure
of the one who haunted by his vision of rock and sea is also haunted by a
desire to express it, that is to get rid of the burden of a sensitive impressionism, to project it from his mind upon a page of print, so that whosoever
may look on that page will assume the burden of sea and rock, sheer and
stark. In a word, the artist (whose club address might very well be 'The
Mercantile').

And all at once a rather singular memory comes to me by way of illustration. Many years ago I read a short article in the *John o'Groat Journal* (over

an initial—I think, uncertainly, 'R') describing some Caithness sea-cliffs in which were a few lines of sudden and quite unusual evocative power. I am not here going to attempt to re-create the writer's vision. Suffice it that in a moment I was back on the cliffheads with the gulls crying cavernously far, far down to the green sea water moving languidly the refluent brown weed … That, however, as a background to the more immediate evocation of a wild white gull that without a wing-beat rises from its echoing chasm and, against the wind-wave that ever combs the cliff's grassy scalp, settles for a startled moment to stare at me with its clear unearthly eye.

Why does the vision from that accidentally encountered passage, whose actual words I have forgotten, remain in my mind, when hundreds of columns since, dealing with scorries and poetry and cliffs and Wick, have absolutely and forever slid into limbo? Perhaps it is impossible to answer that question precisely. It is not altogether that the person who wrote the words was an artist, or that he (or she) observed rather particularly, or that he was susceptible to impressions, or so on; is it not rather that he got a sudden vision of life in nature which he 'translated' on to the plane of Art? Art is not a precise reflection, a cunning reproduction, of life. That is realism. Art, in translating life, heightened it. It raises it to art's plane, where it is discriminated and made forever memorable. Let us say that this writer captured for me and transfixed what I could evolve in only a hazy general way; and what he transfixed was not 'funny' or forgettable; it was uncaring of me and unforgettable.

Perhaps I seem to overstress here his few lines, but I do it with this end in view, namely, that what that writer did with his cliff-head is what the Scottish Literary Renaissance Movement wants to do with all Scotland in her myriad aspects. And if that seems rather a sudden thrust, let me put it in another way. For it is just this point that is the most vital for the young Caithness writer or artist, with whom my mind (in spite of me) is really concerned.

The homely stuff, then, that moves us to varied emotions at a soirée of our kindred, that occupies the poets' corners of our country press, that maunders through columns of reminiscence and is made 'humorous' and entertaining for our benefit, is all very excellent in its way, but its interest is essentially local and associative. The subject-matter, the style, is fine for a crack, the very thing for a friendly ceilidh, indispensable to a pint of beer, but beyond that—and this is my point—it has no value, no reason for existence. It is not literature. For example, to the Wick boy the word 'scorries … the Ould Man' evoke a real scene; to the Dunbeath boy, in the same county, the word 'scorrie' is unknown and the term 'ould man' merely evokes the Gaelic 'bodach'. But to the Wick boy and to the Dunbeath boy and to every lettered mind all the world over, the scene on the cliff-heads by Wick, as described by the writer in the *Groat*, is vivid and arresting in a way that is absolute and unconditional. From being a parochial observation it has been translated on to the plane of art where it becomes a universal possession and a civilising and cultural power of unguessable potentiality. Thus it provides not merely a thrill for the Wick boy; it provides a thrill for humanity. At the best, the parochial or kailyard provides not a thrill but a chuckle—or a tear ... estimable manifestations, though in public inclined to be produced by a trifle too much pepper on the cabbage.

Now if one has got the distinction here in the two possible ways of treating a rock scene, one has at the same time got the difference between the old Kailyard and the new Renaissance Movement. The Renascent Scot is—must be—intolerant of the Kailyairder, that is, of the parochial, sentimental, local-associative way of treating Scotland and the Scots. He wants to treat of Scotland as rock and sea and land—a unique and wonderful rock and sea and land—and he wants to treat of Scotsmen as real projections of *homo sapiens* (rather than as kirk-elderish grannies), and he wants to complete his picture in a way that will not only make self-satisfied Scotsmen sit up but will make the cultured of the world take notice. That may sound rather a big claim. But considered in its creative aspect, it is merely the modest claim to serve the ends of Literature.

But I can assure my lonely walker of the cliffs now that if he takes to his task a fine vision, a sensitive discrimination, an artistic integrity that will not be satisfied with anything less than the best that he can do, the chances are that he will find himself lonelier in print—I mean, in manuscript—than he is on the cliffs. Editors will have no space for his work. Publishers (in our case, as a rule, English publishers) will demur. By forced compromises, by parleyings with his soul, by frank journalism, he may ultimately find a way of winning out here and there. But the mass will not take the slightest interest—except now and then to deride. Take courage, and humour, accordingly! The only thing that impresses the mass is Success—material success. And if that sounds platitudinous—well, it is rather a terrible platitude. Or, if you must have a concrete case, take the work in Scots of C M Grieve, that is, the poetry of Hugh MacDiarmid, which is the most distinctive work the Scottish Renaissance has yet produced.

In a column of the *Groat* some months ago I observed a contributor writing about this extraordinary figure, who refuses tamely to be silenced, as 'tootling on his penny whistle'. Well, my own cool opinion of Hugh MacDiarmid is this, arrived at after careful study of all his work and with a fairish knowledge of the trend of world poetry today, that he is not only the finest Scots poet since Burns but that he has poetically penetrated dimensions of the spirit that Burns never even conceived. That doesn't mean that I am asserting that he is *greater* than Burns. Comparison of that sort is meaningless, as though it were being said that an orange is *greater* than an apple. But I do want thus to stake my critical faculty for what it's worth against those who find nothing but 'a tootle on a penny whistle'. Such a discrepancy in judgement would seem incredible, impossible ... and yet, come to think of it, provides for my purpose perhaps the best illustration of any.

Meantime let me ask the young aspirant to be affected by neither judgement, but to get down to the work itself, and not to a casual reading but to a close unprejudiced study. Older men and women, with fixed beliefs and standards, naturally enough react to MacDiarmid adversely. But my concern here is with the younger men and women who must carry on the fight for the free fine ways of the spirit and Scotland's place in the literature and culture of the modern world.

THE SCOTTISH RENASCENCE

SM, 1933

In the following essay, Neil Gunn, using a pseudonym, replied to an article by Gordon Leslie Rayne, which had appeared in the previous issue of *The Scots Magazine*, entitled 'This Scottish Tongue: the Renascence and the Vernacular'.

IN HIS ARTICLE in your last issue on 'The Renascence and the Vernacular', Mr Gordon Leslie Rayne has the disarming suavity of one who would present his keenest barb sheathed in cotton wool before shoving it home by inadvertence. The operation is courteous, if more than a trifle obscured. Indeed through the final 'woolliness' I find it difficult to assess what exactly has taken place, or even, with clearness, what it is that Mr Rayne designed should take place, for he is all for encouraging every man, such as he is.

Broadly, however, his charge would appear to be that there are those who proclaim a Scottish Renascence when in reality there is no such thing. Or, as he puts it himself, he has been 'slightly puzzled by the vociferous heralds of a Scottish Renascence which somehow I seem to have missed,' and then attempts to show that what he has missed can hardly be held to have existence in fact.

Now this is the true national game, for it allows the ironic off-taking of our neighbours without which no Scot among us ever really feels properly bedded or safe. We rise to this lure almost before it lands, and leave our surface chuckles to ring the inane. Observe, for example, that Mr Rayne uses the words 'vociferous heralds'. Others on the same quest have used similar lures. There has thus been created the impression of a host of clamant individuals (little higher than the angels) heralding the miraculous rebirth in letters of Scotland's spirit. It sounds good fun straight away. It ensures for Mr Rayne his 'deep chuckle' before he has right started, thus aligning his technique with that of 'the genius of Sir Harry Lauder'. Sense and sanity are immediately enthroned upon that guid conceit which is going to have moderation in all else, and particularly in everyone else (leaving the Lord to appraise exceptionally 'me and mine'). Yet all we have to do to destroy the good old game in this particular instance is to ask Mr Rayne to produce his 'vociferous heralds'. It is as simple as that. Here is a book, for instance called *Scotland in Quest of Her Youth*, in which this very matter is touched upon by half a dozen of our known younger writers (Catherine Carswell, Naomi Mitcheson, James Bridie, George Blake, Eric Linklater, Neil Gunn). They are not only not vociferous heralds, but on the contrary severe critics of what has been accomplished, using an irony ruthless enough to indicate that very spirit they seek. Among the other younger Scottish writers of note, where are the 'vociferous heralds'? I have studied this modern 'Movement' as closely, I hope, as Mr Rayne, and I can think of only one writer to whom this appellation might be attached (and then only with a certain significance), and that writer is Mr C M Grieve. Those who have followed the early work of the Movement will understand the reason for this, but it need not detain us here, for my purpose may be served by asking Mr Rayne whether out of those recent generations of writers with whom he has been in touch there is one he can place against Hugh MacDiarmid (Mr C M Grieve) as a poet? There is none (surely none amongst those names he has mentioned), and I presume he must allow it. And poetry is the very flower of literature.

Now if I have dealt with this epithet of Mr Rayne's at undue length, it is because the whole attitude of mind in and behind it is very revealing. Indeed, it is the analysing of this attitude of mind that would probably be the swiftest and surest way of arriving at the heart of our quest. If we can show that the attitude to literature in its Scottish expression by what we may call the renascent writers is radically different from that shown by Mr Rayne's previous generations, then at once we have established a spiritual distinction. If the kailyairders were sentimental and deliquescent, and the new men are vital and life-giving, the change amounts to renascence or rebirth. Quintessentially it is not a matter of whether we are producing great writers so much as whether we are producing writers quick with this new validity or vitality. That is the real issue.

For manifestly it would be a useless dogmatic game to go on assessing one writer against another. Time is needed, apparently, to give the perspective that permits Shakespeare a higher place than Ben Jonson (to how deep an astonishment on the part of rare Ben—and of his friends!). Furthermore, if there is a Renascence, then clearly it has had very little time to get over the birth pangs; a very short time compared with, say, the reign of Robertson Nicoll (to cite one of Mr Rayne's 'mighty men'). Altogether let it be emphasised that renascence does not necessarily imply or demand the emergence of one or more great figures (though it nearly always coincides with this emergence), but rather a reawakening or rebirth of spirit amongst many people, ultimately discernible even in the minor social manifestations of a whole people.

I am tempted, however, to pause over that name, Robertson Nicoll, and to place against it one of our critics of to-day, who has shown concern with the Renascence and is himself one of its significant figures, Edwin Muir. As critics, they have both been concerned with assessing literature, and however we may dispute their individual merits, I maintain that their attitude, their approach, their criteria or standards of judgement, exhibit a fundamental difference or divergence. This may be difficult to define in a sentence without seeming unfair, but, that granted, it might be said that Nicoll was concerned voluminously in his journalistic manner with what appealed to his personal idiosyncrasies, against a given local religious background, whereas Muir is concerned with the isolation of pure or permanent values by applying literary standards of a high, exacting kind. The most cursory study of Muir's work will show the plane of his debate and its remoteness from Robertson Nicoll's. I am not here concerned with personal gifts or abilities, but merely with indicating this difference or divergence, because appreciation of it is essential before what underlies any renascence claim can possibly be apprehended.

Let us take another example. 'The genius of Sir Harry Lauder,' writes Mr Rayne, 'is part and parcel of the kailyard tradition, and since then our younger people have lost the gift of eliciting the deep chuckle and provoking the postponed, but persisting, grin of inner merriment. They are so desperately sober-sided. ...' When Sir Harry tells his 'best one' about a Scotsman's meanness, and has the added joke of making money out of the transaction, the young renascent Scots have their chuckle all right, and, let Mr Rayne be assured, the grin of merriment persists. True, it is merriment with a difference, anything but sober-sided, positively Rabelaisian in its sweep, and any day it may burst out. Much as George Douglas Brown burst out, though I observe that Mr Rayne does not include that name amongst his mighty.

And so one could go on. Poetry I have already mentioned. In this Magazine there is verse (by William Soutar, for example), which has all the characteristics of the renascence temper, and is as different from the Magazine verse of a former generation as a divining rod from a Lauder crook. In fiction one could make, perhaps, the clearest claim of all.

Mr Rayne perceives there is something in all this, for he says the 'revolt' from the standards and ideals of the past 'is not peculiarly Scottish, it is essentially modern and current throughout Europe.' Yet further on he tries to ridicule the revolting Scot for *harking back* to Dunbar's pedantic tongue! Nor is our confusion clarified by his exclusive reference to tongue. He should know that the harking back to Dunbar is professedly not a harking back for language so much as a harking back for greatness. Dunbar is great in breadth, in variety and ingenuity, in largeness of conception and utterance, after the fashion that Chaucer before and Shakespeare after him were great. It is this lost greatness that the renascent Scot would strive to see restored, recognising that its manifestation in a nation at any time is due not so much to the odd appearance of an individual genius (generally forced to dissipate his best energies in rebellion), as to the existence within the nation itself of that aptitude for greatness out of which genius naturally flowers.

Finally, that the development of the Scottish nationality 'has nothing whatever to do with the continuance of the Scottish vernacular', may be correct. Scottish nationality may have nothing to do with the Gaelic tongue and literature. Having at last acquired English, it may be able to dispense with all history and tradition; it may indeed develop all the better for the lack of roots of any sort. Something of this parasitic conception of Scotland is common enough. All that can definitely be said is that the greatest poetry produced in Scotland since Dunbar has been in the Scottish tongue, that our only poetry to-day of European importance is being written in that tongue, and that, with all due deference to Mr Rayne, great poetry in whatever tongue makes a nation neither ridiculous nor ludicrous. For the rest, it would appear that Scotsmen have the chameleon-like quality of 'adaptability to the habits, the thoughts, and the speech of other nations'. Yet, adds Mr Rayne, our nationality is irrevocably bound up 'with the preservation of qualities and gifts of which the glorious company of the self-styled revivalists have yet to learn and think'.

If only Mr Rayne had helped us by explaining when his chameleon is not a chameleon and how! Unless, of course, all the 'qualities and gifts' had already been summed up by him in our genius for music-hall comedy, complete with deep chuckle and grin of merriment (continuing).

SCOTTISH RENAISSANCE

Scottish Field, 1962

WHEN I WAS ASKED to pay this personal tribute to Hugh MacDiarmid, my mind went back to the early days of our association, and I thought it might interest readers if I said something from my own experience about what has been called the Scottish Literary Renaissance and of Hugh MacDiarmid's connection with its beginnings.

I seem to remember that the appellation itself was of French origin, and certainly MacDiarmid in these years, the twenties, was in contact with French writers like Denis Saurat, and generally was very much aware of what was going on in literary affairs, particularly of a new or revolutionary kind, on the Continent. Also, of course, he had his English contacts, as I have just verified by looking up *Contemporary Scottish Studies*, by C M Grieve, and finding that the volume had belonged to Gordon Bottomley (who bequeathed his Scottish books to me), and finding further, behind the front cover, some cuttings from Glasgow newspapers showing Grieve on the warpath and dealing out everything but mercy to those who had dared question his critical judgements on contemporary Scottish writing. Clearly, then, there was one English poet of the time whose interest in Hugh MacDiarmid even went beyond the Lallans.

These cuttings had me laughing once again when, in his reply to William Power's high challenge to formulate 'a canon of criticism', he writes that, while agreeing with the need for such a canon, 'I cannot conceive of one which, to say the least of it, is simpler to expound than the theory of Relativity, and I could not attempt to formulate one myself in less space than a complete issue of the *Daily Record*'. Even as it was his reply was spread over three columns. But the exaggerated humour, the wild gesture for its own sake, was part of the adventure of that time, and the adventure was young and full of life and noise and hope.

However what I found among the cuttings and had quite forgotten was a leaflet published by the *Scottish Educational Journal* announcing a series of articles by Mr C M Grieve 'which would discuss in all the work of no fewer than three hundred men and women of Scotland in Literature, Music, Art,

Drama, Education, and other branches of cultural activity ... a real achievement in nationalistic integration'. How far the promise in that formidable
announcement was fulfilled may be judged by the contents of *Contemporary
Scottish Studies*. For I am not concerned now with critical assessments, but
only with the desire to point out and emphasise something truly astonishing,
namely, the amount of sheer hard labour, of tireless discriminating research,
that the completion of this work had involved.

Then let it be remembered that in these early years he was also producing
Scots poetry on the level of the old Scottish masters, not to mention editing
periodicals like *The Scottish Chapbook, The Northern Review* and *The Scottish
Nation*. Over all, then, is it any wonder that to many Hugh MacDiarmid *was*
the Scottish Literary Renaissance?

Yet that would be to exaggerate, if not to nullify, the true situation as
Grieve saw it then and tried to make it clear. Indeed his articles and editings
would have been pointless, unless there had been in Scotland sufficient
activity and accomplishment in cultural affairs to warrant his use of a word
like Renaissance. As the *S E Journal* leaflet put it: 'The synopsis given overleaf
lends substance to Mr Grieve's claim that Scotland has at no time in the past
had so remarkable a body of writers and artists as at the present moment,
and the youth and ascending aim of the great majority of these justifies the
hope that we are on the verge of a genuine awakening.'

In how far the hope was realised may be a matter for discussion (as it so
often has been), but once again I wish to stress here what one man indubitably *did* to help to justify the hope and bring about a genuine awakening.
Amid the national tendency towards arguments and flytings, how rare to
find the doer, and particularly on so high a level over so wide a field.

But there still remains one more aspect of this unusual tale of achievement,
which to-day may need special emphasis, and this is the earnestness with
which at that time he strove to discover and praise good work by his contemporaries. Some of his assessments and prophecies may well be considered over-generous, as when he said somewhere in these *Studies* that
there were ten living Scottish poets who were immeasurably superior to all
but the ten greatest poets our race had produced throughout the past. And
he named the living ten. Acclamation could hardly have gone further.

If at times denunciation went equally far in the other direction at least let
it be remembered that his critical standards were indicated and that in any
age indifferent work is much greater in quantity than fine work. But, that
apart, what always springs spontaneously out of his research is his pleasure
when he finds what he likes, first for its own sake and then for its strengthen-
ing of the Scottish national tradition in literature over against all other
national traditions, particularly the one south of the Border.

Perhaps if one could define 'what he likes' some understanding might be
gained of the counter-attacks he naturally enough drew upon himself. To do
this briefly would be difficult. But at least it can be indicated that in the
twenties a profound revolution was taking place in literature, and that it was
possible for writers living in even the remoter parts of Scotland to be aware
of it. One can remember reading the Parisian magazine *Transition* in the

Highlands, when James Joyce's *Work in Progress* was appearing in its pages, and memories of some of its more intolerant avant-garde verse and denunciatory attitudes can still spill over into mirth. But it wasn't even necessary to go abroad, for T S Eliot and Ezra Pound were publishing their poetry and criticism in London. The revolution was in fact so widespread and relentless that it did not take so very long for many to feel something like a sense of secret shame for once upon a time having wallowed in Shelley or Tennyson. I knew no one in Scotland at that time who was more aware of this and more attracted by its innovations than Christopher Grieve.

So far I have been concerned with describing events that happened in these early years of the Renaissance Movement and showing how closely our poet, critic, and controversialist was identified with them. But all along at the back of my mind has been the desire to pay him, on this special occasion, a more personal tribute out of abundant memories of our joint doings and discussions, of all-night sessions when the speech organs had to be wetted now and then with a drop of old malt. His happy references to these sessions in a recent broadcast stirred the memories up, and I confess that what astonished me most, on reflection, was an absence of any real disagreement between us that I can remember as though some kind of overriding harmony held us both. Perhaps he explained at least one aspect of this when he said that our concern was to try to bridge the gulf between the Gaelic and lowland elements and so bring on a modern Scottish literature. Though no explanations can ever evoke the warm spirit of fellowship in adventure.

NATIONALISM IN WRITING

I—Tradition and Magic in the Work of Lewis Grassic Gibbon

SM, 1938

This article, on an aspect of the work of Lewis Grassic Gibbon (J Leslie Mitchell), was written by special request, shortly after that writer's death, for a projected book of similar appreciations by other writers. Gunn heard no more of the project and allowed *The Scots Magazine* to print it as the first of three articles on the general subject of Nationalism in Writing.

THE TWO QUALITIES in Leslie Mitchell's writing that move me to delight are his profound sense of Tradition and his eye for, and power to juggle with, Magic. These qualities I find at their most potent in *Sunset Song*; less so in the succeeding two parts of the *Quair*; and scarcely discernible in such of his purely English fiction as I have read.

Why this should be so in the case of the normal or orthodox use of English raises perhaps one of the most interesting speculations in literary practice known to our age. I am aware how unfair and misleading it can be to try to get at an author's own convictions or disabilities by way of what he has placed in the thought of one of his imagined characters, and accordingly I quote the following description of the division in the mind of the girl Chris Guthrie rather as a condition applicable to every mind that is trying to be creative in the fundamental world of the senses.

> Two Chrisses there were that fought for her heart and tormented her. You hated the land and the coarse speak of the folk and learning was brave and fine one day; and the next you'd waken with the peewits crying across the hills, deep and deep, crying in the heart of you and the smell of the earth in your face, almost you'd cry for that, the beauty of it and the sweetness of the Scottish land and skies. You saw their faces in firelight. ... You wanted the words they'd known and used, forgotten in the far-off youngness of their lives, Scots words to tell to your heart how they wrung it and held it, the toil of their days and unendingly their fight. And the next minute that passed from you, you were English, back to the English words so sharp and clean and true—for a while, for a while, till

99

they slid so smooth from your throat you knew they could never say anything that was worth the saying at all.

Thus one comes to appreciate not only the problem which Mitchell the realist posed to himself, but his brave effort to solve it. For manifestly the difficulty that here confronted him in all its terrible simplicity was to evoke the living girl in that absolute way that would make her known not only to us but to herself. The 'sharp and clean and true' refers not to evocation of such living reality but to description in exact terms of an outer apprehended reality whether in economic or social conditions or in the world of all the sciences.

It is a basic distinction, and one that may reasonably be taken to indicate Mitchell's own preoccupation with life; on the one hand, the concern of the creative artist; on the other, the concern of the man for the iniquitous conditions of the poor, strengthened by knowledge gained from his studies in archaeology and anthropology. Accordingly it might broadly be suggested that when Mitchell is using orthodox English, he is manipulating intellectual rather than blood values, and consequently in the realm of the emotions such English does not move us with a sense of the unconditional magic of life or of that life's being rooted in the breeding soil of tradition.

Before going on to consider more particularly the rather rash terms, Tradition and Magic, perhaps I should look for a moment at the nature of the effort he made to solve his problem, because it involved the use of the English language in a new pattern. To a writer, and particularly to a Scots writer, the problem is not only fascinating but still for the most part awaiting individual solution. Any effort at logical analysis would, of course, require much more space than this little essay will occupy, but if I may be allowed to cut the reasoning and come to my conclusion, I should say that what Mitchell achieved was not a new language but an old rhythm. Apart from a handful of Scots words, the medium used in the Scots novels is English, but the effect produced by the rhythm is utterly un-English. Indeed it is so profoundly of the soil of which Mitchell writes that in an odd moment of reverie the illusion is created of the soil itself speaking. The girl Chris realises she must have this rhythm of words or she will not know herself; Mitchell realises it; and the earth is fecund with it as with the peewit's cry. Mitchell makes the bold stroke of using it, and *Sunset Song* will justify him till the peewit becomes *vanellus vulgaris* in that language of Cosmopolis towards which he saw the whole world move.

Yet what a troubling division was in him just there! For he never imaginatively realised this Cosmopolis; he merely accepted it, like Tennyson or Mr H G Wells, as something in the nature of 'Progress' that is inevitable; and it was inevitable for Mitchell, I feel, not because of any ultimate need for it *in itself*, but because it was for humanity's final good *on the material or economic plane*. When we attain Cosmopolis, economic slavery and physical want will have vanished (though precisely why—as apart from piously—is never explained by any Cosmopolitan). It was not his anthropological studies, his scientific visualisations, if I may use such a phrase, that moved him here so much as his genuine, profoundly sensitive concern for the downtrodden; not that this concern expressed itself in the natural positive terms of love or kindness or Christian charity, but, characteristically (of himself and of his age), in a hatred of the oppressors—individual and system—that drew from him so often language of scathing directness or of obliterating irony. His sympathy is with 'the lowly, the oppressed, the Cheated of the Sunlight, the bitter relicts of the savagery of the Industrial Revolution', and he 'would welcome the end of Braid Scots and Gaelic, our culture, our history, our nationhood under the heels of a Chinese army of occupation if it would cleanse the Glasgow slums, give a surety of food and play—the elementary right of every human being—to those people of the abyss'.

This conjunction of social reformer and literary artist is generally held by the critics to be disastrous to inspired imaginative creation. And on occasion it certainly betrays Mitchell, as, for example, when he brings Ewan back from an ordinary training camp in Scotland to behave to his wife in so perverted and brutal a fashion that the reader can make less of it than Chris herself; a Ewan, too, reared amid all the healthy realities of the farmlands of the Mearns and already acquainted with most human experience between seduction and self-preservation. But I feel that Mitchell's concern for the poor and his hatred of any brutalising machine of the economic oppressors are factors of such importance in his make-up as a writer that any literary lapses to which they may lead him—often through restraint arising from excess of sensibility or through the taking of the social evil for granted—are relatively insignificant. Writers of the first class can no more escape the spirit of their age than they can stand detached from its struggles. With his sympathies already committed, for a writer to think he can justly hold the balance between the revolutionary and the reactionary may no doubt flatter him into the belief that he is acting like a god, but into his judgements or descriptions falsity will inevitably be woven.

In this respect Mitchell was never static, weighing 'literary values' as if they were eternally divorced from life and change (critics who do something like this fulfil a very necessary if secondary function), but dynamic and deeply committed to human life as it was lived around him, and facing fearlessly and courageously the ominous darkness of the future. In that sense, he was a portent on the Scottish scene and to me at least a portent of incalculable potentiality.

Now, all that being wrapped up in his idea of Cosmopolis, it naturally leads him to assert that he would destroy civilisation itself if it meant food and fun for the Glasgow slum dwellers. But to whatever exaggerations or sentimentalities it may have prompted him, the *cri-de-coeur* had justice at its core, and, for that matter, if we could see the whole actuating motive, probably the dream of that Golden Age which he believed the hag-ridden rites of civilisation strangled so long ago.

From that economic-ethical standpoint it is impossible to divorce the creative writer. Nor is there any need to, for the dichotomy is apparent only, even if Mitchell does not always appear to have realised as much himself. For to us the fact is that when he came to do his first creative work he deliberately chose not a language of Cosmopolis, not even orthodox English (which is near enough to cosmopolitan size for all practical purposes), but a particular use and pattern of English applicable to a small part of the small country of Scotland, a regional rhythm—and dying at that!

Not only so, but he (in *Scottish Scene*) has a characteristically fierce on-slaught on all living Scottish authors writing in English, for him they are not Scottish authors at all, but, at the best, 'brilliantly unorthodox Englishmen writing on Scotshire'. Quite apart from the 'heights of Scots literature' they do not attain even its 'pedestrian levels'.

From *economic* Cosmopolis to *creative* Nationalism, the turnabout is absolutely complete. And by his own work, it is absolutely justified. From the last ever-widening ring, he has come back in a rush to the heart of the disturbance. His rationalising of this may be faulty. In *Sunset Song*, for example, he justly recognises himself as a Scots writer attempting Scots work. But his use of English is similar in kind and creative intention to that of a considerable number of modern Irish writers, whose reputations are worldwide; to what is being produced in America; and possibly to what is being attempted in Scotland, if the mannerism was not always pronounced enough to take his fancy. But if his reasoning is inadequate here, the urge that moved him to it is sound. In a similar way his professed readiness to accept the Chinese army of occupation is sound, though at the same time palpably fantastic, simply because the Scots people, reforming and running their own social system, could cleanse the Glasgow slums without help either from the Chinese or from Cosmopolis. Why a Scot may not consume the surplus he produces until he has got the permission of an Asiatic or Cos-mopolist is a mystery that is not going to remain for ever dark. I would have had more faith in Mitchell's Cosmopolis if Mitchell had shown more faith in his own Scotland, and that for the obvious reason that the chance of reform-ing the world becomes possible only in so far as we show a disposition to reform ourselves. If a Scot is going to help the world towards Socialism, then the place for him is Glasgow or Dundee; if towards Cosmopolism, then still Glasgow or Dundee; if towards some still finer conception, yet again his native heath. History shows that the manner in which the peoples of the world have created new systems, from the Pharaohs to Lenin, is not likely to be upset by a sudden crystallisation of that Wellsian vagueness towards some universal good which has been, very properly, the theme of dreamers in all ages.

The intention here, however, is not to argue such discrepancies in belief or logic, but rather to indicate that Mitchell's hatred of human evil in our social relations and love of human good were fundamental and inalienable, and occasionally had such an intensity as gave his spirit a singular radiance.

It is because, then, of this real knowledge of, and revolutionary attitude towards, world affairs, that Mitchell's return to the Mearns in the narrowest, most absolute way, to perform his greatest creative act, is so striking and so important. And when he came back to write out of the tradition that was native to him, he inevitably became more truly traditional than the most ardent provincial charged with local pride. The sense of our Tradition is richer in Mitchell than in almost any modern Scot I know. For he is not primarily concerned with any particular phase of it, with whether we have sprung from Ossian or Dunbar; he is not the conscious craftsman continuing and enriching some particular past greatness; he is something newer and older than all that; he is the last man bred out of the Mearns earth, and at the same time and just as realistically he is the vanished Pict; in some curious but potent way, he is himself and his own reincarnation.

Thay may sound vague, but, taken in conjunction with what we have already said of his social ideas, it illuminates, I hope, his attitude to the whole range of Scottish history. For, above all, Mitchell feels himself as the man who roamed and tilled out Scottish land, its 'common man', who endured the conqueror, the tyranny that bred war and famine and plague, from century to century, epoch to epoch, but through it all turned to earth and sea, and from what was everlasting bred what is everlasting in us.

Accordingly it becomes easy to apprehend his meaning when he sees the Celts as 'a conquering military caste not a people in migration ... They survive to the present day as a thin strand in the Scottish population ... They were and remain one of the greatest curses of the Scottish scene ... It is one of the strangest jests in history that they should have given their name to so much that is fine and noble.' And: 'If the Kelts were the first great curse of Scotland, the Norse were assuredly the second ... And yet those dull, dyspeptic, whey-faced clowns have figured in all orthodox histories as the bringers of something new and vital to Scottish culture. ...'

No doubt his method of expression is deliberately meant to provoke complacent Scots, and, in any case, there are other historic readings of Celt and Norseman. M Hubert, for example, in two exhaustive books on the rise and decline of the Celts, shows them as being driven continually to the West, because 'they were not conquerors, they were civilisers'. But again, as in the dream of Cosmopolis, the debatable points are unimportant over against the validity of what Mitchell is striving to establish. And here is its picture: 'The peasant at his immemorial toil would lift his eyes to see a new master installed at the broch, at the keep, at, later, the castle: and would shrug the matter aside as one of indifference, turning, with the rain in his face, to the essentials of existence, his fields, his cattle, his woman in the dark little eirde, earth-house.' And when Christianity came he 'merely exchanged the bass chanting of the Druid in the pre-Druid circles for the whining hymnings of priests in wood-built churches: and turned to his land again'.

There is something deeper in all this than sympathy keyed to violence for the common man who has eternally to endure. For Mitchell believed, in common with a modern school devoted to scientific research in anthropology, that before civilisation came to ride us, there did exist on earth what the poets have called a Golden Age. That belief was at the back of his mind giving it poise and philosophy, impetus and wrath. And whether (as with his Cosmopolis and racial judgements) it is right or wrong again does not greatly matter to our purpose, for man has in him to this day a positive intuition of that far-back primordial goodness. Mitchell knew it not only scientifically but in the marrow of the bone.

Tradition is, then, for him at once a living embodiment of racial history and of his own history; and its settings (as in Chris's innermost thought) is 'the sweetness of the Scottish land and skies'. True to his instinct, he sets down the tale of it in the speech, the living rhythm, of the common man who in that land still endures.

Yet, however true his knowledge and intuition of Tradition, that tale would be unexceptional as literature if not touched, as we say, by creative fire. And so we arrive at last at what I may too spontaneously have called Magic. But this is where I want to please myself and to admit my own delight!

It is easy to say that Mitchell is a poet; and only a trifle less easy to argue that the degree of poetic inspiration is the measure of the novelist. We have the orthodox English conceptions of character-creation and descriptive narrative, and these are used by Mitchell as a matter of course and superbly well; but I maintain that the delight he communicates is something beyond this, beyond narration of seedtime and harvest in earth and brute; beyond a last human concern for the girl Chris Guthrie even; it is the transfusing spirit or essence of these and all that goes to give them substance and texture in a living and eternal pattern, and it is evoked by what I can only think of at the moment as incantation. And it is because (even to the precise degree in which) this evocative quality is lacking in *Cloud Howe* and *Grey Granite* that they fall short of *Sunset Song*. Any critical concern for exaggeration of fact or overstatement of brutality or limitation of style or other arguable detail of his work is here of quite secondary importance, is indeed almost beside the point. By virtue of this particular vision Mitchell gave reality to his earth and all that moved thereon against the eternal background. And if this savours of the easy phrase, *sub specie aeternatatis*, let me again repeat that the eternity was quite specifically the Tradition which I have so inadequately tried to suggest. For example, he is never overcome by fear or curiosity or mental blankness in the middle of a Stone Circle. He sees himself moving there in the twilights beyond recorded history, and occasionally seems to convey the scene by his very presence, without a word. He calls a place the 'den of Kinraddie', and the syllables are not only troubling in an evocative, prehistoric, wild-beast fashion, but cunningly draw into them, like prey, the starkest cries from the ballads. The Grampians are seen through a dip in the ground or a pass in the trees, and the face of the girl bears the wonder and strange delight and half-fear of all the faces that have so gazed since time began.

Finally, in this apprehension of what our Tradition is and what its evocation may mean in the way of delight, there is 'something still more deeply interfused'. I can only refer vaguely here to a richness, a fecundity, out of which life itself is born and will go on being born. For meaning, we should have to get contrasts—with, for instance, what it is that keeps some of our moderns burrowing among the roots. Whatever of darkness or sourness is in the Mearns soil, however the roots twist or knot, the white shoot of life pierces upward to the sun. There need be no lack of complexity, of thought coiling on itself like a druidic serpent, but the inherent principle is always that of life, never of the perversity that leads, by convolutions fascinating because personal, to the sterility that is ultimate death. So obvious a statement of opposites does not naturally permit mention of D H Lawrence, yet a profound study might well be made of what Lawrence hunted for in the deeps and contrasted with what Mitchell at least indicated might be born out of our Scottish soil in all its long pedigree from the sun circles of the pre-Druids: indeed, from long before that, when the life principle, working through perfect health, had for a spell its Golden Age.

Some time ago a distinguished Scottish writer, broadcasting on the efforts of his brethren, suggested that our Scottish countryside had nothing more to give the indigenous novelist. As if it were a place that had been skinned, leaving the void beneath. How effectively Mitchell proceeded to show that so far hardly even the skin had been affected! How supremely tragic that the demonstration should then have ceased!

NATIONALISM IN WRITING

II—The Theatre Society of Scotland

SM, 1938

I HAVE JUST RECEIVED a circular from the secretary of a new association which is in process of being formed with a view to establishing 'an endowed professional theatre in Scotland'. I have been interested from time to time in so many new 'movements' within our country, and have got so used to seeing them run their short race and fade out, that my first approach to still another effort is inclined to be tinged with scepticism.

I think I am expressing there a general attitude, an attitude which is almost instinctive and therefore rarely analysed. For, in the first place, why should Scotland be suffering this lust for new movements, and, in the second, why should we approach them with a touch of scepticism or despair?

To answer these two questions with anything approaching fullness or adequacy would require at least a whole issue of this magazine, because obviously it would entail a careful and realist investigation into what the word Scotland sums up in itself; and only when we arrived at that should we be in a position to appreciate what elements of the whole were so being denied or inhibited that every now and then there had to be efforts at easing or evacuating the congestion by 'movements'. This may have the air of being a too physiological parallel for what may appear to be a psychological affair. But in fact it is not so, for associations or parties, aiming at the freedom of the body politic, have been more strongly at work, have received greater publicity and have been better organised than any associations working for a cultural expression. I do not say that they have been more important, for body and mind make a single working unit and neither can function without the other.

But manifestly I cannot go into all that here. Even if space permitted, we should very soon hardly be able to see the green for bonnets! For the last thing we are prepared to do in a matter of this kind is to regard it scientifically. When a doctor sees a man suffering from nerves or on the verge of a breakdown, he does not consider it unnecessary to ask him a few questions about his bodily health. Yet that same doctor, if he is a literary gentleman, aware of Scotland's mental or artistic deficiencies, will at once pooh-pooh the very idea that the causal factors may lie in the governance or functioning of poor old Scotland's body. He affects to be superior to those who do consider the body, deems them cranks or quacks, and wise-cracks at their expense. All of which is very easy and entertaining, but of no earthly use as diagnosis. For he dare not face up to a scientific diagnosis. None of us really cares to be told the truth if it is going to be in the least uncomfortable. Better let us slide on as we are doing, and if we can be eased now and then by a new 'movement', particularly if it is cultural, why we are doing fine!

That, as far as I can make out, is the general Scottish attitude to-day. That it is an uneasy attitude, covering a feeling that something internal and deep-seated is far wrong, is, as I suggest, manifest from these sporadic ebullitions of energy that every now and then conceive a new weekly, monthly or quarterly journal, a new amateur, national or repertory theatre, a new political organisation or link-up of existing organisations, a new analysis, a new poetry, a new Highland League, a new rebellion, a new desperation of some sort. These symptoms are known and declared. They are not fanciful.

And the latest is this effort to form a 'Theatre Society of Scotland'. Those who first conceived the project obviously made up their minds that it was to be no hole-and-corner affair of parochial enthusiasm. Apparently the conception of Scotland is widening. Even in 'movements', there is no avoiding the general law of learning from our mistakes and defeats. After all, presumably it is a big affair or nothing; it is of national size, with inter-national implications, or it isn't worth bothering about. So amongst patron advisers, we find names like Ashley Dukes of London, Hilton Edwards of the Gate Theatre, Dublin, Tyrone Guthrie now of the Old Vic; in organisation, names of University principals, and of city fathers like Will Y Darling and P J Dollan: in playwriting, Bridie and Robins Millar; in literature, Eric Linklater, Hugh MacDiarmid, Edwin Muir, to select a contrasted trio; and so on for painting, sculpture, and the learned professions. Of the long list of printed names, only a small minority is Scottish Nationalist in politics. It is as if it had been decided to approach the national problem from the inter-national point of view.

Now, let me make it quite quite clear that the promoters do not explicitly recognise a 'national problem' at all. In their prospectus there is no sug-gestion that Scotland needs a theatre through which she may express her essential self. They merely want to 'bring together all who believe in the social and artistic value of the theatre, in order that a united effort may be made to establish an endowed professional theatre in Scotland.' This theatre 'would form a permanent centre for the pleasure of audiences and the advancement of the art of the theatre'. Amongst its services to the com-munity, it would 'explore the theatrical possibilities of Scottish intonation and movement, as shown in national speech and dance' and 'interest Scottish artists and art students in the work of scene and costume design'. 'Plays of all nations, types and tendencies' would be performed, as well as ballet, opera, and even the right sort of revue.

In short, what is envisaged here is a professional theatre for Scotland, through which the whole art of the stage would be made manifest; a national theatre such as countries of less population than Scotland, and with very much less material resources and educational endowment, possess normally in Europe. Even down in the Balkans, where a city may not have half the population of Edinburgh and a tiny fraction of its wealth, one naturally looks for its Opera House or its National Theatre. From the Balkans to Norway, where every budding dramatist thinks in terms of Ibsen. And from Norway to Dublin, where the endowed Abbey Theatre has produced drama that has had no small effect in recent years in revivifying the English stage and in setting a certain fashion to Europe.

Surely it should be possible to endow one such theatre in Scotland. Think of Glasgow with its enormous population and industrial wealth—the boasted second city of the earth's greatest empire—and then think of it or its citizens unwilling to endow one small theatre. For the moment, do not let us quarrel over the reason for this. Let us simply realise the fact, and see in this Theatre Society a body of Scottish men and women, representative of all the arts and of learning, endeavouring to bring an endowed Scottish theatre into being. Anyone can join this Society by paying half a crown and so help to realise the great aim. Are we capable of doing it?

As I began by saying, my first reaction was one of scepticism. But there are factors undoubtedly favourable to the scheme. The idea of Scotland as a unit for such an experiment is emerging. The swift and vast spread of the Community Drama Festival Movement implies that we have been starved of true dramatic nourishment. And there is, in satisfaction of what I have called the general Scottish attitude, the negative factor that the scheme is not 'nationalist'. For all those who assert that political nationalism is nonsense, and that what we want is a purely cultural revival, then here surely is their perfect opportunity to prove their case in at least one direction, that of the drama. Will they do it? Those of us who incline to scepticism, because of an analysis of the Scottish situation such as I have earlier indicated, shall await the results with interest: and meantime, let it be said, shall assist in every way possible.

For we in Scotland are labouring under difficulties. In Dublin, Irish national life was so strong that it created a drama out of itself. It had not to appeal to patrons by promising foreign plays and ballet and opera. It did not say: Endow us so that we may give you artistic satisfactions. It said: We will show you your own life translated into drama, and make you sit up, and look at it, and realise it as you have never done before. Here is Ireland, here is Cathleen ni Hoolihan, here are your conflicts and your slums, the plough and the stars, and there goes the all-wise Juno, and there her drunken Paycock asking: 'What is the moon; what is the stars?' I have seen most of the great Abbey plays in the Abbey, and remember vividly still the shock I got when, at my first visit many years ago, I heard the Irish voices in the 'Shadow of a Gunman' coming over the footlights into the darkened auditorium. I had forgotten, if I had ever known, that contemporary drama could act on one like this.

But we cannot expect anything like that in Scotland, because there has been neither a sense of national conflict nor of national travail; there has not been that high movement of the country's spirit out of which great drama is made. That is not a vague emotional statement; it is simple fact, and can be checked, as I say, by reference to the experience of Ireland and, even still more recently, by the experience of Russia and the remarkable drama that is appearing in that country, a drama that makes most of our British pieces look like sophisticated trifling about sweet or nasty nothings.

How, then, can an endowed theatre in Scotland be of any real use to us, apart of course from providing those so-called artistic satisfactions? Where dramatic conflict is lacking how can real drama emerge? What do we want a national theatre for if we have nothing in ourselves, nothing national, to express there?

In a sentence, is this to be another petit-bourgeois effort at keeping abreast of other peoples' conceptions of the drama of life? Looking ahead, I think not. Because of our position, as I have attempted to hint at it, we need a theatre first, to which Scottish writers may bring their conceptions of life, born out of a heredity and environment peculiarly their own. These conceptions may be defeatist, disruptive, rebellious, constructive, but at least they would refer to elements of conflict in our country that are profoundly real, from the tragic and heroic sea-fisheries of the north to the desperate industrialism of the south, from the Highland glen to the Lowland farm, with all the vital inter-play of character and thought and aspiration such scenes inevitably imply, for portrayal through the essential Scottish conception of fantasy, comedy, and tragedy. At present a Scottish writer has no theatre to which he can take any such drama. Just as his country suffers from having no focal point, no vitalising heart, so the native playwright suffers, in this single element of the drama, from having no central stage, no national theatre, to which he may bring the fruits of his talent and have them read and judged as drama, not as hopeful commercial efforts at understudying the London stage. Even in the immense growth of the Community Drama Festival Movement, he has proved to himself already that only a certain type of play is preferred for competitive purposes. To a large degree it has become a game of acquiring marks, and the more cunning amateurs have become expert at the game.

What the Scottish playwright, who feels he may have something to say or to evoke, needs is a theatre, run by professional players, to whom he can entrust the expression of adult thought and irony and imagination. Without such a theatre he is crippled in expression or simply does not write plays at all and turns to some other medium, like the novel. Such a theatre needs to be endowed, if we are going to get the best.

Again let it be said that this Theatre is not being founded with a view to encouraging the Scottish playwright. It will encourage him for all that, and the seeing of first-class foreign work will be no disadvantage to a developing technique. If he comes away with plays, as the Irish and Russians have done, there will be much more fun going around than is usually found in a milieu for providing social and artistic values. But that smile must remain directed towards the lap of the gods.

Meanwhile there are doubting but still hopeful Scots who will watch with considerable interest what is going to happen to the Theatre Society of Scotland.

NATIONALISM IN WRITING

III—Is Scottish Individualism to be Deplored?

SM, 1939

HOW OFTEN IT IS STATED in these days that what is wrong with the Scot is his individualism! Because of this characteristic, this inbred desire to gang his ain gait, he is the notorious creator of schism. The history of his Church appears to show it conclusively, for surely if there is any realm in which a people with a long tradition should tend to be at one it is in the religious, where no personal privilege should intrude and all vanities be forgotten; yet the divisions and sub-divisions in the history of Scottish worship have been more numerous and bitter than those in the history of almost any other country. Again, in the temporal sphere, there is much the same record of sporadic communal endeavour destroyed by internal bickerings or lack of faith, whether it be a scheme of co-operation in the Western Highlands that runs its short course and dies, or the effort to-day at a political and economic reintegration of the whole nation which can hardly be said to have roused popular enthusiasm. Indeed, it has become a common saying that the Scot can govern anyone but himself. Even when he did combine, as the crofters combined towards the end of last century to fight for a common aim and had their victory recorded on the statute book, what was won was the right of each *individual* crofter to security of tenure. That end ensured, those concerned immediately reverted to an individualism which can hardly be considered to have saved the Highlands economically or spiritually.

So much has all this been the case, that our best Scottish writers to-day not only deplore it, but turn away from any particular consideration of the Scottish scene towards more hopeful movements of the human spirit in other countries.

The whole theme is one of great interest and deep importance. In fact, it may be said that the conception of individualism, of individual freedom, is occupying the mind of man to-day more sharply than at any other period.

Freedom is a word that is used frequently, yet seldom defined. Its meaning is taken for granted. Now the danger in taking anything for granted is not altogether that it may produce a confusion in thought. We may all have approximate agreement in the meaning. The danger lies in assuming as inevitably correct those basic conditions—the premises—out of which the meaning or accepted conception is born.

In the ancient agrarian system there was the relationship of the master and the slave. To us, more familiarly, there were the fuedal lord and the serf. Here was a human relationship in a form of society so circumscribed that it had a clear pattern, with laws of conduct and social obligations very simply defined. The serf found his freedom in complete dependence on his master, much as soldiers in a modern army are said to find freedom in dependence on their officers (that is, in getting rid of all responsibility for personal decisions), or as members of a Church may find freedom by resigning the purpose of their lives into its absolving and saving hands.

Now the ancient agrarian system might have continued indefinitely, for it was essentially static, were it not for that discontent in man which is sometimes called divine. Man began to adventure, to trade, to gather wealth that he held on to as his own. In thus adventuring and trading he found the horizons of the world opening out before him, and the inner horizons of his thought widening beyond his dreams. New speculations, new beauty, and, in particular, a new and thrilling conception of personal freedom. It was as if he had been born again; and, in fact, this new attitude to life came to be called the Renaissance. Enter the trader, the merchant, the financier—the new bourgeois class.

The old personal relationship in the agrarian state was now seen to be intolerable in its human compulsion. No man should have absolute power over another man, as the master had over the slave, or the lord over his serf. The consequent servility denied the God-implanted spirit in man and lowered him to the level of the beast of burden. Man had been born free, but everywhere (as Rousseau memorably summed it up) he was in chains. The chains must be broken and man emerge as master of his fate and captain of his soul. Man's high destiny was to be independent of any man's compulsion, and he was, in fact, completely free only when he could withdraw from society altogether and pursue his thought or his wild flowers or his loves in some happy bower far from the multitude's ignoble strife.

This bourgeois society which followed on the gradual break-up of the agrarian or feudal system, and which is still with us, has been for man the most brilliant period in his history. It brought tremendous gains in speculative thought, wealth, diversity of art and applied art, diffusion of knowledge, travel and adventure, but particularly in science and mechanics, and to such a degree that it fully discovered and in no small measure changed the surface of the earth. The enterprise and energy expended were stupendous and in result often magnificent and sometimes marvellous. It is doubtful indeed whether the tyranny that underlay the old feudal system could have been broken by any less powerful force. It certainly was broken, and man emerged, a free individual with control over his destiny.

Of course, there was one respect in which he was not free, namely in his economic relations, but then he never can be free there so long as his animal body needs food, shelter and clothing. That had all along been realised. But bourgeois society had provided in some measure for that difficulty, too, by offering the opportunity to a small percentage of its members to amass wealth or property, so that without toiling or spinning themselves they could yet be housed and fed. The right to achieve this happy state was denied to none. The basis of the whole system was equal opportunity and equal right under the law. No man could compel any other man's labour. Every man was free to offer his labour or to withhold it, to stay at home or to adventure abroad. The old relationship that had existed between the lord and serf was dissolved and its place taken by a cash relationship.

This change from the personal to the impersonal was bound to be fraught with striking consequences, because the one fact about economic or social relations is that they are social; that is, human. If they are dehumanised, then the emotional forces of man are interfered with and, lacking normal expression, will in course of time, and after many rumblings, find abnormal expression; particularly if, behind them, is the growing compulsion of economic necessity.

And this in truth began to happen. Man had won free from the direct tyranny of man by accepting the indirect tyranny of cash. But because the tyranny of cash appeared indirect, it was no less compulsive than the tyranny of the slave owner, for without cash in this fine new world, man dies. In truth, the machine that employed him, when it was glutted, threw him aside—unlike the old master who continued to look after his slave because, at the lowest, he was of value to him, as was his horse.

A strange new world indeed, where man in theory was completely free and where yet in practice he found himself tied by invisible chains to a machine. If he threw off the chains, he starved. He was free to starve. But no man wants to starve, nor does he want his wife and children to starve. And then a new horror invaded this hitherto expanding and adventuring society: the difficulty of finding a machine to which to chain himself. Slumps, unemployment, war.

II

So this new society began to be examined with some care. It professed the complete freedom of the individual, a freedom that was as much his birthright as it was that of any noble animal of the forest. Free trade. Free thought. There seemed no end to this freedom—until one man came up against another man's property and found that (unlike the noble animal of the forest in parallel circumstances) he was not free to attempt to acquire it by stealth or force, however much he required it and however little the owner did. A man—every man—had not only the right to hold to what was his own, but was supported in that right by the laws of bourgeois society. The machine might appear a very impersonal thing, but it was private property. And the man who owned it had as much power over the man who worked it for him as ever lord had over his serf—but not a direct, personal power, for the human relationships had been lost in the cash nexus. This was a very interesting discovery and gave rise to all sorts of political doctrines and economic analyses. To 'blame' the man who owned the machine was absurd. It was implicit in the system that men should own the machines and that men should work them.

Once again then it seemed that, though man had been born free, he was still everywhere in chains. Bourgeois society had, in fact, failed to give man the individual freedom that it conceived of as his birthright. What had gone wrong? Or was bourgeois society doomed by its very nature to be unable to give it to him?

The answer to this, from the new school of thought that now divides the world, was the striking one that bourgeois society could not give it to him because its very conception of freedom was itself a myth. Man was not 'born free' in the Rousseau sense. Man was not a lonely, splendid being who 'found his soul' only when he withdrew from society and all its dealings. Man, as we know him, could fulfil himself and find his highest measure of freedom only in and through society; man was a social animal, not a detached and noble individual independent of all restraint.

This was indeed revolutionary doctrine, hitting not only at our bourgeois conceptions of society, but at some of its finest literature, at most of its speculative thought, and at not a little of its scientific research. Its argument against being 'born free' for example, was as simple as this: Take the child when he is 'born free' and send him out to the wilds to be suckled by goat or ewe, and then visit him after twenty years to see what sort of man he has grown into. Even the most optimistic would hardly expect him to have speech, music, art, science, poetry, in any developed form! In short, that which distinguishes us from the animal, that which gives us the very power to contemplate freedom as a possible possession, is received from society.

This was the new doctrine, derived from Karl Marx. It was not only an economic creed: it was a whole way of living, a philosophy of life, and many of its devotees profess their faith with a religious zeal. Bourgeois society, with its private ownership of the sources of production, had not only failed to satisfy the economic needs of society, with consequent slumps, unemployment and war, but in the process had driven man into a tyrannical impersonal relationship to a machine instead of into a warm, human relationship happily held together by common economic necessity. Absolute freedom was a myth. Even the owner of the machine was not free. His economic privileges were the result of a constant watchfulness, and often indeed of slavish, fear-driven hard work.

The important psychological element in this new doctrine was, of course, the tender social relations that would exist between men who in common owned the means of economic production. To satisfy a common need there would be a common endeavour, divorced from any possibility of private tyranny. In this endeavour man would find his freedom, the greatest measure of freedom he can ever hope to find; for as an animal he must always be under the compulsion of economic necessity and as an individual he can get his culture only from society. The economic relations that are the basis of society thus became of supreme importance. An individualism which tended to disrupt economic relations, which challenged this new social doctrine, had to be squashed for the common good. And the proof of the doctrine was always to be discovered by working it out in actual practice. That was part of what was called its dialectic: one thinks and then one acts, and the validity of the thought is proved or otherwise in the action.

If in bourgeois society the important element was the individual, in this new conception of society the important thing was society itself, based always and forever on economic relations.

III

Now this new doctrine came to be tested in actual practice in Russia and with results that have in many ways been remarkable. But it is not the intention here to enumerate economic achievements, or to express a personal attitude to the Russian experiment. Our immediate point of interest lies in this matter of individual freedom, and it has to be recorded that, more and more, responsible critics are beginning to wonder whether in this particular respect the doctrine is really proving itself in practice. I refer particularly, perhaps necessarily, to critics who themselves were favourable to the experiment and anxious for its fulfilment, such a critic as Mr Herbert Read, who, in his recent book, *Poetry and Anarchism*, has come to the conclusion that all is not well in Russia so far as this personal freedom is concerned. He makes allowances for the necessary suppressions of the 'transition period', but regretfully finds that after twenty-one years the suppressive and repressive influences are still at work, and twenty-one years is a long time. For it was a cardinal part of the original doctrine that after the transition period, after a classless society had been achieved, then the conjunction of forces which had achieved it would naturally tend to disappear; or, as it was graphically put by Engels, the State would gradually 'wither away'. But Mr Read finds that the State in this case, instead of showing any signs of withering away, is, on the contrary, growing stronger, with everywhere its bureaucratic forces becoming more solidly entrenched. Freedom of individual expression and action remains restricted, and the tragic fate of some of the Revolution's best poets and writers leaves him deeply troubled. For, unless the State withers away, Communism to Mr Read is merely another tyranny, the tyranny of the bureaucrat over the worker, and he finds it difficult to believe that the tyranny is likely to grow less, because of the psychological factor that *power corrupts*.

And no matter how perfectly in these circumstances the economic life of the country is arranged, such a critic as Mr Read would still be unimpressed, because the best example of a perfect functioning of economic relations is to be found in the beehive—a conception of efficiency that applied to human society would be utterly repulsive.

The freedom of the individual would thus seem to be an elusive quality! Yet nothing is more certain than that individual man, with his capacity for rational decision, is the highest-known achievement of the evolutionary process. First the single cell, multiplying itself by fission. Then the grouping of cells in a single organism in a relationship that may be regarded as rigidly economic. The increasing complexity of the organism, with functional specialisation of parts, until man arrives on the scene, and adds to the economic relations the new element of self-consciousness, the human mind. This new element, this 'extra dimension', of the organism, is particularly distinguished by its capacity to discuss 'free will', to contemplate itself and ask in how far as an individual it is 'free'. Even from a purely scientific standpoint it is no wonder, then, that man should be so preoccupied with this notion or problem of freedom, for it is the flowering of the whole biological process.

Thus is set up the stress between economic relations on one side and freedom on the other. As they are interdependent, or as one arises and can only arise out of the other, there should ideally be no stress, or as little stress as possible, and so man strives to found his 'perfect State' where such a happy arrangement might be consummated. But because of the complex nature of man's mind, of its many elements destructive as well as constructive, and because of the basic need for economic security (with the strife and consequent greed and hate hitherto arising therefrom), he naturally finds it difficult to achieve this happy arrangement. But he goes on striving; and the business of the artist or creative writer is to see that, whatever permutations and combinations of economic relations may arise, the flower of freedom must be preserved; and not only preserved, but cultivated. In its many forms and colouring, and in the irrational subjective fantasies to which it gives rise, he finds what he calls beauty. This is the true function of artist or poet and perhaps explains the reason for the remarkable importance he has had in human history. He is the jealous guardian of the latest manifestations of individual life in the biological process.

Accordingly it would seem that he cannot become the politician in the accepted sense. He can belong to a political party and work for it in the hope that it may so arrange economic relations as to help towards human freedom, but at the same time he must forever be critical, and when he sees his party laying so much stress on economic relations that the flower of freedom is endangered, then he must protest.

IV

If, after this somewhat lengthy over-simplification of certain historic processes, we return to our original question, whether Scottish individualism is to be deplored, we may perhaps get a slightly clearer idea of the scope of the answer. At once, then, we may agree that an excessive individualism tending to neglect and disrupt the economic relations of society is harmful ultimately to individual freedom. And this, in fact, is what has happened in Scotland. But—and now the point has to be emphasised—that does not mean that individualism (the expression of individuality) is bad in itself. On the contrary, as we have seen, it marks the highest point in biological evolution, and to attempt to 'sink it' in an earlier phase—and a purely economic relationship is the earliest phase of all—would be to retrogress. In short, it is not the Scot's individualism that is at fault, it is his failure to deal with the abiding problem of economic necessity in such a socially co-operative way that he would attain the maximum freedom to develop that very individualism which as things are, seems to be his curse.

Why has he failed to do this? Does his history show him to have lagged behind in social evolution, compared with his European neighbours? The answer is very definitely in the negative. Scotland was perhaps the first country in northern Europe to give clear expression in a political instrument to the modern conception of democracy, of the 'liberty which no good man loseth but with his life'. (The Declaration of Arbroath, 1320 A.D.) Even in that earlier form of agrarian society, characterised elsewhere by the master and the slave, or the feudal lord and the serf, Scotland had a relationship between what we may loosely call chief and clansman that was not only warm and human but remarkable for a high degree of individual independence and absence of personal compulsion or tyranny. Nor was that merely 'a tribal stage', as has been made clear by those who have studied what is called the old Gaelic Commonwealth. Accordingly the institutions that grew out of this background were at an early date democratic in form, as the constitution of her Church and her legal and educational systems clearly show. What then went wrong with the evolution of Scotland *along her own natural lines* towards a higher communal integration of economic relations and a clearer expression of individual freedom? How were the chiefs debauched and turned into bad feudal lords? (for feudalism proper had a clear philosophy of its own). Why should a Clydeside communist have to turn to Russia—to Russia that, a generation ago under the Czars, was still largely at that agrarian stage of master and slave which had been transcended by Scotland before the beginning of her recorded history (if indeed it ever obtained)? Why should the Scot have retained in so marked a degree his individualism, his uneasy individualism, and lost his capacity for economic co-operation?

Does the logical answer lie in the possibility that the Scot was inevitably doomed to lose his capacity for co-operation from the very moment that he abdicated his power to deal with his own economic relations?

But that would require a searching inquiry into comparatively recent history, and so here for the time being I must let the matter rest.

LITERATURE: CLASS OR NATIONAL?

Outlook, 1936

THOUGH I HAPPEN to agree with much that Mr Lennox Kerr wrote under the above heading in your last issue, I must say that I feel he failed completely to make out his 'case against the claim that literature is national in origin'. In fact, in his provocative article he does not discuss the origins of literature at all, and his reply to the PEN's 'Literature, though national in origin, knows no frontiers and should be a common currency between nations ...' takes the evasive form of a discussion of class differences within existing political organisations.

The simple truth of the matter seems to be that literature is national in origin and has found its subject-matter or drama precisely in those class differences and other distinctions or inequalities which together make up the life of a nation. That such has been the case may—or may not—be unfortunate. That it is a fact is surely unquestionable. If we regard poetry as literature's highest expression, then literature still remains a national affair, for to this day great poetry does not bear translation from its own tongue into any other. Even in a country like Scotland, which has been doing its best, or worst, with English for some centuries, we are forced to recognise that the poetry, which has achieved more than a national reputation has been written in Scots.

And it may be interesting for Mr Kerr to reflect further that what we consider in Scotland our finest literature is largely an expression of the people, whether of yesterday in the *Scots Quair* of Lewis Grassic Gibbon, or the day before in Burns or Mary Macleod, or earlier in the Ballads, or earlier still in the ceilidh-house tales and poems; the expression of a folk who together make a unique nation. Burns is as well known in the Highlands as in the Lowlands. A Skyeman assures me that a generation ago he was the only poet, other than the Gaelic bards, known—and loved—in the Island. I can myself vouch for the far north. And decidedly the best of Burns is not a poetry produced to pander to the tastes, social or possessive, of those in power, any more than were the satires of the northern bards. It is not a mere accident that made *Sunset Song* so significant and stirring as literature compared with the English novels of Leslie Mitchell. In both his English and his Scots novels, Mitchell was always for the people, for the classless folk. No one hated more bitterly the social inequalities and tragedies resulting from the present organisation of society. But Mitchell had to come back to his own country, his own people, before what moved him so deeply received in profoundest expression. In the absence of any evidence to the contrary, that is what we have got to accept; and that is what, I take it, is implied by 'national origin' in the PEN declaration, or, if one likes, by the 'culture pattern' of our modern anthropologists. The culture pattern is susceptible of change, of course. What Mr Kerr has really done in his article is to indicate the form such a change may or should take.

Yet at this point I again feel that Mr Kerr evades the real issue by an attempt to 'escape' from it, like his middle-class artist, into a realm of political theory where literature's individuality is sunk in the major dictum, 'all art is propaganda'. I hope he will not misunderstand me if I say that this dictum is becoming intellectually fashionable, particularly amongst those—mostly *bourgeois*—who consider themselves as political rebels deriving from Lenin. Not nationalism but internationalism is their phrase. Not merely the steve-dores of Glasgow and the stevedores of London (to whom Mr Kerr refers), but also the stevedores of Hamburg and Jibuti and Singapore and Venice. The culture change can be brought about only by the working classes of all nations making common cause against the capitalists of all nations. This is the sort of facile conception of direct action that may well be subversive of the very idea it carries. However, as it is possible to theorise endlessly, let us be realist or concrete; let us choose two cases: one, where such an economic change has taken place as realises more or less the classless order or working-class order of society desired by Mr Kerr; and, two, a country where a literary renaissance has actually resulted from a national rebirth. Let us take Russia and Ireland.

Now the first outstanding fact about Russian Communism is that it was built on a national basis. Lenin manifestly did not make it a *working* maxim that it would be impossible to get the stevedores of Archangel into a classless State without first of all getting the stevedores of Glasgow, London, etc, to link up with them in a revolutionary struggle. Although Russia was over-whelmingly peasant, Lenin did not approach the crofters of Wester Ross before collaring the land of Russia for the Soviet Republics. The social dif-ference between a Russian landowner and the slave who bore the weals of his knout was vastly greater than the difference between Mr Kerr's Duke and his Communist MP in modern Scotland. But such differences did not deter Lenin: on the contrary, they spurred him on all the more strongly to realise his classless society in that place where he could plan and function most naturally and satisfactorily, namely, in his own land. A stevedore in Glasgow is in the same relation or proportion to the Scottish people as a stevedore in England to the English, or as stevedores elsewhere to peoples elsewhere. Increasing the unit does not mathematically alter the proportion. As a realist, Lenin saw this and so went into action on the basis of the organised political unit or nation of which he himself was part. He must first remould his own culture pattern and leave it to other nations to realise how valuable or otherwise the change might be.

This is the sort of fact that our more romantic internationalists do not care to face. It is so much easier to grow eloquent over the world brotherhood of the workers, their similarity of interests, and to point out that as a stevedore in London has much in common with a stevedore in Glasgow, therefore all talk of the nation as a basis for economics or art is 'nonsense'. Whatever else Lenin did, he gave the knock-out to all that. And it is only too easy to imagine a Russian today saying, 'Russian Communism, national though it be in origin, knows no frontiers and should be a common currency. . . .' In such a light we can see the enormous importance of the Russian experiment. Should it work through to a permanent solution of the present appalling economic conditions in capitalist States, then humanity's indebtedness to it will be very great—and for generations literature and art may well be concerned with its spiritual interpretation and praise. Indeed, in Russia, literature and art have already been powerfully affected by the social change, though unfortunately there is no space to consider the results here, nor to look into the rebirths of arts and tongues in the various Republics. One word more in this connection. Mr Kerr says that politics and art 'are both products of contemporary life and thought', both 'no more than expressions' of the age. In an immediate sense, yes. But actually this age is the result of all the ages that have gone before. The new virile art of the working classes that Mr Kerr foresees will not be divorced from past expressions of art, but, on the contrary, will be added to them, affecting them all by its presence, as it (and they) will be affected in turn by the art of a later age.

In Ireland, the significant feature for our purpose is not economic but literary. Joyce and Yeats are not accidental portents any more than the rise of the Abbey Theatre, which responsible dramatists call the mother of Repertory in Europe. The plays of Sean O'Casey that took the theatre by storm were plays by a Dublin working man dealing realistically with the effect of a nationalist uprising on the common people. Out of conflict in the national spirit, he created his vivid drama.

There are those, of course, who put down Scotland's failure in the arts not to the loss of any possibility of conflict in the national spirit (Scotland having surrendered her nationhood and therefore all responsibility), but to the introduction of Calvinism. Could anything be more fantastic? For it only requires a moment's thought to realise that an even worse failure occurred in Ireland, which has remained Roman Catholic throughout. In metaphysics, experimental science, painting, and even in architecture, Scotland struggled along to give some sort of account of herself. By comparison, Romanist Ireland remained deep in superstition and despair. The magnificent outburst of literature in recent years in Ireland synchronised precisely with the national uprising of the people; and it is a fair assumption that had the national spirit not raised its head, the literature would not have appeared. Religion in either case was not one of the profound factors in the matter. Excess of Calvinism was a symptom, not a cause. If the loss of Catholicism was Scotland's undoing, then the history of the Scandinavian countries with their brilliant progress in literature, sculpture, and architecture must remain one of the world's great mysteries!

So far as social evolution has gone, then, it would seem that a man creates most potently within his own national environment. Outside it he is not so sure of himself, not so fertile, not so profound. That appears to be the accepted anthropological fact. Lenin recognised it. So did the Irish writers. If a man feels that he has no longer a nation of his own, then he will hang on to some other nation, as the Scottish Labour Party, for example, hangs on to the English Labour Party. Unless the English Party may be cajoled into doing something about Mr Kerr's working-class ideal, the Scots of themselves can do nothing. The relationship is essentially parasitic, working at second-hand, and provides the mechanism of escape for those who have not the courage to assume direct responsibility. For, whether we like it or not, the nation is still the basis of all large-scale creative human endeavour, and in that sense, it seems to me, it would be difficult for a Scot to show up impressively before either an Irish dramatist or a Russian of the classless State.

REVIEW OF SCOTT AND SCOTLAND

SM, 1936

LITERARY CRITICISM of the quality of Mr Muir's is rare in any country; in Scotland even its tradition seems to have got lost. In saying as much, I am not concerned with particular attributes of penetration or insight, with individual gifts of paradox or brilliant exposition, but with that rare power of lifting criticism on to a plane where its observations and judgements combine in a synthesis that induces in the mind a state of harmony. His writing has, in fact, no tricks at all. It is quiet and lucid, and eschews colour and personal whim to the point of seeming cold. Nor is this the clarity of intellect alone. Metaphysicians are common enough. Behind Mr Muir's assessments is not only a fine intellect but an imagination of a very pure kind, and it is with the help of this imagination (or in its light) that his intellect is able to select all important factors (an intellect that included everything would describe nothing) and to combine them with the same sort of satisfying or harmonious effect as is achieved by any truly creative work. Whether his intellect is powerful or his imagination profound does not arise here. It is enough that his literary criticism is of this creative kind, because in Scotland we had almost forgotten that real criticism was anything but a collieshangie or a fight.

Accordingly what Mr Muir may have to say on Scott and on Scotland will not only command our respect, but—more important—move us beforehand to an agreeable expectancy. If therefore I find him at the end of his present task stumbling and uncertain, it is with a feeling of dismay. It is as if when he leaves the realm of literary criticism, where his judgements are so sure and illuminating, and faces the common light of our political day, his powers of apprehension desert him. This is so curious a phenomenon that it justifies, I hope, particular attention. For the rest I can but trust that any remarks of mine may serve the one purpose of sending readers to this searching and original study of the predicament of the Scottish writer.

At once Mr Muir sees that the line his enquiry must take is not what Scott did for Scotland but what Scotland failed to do for Scott and why. How does it come about that 'by far the greatest creative force in Scottish literature as well as one of the greatest in English' leaves a feeling of 'curious emptiness' behind all the wealth of imagination? 'Many critics have acknowledged this blemish in Scott's work,' and Mr Muir sets himself out to account for it by considering the country in which Scott lived, a country 'which was neither a nation nor a province', and had, 'instead of a centre, a blank, an Edinburgh'. Scott had no country and no continuing tradition in the way that an English-man or a German had. To this day, if a Scots writer wishes to add something to his native literature, 'he will find in Scotland, no matter how long he may search, neither an organic community to round off his conceptions, nor a major literary tradition to support him, nor even a faith among the people themselves that a Scottish literature is possible or desirable'. In this, Mr Muir is more or less summing up what has been said by nearly every modern Scots writer of importance, and shows in due course how Scott himself, in a moment of moving self-realisation, cried out against the historical material he dealt in, calling it 'stuffing my head with the most nonsensical trash'. Scott was so great a genius that what he dealt in must have some reality to the mind of living men. It is not that the history was untrue or was inadequate subject matter for his genius; it was that it no longer enriched or influenced a living national tradition; it had not even the potency of pure legend; it was story-telling or romance set in a void; it was seen backwards as in the round of some time spyglass and had interpretive bearing neither upon a present nor a future. Only some such intuition from Scott's 'secret world' could have drawn from him in his latter years these bitter words.

Mr Muir's great service to us here consists in analysing the meaning of this tradition; that is, he first isolates the elements that go to make a living tradition and then shows the inevitable result of their loss. Language, criticism, comparisons of Scottish poetry before and after the dissolution of Scots, the failure to achieve poetic drama, particular expressions of the Scots spirit as in Fantasy—each element is treated in turn with a fine precision. This section of the book is an original contribution of high value. The matter, however, is so condensed that an adequate resumé here is impossible. It may suffice for my purpose to indicate the trend of the discussion.

'The pre-requisite', writes Mr Muir, 'of an autonomous literature is a homogeneous language', Scotland had this language until 'sometime in the sixteenth century'. While it had it, it produced a literature that bore com-parison with other national literatures; when it lost it, its literature decayed, because writers in Scotland were left not with one medium but with two: English for the expression of thought and Scots for the expression of emotion. Poetry of a major kind cannot be created by a mind thus divided. Great literature results from the fusion of thought and feeling on the highest plane. Where this fusion does not take place, poetry tends to become an irresponsible outburst of emotion and thought an arid expression of disapproval.

That Scotland had a homogeneous language, a single tongue for thought and emotion, up to the seventeenth century, we already know from the works of poets like Dunbar. How rich and varied the expression of this early period must have been, most of us are only beginning vaguely to realise. Mr Muir quotes an anonymous poem from the Bannatyne MS (1568) which he considers one of the supreme lyrics in Scottish literature. Its first lines evoked for me a memory of Donne's 'Ecstasy'. Yet it was written not only before the 'Ecstasy' but possibly long before Donne was born. He quotes other poems representing 'a quality in Scottish poetry which has been lost for good, a quality which has not been striven for since, even unsuccessfully'. He concludes this section with the sonnet by Mark Alexander Boyd (died 1601), which Mr Ezra Pound writes of as 'the most beautiful sonnet in English'. Altogether a remarkable period, of which we know only a few figures and 'a few scraps'. As Mr Muir points out, of the twenty-two poets Dunbar mentions in his 'Lament for the Makars', only four or five are known to us by their works.

It is supremely important that we realise not merely the richness and power and promise of this period, but its wholeness. These poets, writing in uninterrupted national tradition, were expressing the minds of a highly civilised society. Only when this is remembered may the disintegration that followed be understood. With this illuminating fact in his mind, Mr Muir has no great difficulty in resolving what Gregory Smith called 'The Caledonian Antisyzygy'. For all that it broadly amounts to is that we are back at the old division of mind again, with the opposites now labelled practical and fantastic, but with the critic attempting to reconcile the opposites by showing that the Scots poet can be at ease in 'both rooms of life' at the same time. Gregory Smith's analysis is brilliant and Mr Muir does it justice, but the truth surely is that you cannot be in both rooms at the same time; the best you can do is to hover in the doorway between, and however humorous, fantastic, and delightful may be your efforts at a double tenancy, the final result is 'a stationary disharmony, a standing frustration. For imagination and intellect do not reach a reconciliation in this poetry, but a comic deadlock.'

This lack of wholeness in the creative mind is seen in Burns and Scott and Stevenson. Mr Muir shows how in the one passage of 'Tam o' Shanter' where Burns 'makes a serious reflection on life' he drops into English. (The lines beginning: 'But pleasures are like poppies spread'.) 'It is clear that Burns felt he could not express it in Scots, which was to him a language for sentiment but not for thought.' In Scott, the division is still there, but—and one has to isolate this with more purpose than Mr Muir has done—it is not now so much a matter of language, for Scott could use English comprehensively, nor of the inhibiting force of Calvinism, for Scott was a Tory gentleman; it is a -matter of the meeting place of all the dividing or opposing factors, in short, his environment, his country. After his first important work, the 'Minstrelsy of the Scottish Border', Scott said: 'Trivial as may appear such an offering to the Manes of a kingdom, once proud and independent, I hang it upon her altar with a mixture of feelings which I shall not attempt to describe.' Scott saw his country's 'manners and character ... daily melting and dissolving into those of her sister and ally'. And Mr Muir comments: 'By his collection of all sorts of relics and mementoes of Scotland's history ... he conceived concretely a broken image of the lost kingdom'. And that last poet's phrase sums up the whole matter. Scott's ordered legal thought was for the established order, for the Union; but his imagination, his vision, was with the broken image of the lost kingdom. The division we have been trying to grasp here reaches its final definition, and Mr Muir's last words are 'that he lived in a country which could not give an organic form to his genius'.

Now though Mr Muir, the literary critic, sees clearly that it is the inner secret knowledge of the loss of a kingdom, 'once proud and independent', that fatally divided Scott's genius, gathering up in its comprehensive truth all lesser considerations of nonsensical trash, of the personal feeling of being 'almost wholly neglected or left to myself', of religious manifestation and Fantasy, even of language itself; though he sees this not merely with a critic's acumen but with a poet's imagination, he yet fails when approaching the suasion or politics of his subject to apply this truth, the only one in the book which includes all opposites, all warring or disintegrating factors, and reconciles them.

The importance of this disability can hardly be overstressed, for it shows that the old division is still amongst us. In the sixteenth century, Scotland was a kingdom, and, for that age, had a great literature. Indeed, according to Mr Muir, 'the most sensitive and intelligent classes in Scotland were far more civilised four hundred years ago than they are now'. While still controlling her own destiny, Scotland was a country whose subjects had the innate power to make literature and to be highly civilised. The disruptive force was thus not native to the Scots character but brought from outside to bear upon it. Mr Muir's attempt, in this book and elsewhere, to find in the Reformation the major destructive force of the old native concord, is finally as unsatisfying as any of his other individual factors.

For what Mr Muir does not seem to see is that the 'rigours of Calvinism' were a symptom equally with other national phenomena like, for example, the rigours of the industrial revolution. England and Germany were reformed countries, yet their literary tradition continued and deepened. Ireland was never a reformed country, yet its ancient literary tradition disappeared with the loss of its nationhood. When Ireland once more fought for her nationhood and regained it, her literature reappeared (and in English, if with a difference) and Mr Muir uses names like Yeats and Joyce for critical conjuring on the highest plane. I am not concerned here with any argument for Scottish Nationalism. I am merely striving to find the principle which includes the facts and reconciles all opposites. The loss of nationhood does this. No other single factor or cause mentioned by Mr Muir does it.

If Mr Muir had faced up to this (as he does every now and then, and particularly in the case of Scott) and accepted all its implications, he would have saved us the last page of this book—surely one of the most signal instances of the Caledonian Antisyzygy run amok. 'I do not believe', he writes, 'in the programme of the Scottish Nationalists, for it goes against my reading of history, and seems to me a trivial response to a serious problem'. That can only mean that any deliberate action for the regaining of nationhood is trivial, for he immediately goes on: 'I can only conceive a free and independent Scotland coming to birth as the result of a general economic change in society, after which there would be no reason for England to exert compulsion on Scotland, and both nations could live in peace side by side'. In other words, we are to lie down under compulsion until other peoples bring about an economic change (whatever that may mean) which may permit a free and independent Scotland to be born. Is the idea, then, of a free and independent Scotland not 'trivial' after all? Apparently not, for Mr Muir at once proceeds: 'But meantime it is of living importance to Scotland that it should maintain and be able to assert its identity; it cannot do so unless it feels itself an entity; and it cannot feel itself an entity on a plane which has a right to human respect unless it can create an autonomous literature'. What do the words 'identity' and 'entity' mean here? Do they mean the nationhood of a free and independent Scotland, or do they mean some vague literary ideal to be perpetuated in a vacuum? How does a country *assert* its identity? And how, in particular, can the broken image of a lost kingdom 'create an autonomous literature' now, if it failed, as Mr Muir has so brilliantly shown, in the case of Scott, our greatest genius? But Mr Muir goes on: 'That sense of unity can be preserved by an act of faith, as it was preserved in Ireland'. Not economics now, but an act of faith! In Ireland, of course, they never troubled their heads about an economic change. They did not even bother about an act of faith; they simply acted with faith. But they *acted*. And their action was concerned solely with the restoration of nationhood. And Mr Muir holds them up as our example! Was ever unreason so varied within such short compass by so eminent a writer? But these obvious contradictions penetrate to an uneasy depth. For example, in his fine chapter on poetic drama, Mr Muir shows how the ancient national concord failed to go on to produce poetic drama, as other nations did whose tradition was not broken. If the essence of drama is conflict, how can there be drama, spiritual or physical, where the soul is prepared beforehand to refuse the issue? Yet here we have Mr Muir deliberately refusing the issue; suggesting that his country lie down to 'compulsion' until some other country or countries resolve the tragedy of its spiritual disharmony by providing for it a new way of distributing bread and butter.

It gives no pleasure to indulge in this sort of controversy. But it is important, I feel, that a writer who faces up to the absolutes in literary criticism should not hesitate over their implications when they are brought into the light of our common day. What was true in the case of Scott must apply surely with infinitely greater force to Mr Muir himself and to the Scottish writers of his time. If Mr Muir is certain in his mind that the dialectic of history has made consideration of Scottish nationhood 'trivial', then he would have been justified in asserting that as his expression of faith, and should have stopped there. But to have done that would have made of his book an antiquarian effort, a species of indulgence in 'nonsensical trash'. And Mr Muir—like the rest of us—knows it is too vital for that.

ON REVIEWING

SM, 1941

A FRIEND ASKED ME the other day if I had noticed how extremely rare is a good review; in his opinion much rarer than a good book.

It is very difficult to discuss with fairness or balance such an opinion, because one's sympathy tends to be innately either with critic or creator. Critics have been thorns in the flesh of what is called the creative writer since writing began, and before the days of writing, poet or story-teller was no doubt pursued by his detractors.

That being said, the good review is rare, and probably has been in any age. If, in these days, it seems rarer than ever there may be reasons for it, such as lack of time. For example, not so long ago I read a review of a novel in which I was interested by a critic who in that same week reviewed eleven other novels. In his assessment of all twelve he was forthright and dogmatic. Now he may have been a fast worker, and the books he reviewed may not have been worth high consideration, but his criticism itself was self-evidently hurried and valueless. For by a good review I mean a review that satisfies the reader by evidence of insight, understanding, and judgement, that warms the reader's own understanding even when he has not read the book. Whether the book has been praised or condemned, in whole or in part, is beside the point, which here is solely the quality of the criticism.

Some six works of imagination for weekly assessment by a star reviewer has become the common order of popular criticism, and the reviewer is himself sometimes a practising novelist. Can the mind keep up its freshness under such an assault and battery by evoked emotions in 'tense moments' and 'thrilling situations'? Or does it go jaded and deal with human values according to some ready-made formula, much as we play an indifferent game of chess, or 'tell off' a detective story writer for not 'playing fair'? Take some of the most exquisite musical themes by the masters and have them mechanically reproduced at intervals to the sensitive ear, and in time the understanding behind the ear would surely go mad, if it could not protect itself by some formula of indifference.

One might think that if the reviewer did fall in with a really original work he would rejoice, he would thank his gods that here at last was something out of the deadly rut, something he could spread himself upon with an earnest cheer. But that is in fact rarely what happens. What most of us mean by an original work is something done along lines with which we are familiar and which we like, but with an unusual cleverness or distinction. But the work of a real original, like D H Lawrence, had something more to it than that; it had the quality of making many reviewers feel uncomfortable, for example, and so instead of praising they condemned it. I saw a review of a novel in an eminent weekly not long ago where the very clever and knowledgeable reviewer used the occasion to have a wallop at Lawrence. The poor fellow who was being reviewed was used, so to speak, as a peg from which to swing the wallop. From this, I got no impression whatsoever of the value of the book, and its author is a distinguished writer.

Now a certain amount of self-importance or egotism is understandable. Many reviewers are men who doubtless would have liked to have excelled in creative work themselves. It may (or may not) be that the quality of their work was too fine, too unusual, too original to find a publisher, and now, as reviewers, they have 'the awful bore' of reading and commenting upon inferior stuff and not unnaturally want to get a bit of their own back when the occasion warrants it. Who would blame them? But the result, unfortunately, is not a good review.

All reviewers, however, are not overworked. For the overworked I have respect and marvel often enough at their fresh approach and generosity. There are the reviewers who with time on their hands work to a theory of human affairs, and they are a different kettle of fish entirely. Mostly they are what is called highbrow, which means as a rule that they have not worked through their high theory to a final simplicity, to ultimate and catholic values. With anything operating outside the realm of their theory, they are impatient, and because of their sincere impatience, they cannot help passing judgement with an air of arrogance. This type of critic is usually concerned with the 'spirit of the age', and in the world of affairs has a distinct political alignment. To this critic the quality of the work remains important, but such importance is merely regretted if to him the 'direction' of the work is wrong. To-day this kind of criticism is very common, and indeed is rapidly becoming commonplace. A familiar instance of it is seen in the critic who spurns all 'bourgeois values' because they do not consciously shape in a Leftish direction.

Often, however, it is the writer who is sympathetic to this kind of critic who yet suffers most severely at his hands. The writer himself may have the Leftish theory strongly implanted in him, but creative work is different in kind from critical work, and is conditioned by the imagination rather than the intellect. The imagination has its own kind of prompting, its own truths and laws, and they are apprehended in a way that makes them more absolute than any ever-debateable criteria of the intellect. Take a simple instance of the Leftish conception of brotherhood. The critic tends to be concerned with the theory by which brotherhood may be attained, but the creative writer by the conception of brotherhood in being. Let us suppose that the creative writer has some knowledge of a society where man to man is, or has been, as a brother. He gives a picture of this society as best he can, with a wide range of human emotion in action and reaction. But he cannot import into this society what does not truly belong to it in order to help out a theory which both he and the critic may hold in our society to-day. In a fully functioning communal society, for instance, capitalism would not be a living issue, just as witch-burning is no longer a living issue in ours. The creative writer apprehends this intuitively and must remain true to his intuition. Whereupon the critic, concerned with the direction of our present-day society, becomes impatient and dismisses the work of the writer as bourgeois or primitive or irrelevant.

But to the writer himself his work is not irrelevant; it may indeed in his profounder depths appear supremely relevant, because he is concerned with what he apprehends as ultimate human values and the possibility of their free and fearless functioning. He sees, for example, theories of brotherhood to-day working through tentative practice to fear, lack of freedom, wholesale cruelty and death. He has read of it before in history, even in that originally supreme conception of brotherhood, the Christian religion. It was when Roman Catholic (in the Inquisition) and the Covenanter (consider the atrocities of Philliphaugh) had the theory of Christian brotherhood most dominant *in the intellect*, that they committed their worst sins against human brotherhood and were least Christian. Their theory for the propagation of Christ's church was unassailably logical. Destroy all heretics and there will be no heretics. But logic is only an affair of the intellect, and this is what the truly creative writer never forgets. He sees, so to speak, that to destroy heretics is not to destroy heretics but to create them. In our society to-day this kind of vision, this imaginative reason, is naturally not welcomed by the active theorists. It never was in any society. The creative writer has to reconcile himself to this and abide his critics; but it seems to me, if his vision is true, that writing of his, dealing with any kind of society, must have a very real bearing on his own society.

There is one other kind of critic which I might mention, if with some misgiving, for now we are entering the region of what has been called creative criticism. Here again, however, just as in the realm of social or political affairs, we find the theorist who has his own 'closed' system of ideas concerning art. To any creation outside that system he tends to be antipathetic. A cursory study of the reactions of some of our most distinguished living poet-critics to, say, a poet like Shelley illustrates in some measure what I mean; though here the matter may be additionally involved by the conscious holding of certain philosophic or religious views on the part of the critic. But without going so deeply into the matter as all that, we can see at once that the critic whose bias is purely intellectual will react adversely to the writer who deals with the evocation of living human emotion. Living emotion to the intellectual is amorphous, without apparent shape or artform, and he is rendered uncomfortable by it, much as a hostess with definite ideas on behaviour can be rendered uncomfortable by a nonconforming guest. So were (and still are) many critics made uncomfortable by D H Lawrence. This kind of critic cannot see the living moment, as it were, until it is dead; not until it is in the past can it for him assume a recognisable outline, a permanent form; not until then does it become suitable for art treatment.

Realist, idealist, sensualist—one might go on attempting to suggest closed systems of ideas and the critical criteria which proceed from them. But finally one would have to deal with the critic who is capable of producing the good review. What quality is it that operates in him over and above any particular system of ideas? As a first guess, I should say the rare quality of magnanimity. Magnanimity is not a simple quality of kindness; it is rather that light in the mind whereby the elements of what has been created are seen purely. Intention and the measure of achievement are thus apprehended and then expressed with a clarity of spirit free from idiosyncratic obscurity. The temper of this kind of criticism is such that not only is the casual reader aware of being enriched by a mutual understanding, but the writer of the book himself rises above any adverse criticism—if not at once then presently—because of the pleasure he finds in meeting one who appears to understand his ultimate intention. What was flawed may be made perfect in a future work, but meantime above all endeavour, and criticism of endeavour, is this fellowship of a mutual understanding in letters, and so in life itself. There is a proverb to the effect that to understand all is to forgive all. Perhaps in the light of a sufficiently fine magnanimity, to understand all is to give all.

THE NOVEL AT HOME

SM, 1946

This article was written originally for an American publication, *The Writer*, whose contributors dealt with a writer's problems.

ALTHOUGH I HAVE written many books, I have never before offered a word of advice to a beginner; not, anyway, publicly like this. I have never myself asked anyone's advice, and I remember the slight shock I got when the first novel I wrote was accepted by a London publisher, and the publisher's reader, a distinguished literary man, made suggestions about certain phrases which I had used. For him these phrases were obviously condensed or intense to the point of obscurity. For me, they were no doubt a final form of clarity. I forget what I did about them—I suspect not much, but I feel pretty certain now that my critic was right: only, and this is the point—it has taken time and experience and some thought about the novel to make this admission a natural and pleasant one.

I doubt if any advice about the need for sincerity, integrity, simplicity, and so on is of much practical value to the beginner, simply because if he is young enough—and he usually is—these are the qualities which consume him: if not consciously then certainly in the form of eagerness and belief. Where belief, impulse, eagerness are lacking, he would be advised to tackle some other way of earning a livelihood. As a writer he just won't succeed. And I am not now considering the highest form of writing, the kind that remains as a perpetual possession, as literature. Whatever the level, the desire to write on that level must be genuine. It must be a desire, not a calculation. Given that, things can happen. It took all the different levels of writing through all time for Shakespeare to emerge.

Now I have been asked to write this article because an American critic said of my book *The Silver Darlings*, that it was 'written by one who lived in kinship with the matter of his writing', and accordingly it was thought I might have something to say about the apparent illusion by which this 'kinship' is produced. This is rather difficult to do, because it goes beyond any question of the mere facts. The novel deals with herring fishers on the northern coasts of Scotland, and I know about them because I was born and brought up there, went to sea in their boats, and mixed generally with all their ways of living. But 'kinship' or authenticity does not come from knowing the facts. Facts can be acquired easily enough. It comes rather from the attitude of the author to the facts. And this is the important thing.

For example, a writer could look upon simple fishermen carrying on their dangerous occupation upon some remote shore as primitives of an interesting kind. They might be for the literary world an unusual 'subject', treated in a certain grotesque or violent way, they might even provide a seasonal sensation in book production. But the novel so constructed would not have that final or residual element of 'kinship' or authenticity. *That* comes, I fancy, from something even deeper than a sympathetic effort at identity with the characters in the novel; possibly from nothing less than a profound respect for them, because they body forth the real men the writer knows—respect and the feeling that they have taught the writer something of the little he has learned about life. How they vary in character and situation is to him, then, of true dramatic significance. He is on a level with his subject, neither above it nor below it. It is more than big enough for him and he tries to do his best with it. His characters create themselves out of the life he knows. They come alive in his mind in their own right and have for him a true kinship.

One of the most mysterious things in writing is how this authenticity comes through to the reader. I know of a brilliant London author and critic who, because he needed money, thought he would have a shot at writing a popular or best-selling romance. Without belief in what he was doing, he yet did his utmost with all the vast ingenuity he possessed. The book, published, fell flat. Now though the simplest working girl could not tell what was wrong with it, she yet knew there was something wrong. She smelt as it were the false relationship of the creator to his puppets.

The heartening thing about all that is this. A novelist does not require to have a wide personal knowledge of the world. What he needs to know is his own region and what he has to be sure of is his own attitude towards it. If he simply feels superior to it and despises it, then he won't write even tolerable satire about it, for somewhere in satire love lies choked or thwarted. But if he genuinely feels that his home town or farm or factory is big enough for him and can be used to express the deepest that is in him, then from that moment his novel can assume a living form, and, if it has the power, will be able to travel through all the countries and cultures in the world.

That, however, is not the whole story. Though a novelist may not know intimately much beyond his own region or state, he will treat of it all the better if he has some real knowledge of what is going on in the different countries of the world. With this extra knowledge, however acquired, his writing will tend to lose a certain provincial note. He does not need to intrude this extra knowledge for a moment. To have it in his mind, even lying forgotten, is enough. To drag it in, however cleverly, is to show off, and we are all sensitive to bad manners.

Perhaps I could illustrate this in some measure by referring to a recent couple of novels of mine, for this is necessarily a very personal matter. Fellow craftsmen can but swop their experiences, leaving it to the professors to be didactic. Well, I wrote a novel about an old man and a little boy living quietly in the Highlands of Scotland (where I live myself). Nothing you would say, could be more removed from the world of war and political theory. No violence, no killings, only simple daily happenings, against a given background and an old Gaelic culture. In a sense it would be difficult to produce anything more 'provincial', and apparently socially dying at that.

But that's not quite the way it struck me. We all follow political movements at home and abroad and argue about Socialism and Communism. But our arguments are necessarily hypothetical; our concept of the brotherhood of man is a theory in the head; realisation must be an affair of the future. Here in the Highlands of Scotland, however, we still have traces of that old Gaelic communal culture I have mentioned. Thinking over it, I began to understand what a true form of communal living might mean. I have thus had intimations of it from actual life. And a novelist must not only know things in the head like a theorist, or from observation like an anthropologist, but he must also know them in his blood. So knowing them, he can check up on the theorist or anthropologist. In short, the little incidents or happenings, the legends and ways of speech and action, the attitude to nature, of the old man and the little boy take on for me a certain significance which is not confined to a region or province. This, of course, may be my fond illusion. I cannot help that. Nor does it matter, so long as it is genuine to me, and, in particular, so long as I have in my writing told the truth (literal and aesthetic) and not been consciously influenced by propaganda.

I hope it is unnecessary for me to say that I am not making any claims for this book as a book. It may be a very bad book. The reader settles that for himself. But I *am* making the claim that a young novelist writing, say, about some lost area in the Middle West can give it universal significance. If he does not succeed, it's not his subject that lets him down, it's himself.

Let me take this contention a step further. Some of the readers of my book about the boy Art and the old man Hector wanted me to write more of their adventures. I refused, because I felt I had written enough of that kind of adventure. And just here the knowledge of what was happening in the world—we were still some way from the landing in France—began to infiltrate. The notion of testing, as it were, the ways of life of the old man and the little boy against the conscious ideology of totalitarianism got a grip on my mind that I couldn't shake off. In actual life we know perfectly well what would have happened; the two simple country folk would have been physically liquidated. But my concern here was not for the physical but for the mental, for that state of mind which produces the physical manifestation. The fundamental conflict is between states of mind. In essence my problem was spiritual, not physical. I knew a little about the Continent before the war. I had books published there. Now I tried to get all the information I could about what was happening inside the concentration camps of Europe. With an ever increasing sense of horror I began to perceive that the human mind could be conditioned, that Hitler's boast of a domination of Europe for a thousand years was a conceivable possibility. Nothing less was at stake, it seemed to me, than the overthrow of two thousand years of our western civilisation. I studied as far as I could the techniques whereby the adult mind could be broken down or conditioned and the young mind moulded. And I'm not now referring only to physical tortures, applied in their infinite and horrible variety, but, in the case of the highly civilised individual, to the subtle attacks upon the inner citadel of the mind by the expert psychologist.

But I need not enlarge on this. A novelist is concerned with the human mind and its values. At the end of the first book dealing with the old man and the little boy I left them heading for the river which the boy had always longed to see. At the beginning of the second book they reach the river, start poaching a salmon, fall through the bottom of a deep pool, and wake up in their Gaelic paradise, called the Green Isle of the Great Deep. This paradise is run on totalitarian lines, and so my problem is set.

But the problem for the novelist is not just to manipulate the clash of ideas or ideologies. His real business is to see how his two individuals in this new milieu naturally react. He can never depart far from them. When God appears he must in some measure be a projection of the old Highlander's highest thought or wisdom. For even into phantasy, the novelist must import some ultimate sense of reality.

Anyway I wrote the book. Intellectual critics said some nice things about it, possibly because it dealt, after its fashion, with ideas. But the interesting thing for us here is that no critic, so far as I know, said it was a poor story. The old man and the young boy were still having adventures. In a word, far from being 'provincial', the place back home can be turned into paradise and include in its talk the basic problems of a planet.

The only advice, then, I can offer to the aspiring novelist is to treat of what he knows with the attitude towards it which I have suggested. If my experience should provide some new impulse or hope, then I shall almost feel justified in having overcome an initial reluctance to write in this personal way.

WHY I WRITE

Gangrel, 1951

WHY DO I WRITE? I haven't the foggiest notion. The mind baulks before the personal question and puts up the shutters. But presently it saunters out round them prepared for a saving game of generalisation. One writes for the same reason as another makes boats or rockeries or horn spoons. Man likes making things. Where I was a small boy, a grown man gave his oath 'before my Maker'. The old Scots poets were called Makars. Why we—or the Makar—should want to make or create things is still to me, despite Pavlov's dogs and materialist psychology, pure mystery.

However, analysis is our game; perhaps a sublimation of the old hunting instinct whereby, in the absence of lions and tigers, antelopes and hares, we hunt atoms and souls through universes and jungles to their inmost lairs. Sex, power, money—there's a simple beginning: a fellow writes for money.

And the first money is bright, incredible. Contrasted with the weekly wage envelope or even the monthly cheque, it is fairy gold, to be thrown abroad as a tree throws its leaves. It equates the act of making, which has been filched from the wage envelope. This is luck. From the essay or short story to a novel. The novel is a Book Society Choice. The golden leaves fall as in Vallombrosa. You walk in at the door of the house you got other makers to build on credit and call it your own. Miracle. And now, besides, there's another book.

But this time, alas, your helpful and courteous publishers look glum. They are prepared to publish, but ... And in a flash you see that if you persist in this course—when you could pursue the earlier one—there are to be no more golden leaves; worse, the 'promising' tree itself will be publicly axed; worse still, you are aware it is not much of a book, perhaps even a bad book. Yet you persist, smiling, pig-headed, incomprehensible. And in due course the publishers' dire prognostications are fulfilled. Actually in the old legend the fairy gold when brought to the light of common day turned into horse dung. And you think to yourself: my God, how did these primitive myth-makers know about money and publishing?

Then a really astonishing thing happens. Something—probably that primitive snake in the grass—grins. *You were nearly had*, he says, *but now you're free again.* And you can pelt him with the sourest grapes you can lay your hands on. It makes no difference. He enters into fathomless conspiracy with you. His arabesques glitter with laughter in the sun.

Meantime that word primitive has put me on the spoor of something (which is why I write). A book on field anthropology—*Sex and Temperament* by Margaret Mead—slips into mind. I remember her admirable description of a poor hill tribe in New Guinea (which the Japs were so occidentally anxious to civilize). They lived in a truly communal way and got the greatest fun from cultivating one another's gardens. A gentle affectionate laughing people who could not understand violence. For certain purposes, however, they needed a 'big man', a leader or fuhrer. So they caught young what looked a likely lad and got him to shout ersatz insults at his opposite number from across the valley. A real Hitler or Mussolini at his declamatory best would have burst into fragments upon their awe and/or laughter. Even their own fuhrer when fully trained remains uncorrupted by power, waiting for the day when he may retire and laugh happily ever after. The day is achieved in the time dimension when his eldest child reaches puberty. So, as we say, it was up to him to get cracking on the sex business.

Primitives, of course. No conception of Progress. But from this aspect of their culture pattern, does no echo of the laugh come through to us? Would a wise old Chinaman smile? A Yogi contemplate? A Christian saint or mystic understand? Where does Marx come in? And the psychoanalysts?

Success, money, Fuhrer, horse dung. Odd notions and contrasts begin to trouble the writer. He is aware that for some inexplicable reason raw material is starting to collect. Arguments like elvers tie knots on their own tails. He even hears beforehand critical jibes about his searching back through diffusionist theories to a Golden Age, a Garden of Eden. But he doesn't worry, for at least he knows a lot about culture patterns; and is primarily concerned with his own amazing one here to-day—and perhaps to-morrow.

And now from everywhere—work, politics, economics, parties, committees an' all—material of a raw relevancy flows fatally in; until the whole thing is a morass mocked by a will o' the wisp, an elusive glimmer of light, for which he has no lantern. No fable. No conceivable book. How superbly lucky are the fellows who get wage envelopes! Up go the shutters. And then one day—only heaven knows how or why—he observes his unfortunate hand beginning to make scrawls on the mud of the morass with a crooked stick.

And then again—for he realises now that it is all pure mystery to his bloody cost—he makes the astounding discovery that what the stick is designing has apparently nothing whatever to do with success, tribes in New Guinea, fuhrers, or Gardens of Eden. Instead, here are fellows sailing a boat, or working at a beach; or a girl tranced by a singing blackbird while she is thinking of something else. Man emerging from the sucking morass to sing again with a vivid spontaneity of the spirit. ... Is that the hidden notion of it all? Or what? And he must be careful (his own culture pattern being what it is) to slaughter the poetry in his prose. Off stage a monotonous Indian voice is intoning: All is a striving and a striving and an ending in nothing. How profoundly right the fellow is! Comforted, you irrationally get hold of the stick again. To hell with poverty, let us kill a hen. You began to write.

SECTION III

LOYALTIES

THE ESSENCE OF NATIONALISM

SM, 1942

IN RECENT TIMES surely more books have been published on nationalism and its horrid implications than on any other subject that affects the destiny of man. A combine of sovereign states to lead and police the world (the dominant-Anglo-Saxon concept); federalism, with its abrogation of certain sovereign rights; a United States of Europe; international Marxism; and so on. Running through the variegated theme is the curse of nationalism, until the ordinary man has begun to yearn towards some vague brotherhood or common-wealth that he hopes may somehow be attained somewhere, and thus a little peace be granted in our time, O Stalin, or O Churchill, or O Roosevelt.

It is all really becoming very confusing. For whereas we read about these grand concepts or pious aspirations on the one hand, on the other we come sharply up against the desperate situation of those who have been dis-possessed of their nationhood. For the dispossessed we have immediate and profound sympathy. In Atlantic charters we vow that the disinherited shall once more possess their earthly kingdom.

The trouble with a great deal of this aspirational writing is its essentially idealistic nature. The longer I live the more I mistrust idealism, not for what may be genuinely implicit in it, but for the lengths to which history has shown me human nature will go in order, as we say, to implement it. Let an idealism, with power, once get the bit in its mouth and nothing will stop it. It becomes capable of cruelty and slaughter on a gargantuan scale. Take the Christian religion, with its concepts of brotherhood and charity and non-violence and tenderness, and then consider what man made of it, how the Inquisitor lit the faggots round the trussed-up heretic or the Calvinist uttered his battle-cry of 'Jesus and no quarter'. There you had devastating and most bloody wars, not for declared nationalisms or systems of economics, but for spiritual subjugation or conformity. Christ's non-violence was turned into active violence by that simple process of logic which declared that if all heretics were destroyed Christ's church on earth would be assured, whereas, if heretics were allowed to multiply, manifestly Christ's church would be destroyed. It is the logic that sits in the heart of such apparently fool-proof reasoning that is so very deadly to man.

Even the most cynical materialist, with the strongest aversion for any form or kind of religion, does not attack Christ's teaching as a cause of barbarity and war. What sardonically amuses him is the way man can in words affirm the holiness of such teaching and in practice deny it in order to achieve his own temporal ends, and always with a righteous show of reason.

If this can happen in the spiritual realm, where all our human divisions should presumably be transcended, is it not even more likely to happen in our ordinary working world? In a word, is it nationalism that is to blame for the condition of the world to-day, or is it the interpretation we care to put upon that word when we refuse, perhaps subconsciously, to face up to quite other factors?

Is it not, for example, just a little bit suspicious that most of the grandiose schemes for federalism and what not emanate from America or this country? When you are sitting pretty on top of the world very naturally you don't want things unduly disturbed. How obvious all that has been in a personal way in the ordinary social sphere! The squire's lady sends a jelly to the sick poor or a pair of rabbits to the local hospital. The squire sits on the bench. The laird does his bit in local government. The landlord, in fact, may presently be at the stage where he will hesitate to prosecute a poverty-stricken peasant for poaching a pheasant. If I had land and folk poached my game I am quite sure I should be very annoyed about it. But I might hesitate to go to extremes, if I felt that I might thereby endanger my possession. It is better to concede certain small privileges than to lose the main substance.

Grandiose schemes do not emanate from the peoples of the Continent who have been dispossessed. They have seen 'a new order' at work. All they want is their own country back, their own land, where they may be allowed to labour and produce in peace. They are not theoretical about this or grandiose. They know what they have endured, and they are either passionate in their attitude or bitterly apathetic.

Ah yes, it may be said, but as nationalism is the root cause of all the trouble, something must be done about it or our whole world will come to an end. Someone must do a lot of thinking about it now.

The dispossessed, both in the national and the personal sense, are beginning to question this whole assumption. They have grown tired of theories and want concrete facts. And the biggest concrete fact they can look at is the emergence of Russia.

Now from the Russian point of view war is brought about not by nationalism but by economics. That, we may say, is merely another theory. But at least Russia put the theory to the test within an area covering one-sixth of the earth. She deliberately set about encouraging her nationalisms, and she had a great number of them, different races and different tongues. In this country, for instance, we found Gaelic one tongue too many and authoritatively set about its destruction. We felt it had been and might again be a disruptive element. In Russia different languages were authoritatively encouraged, grammars being specially written for those that had none, and the folk-life in each case was deepened and enriched. Where we saw that nationalism might be a disruptive and violent factor in the whole body politic, Russia saw that it would be a cohering factor, making for peace and harmony. And, whether we secretly like it or not, Russia has proved herself right to a degree that continues to admonish us.

Now this is no veiled plea for communism or any Russian interpretation of it. It is an effort to look straight at this somewhat baffling affair we call nationalism. Whether wars result from basic economic causes we may debate. That some of our bloodiest wars did not result from national rivalries we know. (Consider the recent war in Spain or the religious wars that cut across all nations.) True, nations are used as instruments in war, but then so are scientific research and pulped poetry books and glycerine.

Let me pause to look at this matter in a personal way, for ultimately if we are going to understand anything we must apprehend it not as a verbal theory external to us but as something internally felt and comprehended.

Some time ago I listened in to a programme of music by Sibelius, broadcasted at intervals by the BBC. I had not heard any of the Sibelius symphonies before and the effect upon me was something that I could not have anticipated, for it was as if the whole Northland of forest and loch and legend came alive before me, evoked out of the blood. I am neither musician nor musical critic, and could not have been led away by any technical considerations. All I know is that the music had for me an evocative power, some extraordinary element of intimacy. I naturally, I suppose, put this down to some degree of affinity between our Scottish Northland and the Scandinavian, to both a personal and traditional apprehension of these northern lands and seas and the legends or myths bred out of them.

Now the next thing that happened, quite involuntarily, was the thought, flashing across the mind: If only we had a composer who could do for Gaelic folk music and our Highlands what Sibelius did for Finland, how supreme a realm of musical delight would be there! For I happen to know the Gaelic folk music as a natural inheritance and find in it movements of the spirit that no other music can provide, that indeed in some unconditional way make me think are extra-musical, penetrating into that ultimate region where myth is born.

And so the mind came critically alive and I said to myself: What a tragedy that the whole creative musical impulse of the Highlands, as exhibited in our folk songs, should have been crushed and inhibited by certain definite historical happenings! What a tragedy, what a sheer meaningless waste!

In that moment of regret, primarily for my own loss and then for the loss to the world, I touched what is for me the whole essence of nationalism; and, I am convinced, not only for me, but for every normal man who looks into his own mind and refuses to be bedevilled by theories or the power-lust which corrupts. To love your own land, from which you draw your deepest inspiration, is as natural as to love the sunlight or a woman, is to understand what moves in the heart of a Pole or a Czech, is to salute Sibelius not in envy or hate but in admiration and gratitude.

Again, recently, I found myself listening-in to one of Edwin Muir's broadcasts, dramatising Scottish history. He was dealing with Burns and the citations he put into the mouths of the actors were spoken in a Scots that had no slightest suggestion of the comic parochial, but that on the contrary came out of a rich tradition, intellectual, metaphysical, aristocratic in quality and humanly profound. Here was the accent of the ballads, of the Court poetry, of the genius of Burns, of a small but great people making their distinctive contribution to a native culture that in its turn enriched world culture.

It is not my purpose in this short article to discuss origins of war. All I am suggesting is that there are forces at work in the world, of many kinds and of different intentions, directing our thoughts to what are called the evils of nationalism in order that our sight and our reason may get suitably befogged. In times past, as has been clearly documented, private armament manufacturers found little difficulty in promoting a war for their own purposes. That is the simplest kind of illustration.

And just as nationalism could be used by armament manufacturers so it can be, and is being, used by power perverts in an effort at world domination. But they also use pageantry and music and science and every fine element that ever the human spirit has produced to further their ends. But the wise man does not become ashamed of the scriptures and throw them over because the devil quotes them.

DEFENSIO SCOTORUM

A Reply to W S Morrison

SM, 1928

In the previous issue of *The Scots Magazine* an article had appeared by
W S Morrison, in which the writer had criticised many modern Scots critics
of Scotland.

THE CONFUSION OF thought in Mr W S Morrison's article, *Defensio Scotorum*,
is such that one must either assume a conscious disinclination on his part
to face the facts as presented with such ruthless logic in Mr G M Thomson's
Caledonia (which he presumes himself to be critically combating), or else consider his article as a sort of impromptu after-dinner oration culminating in
the emotional glass-tinkle of 'Highland honours'. England may have her
praises incomparably chanted by such as Swinburne, may be made the over-
note, of the greatest cycle of song in the world, but Scotia—ah, Scotia 'has
no classic dignity'. And forthwith our hearts must thrill at the very parochialism of the thought! 'She is to us,' pursues Mr Morrison, 'the old, imperfect,
harassed, homely, gallant old dame. Her tartan shawl incompletely confines
her grey locks. Her arms are akimbo in defiance of all the great ones of the
earth and their works. Her heart is unconquerable and true as steel to her
own. "Scotland! my auld, respected mither!"' And involuntarily one looks
round for the stirring rumble of the kettle-drums, for manifestly that is the
sort of thing to give the tartan troops. ... And here they come, marshalled
by *Caledonia*, to pay tribute to their gallant old dame, having inscribed on
their banners in letters of fire—45 per cent of us live more than two in a
room; we have the highest death-rate, unemployment rate, sick rate, infant
mortality rate, emigration rate and immigration rate in the British Isles; for
all that spells denationalisation, the destruction of a great tradition, the
defeat of a whole people, we stand; our slums are the blackest in Europe,
our famous Highlands have become the sporting preserves of English and
Yankee money kings ...

But the banner legends are too numerous for even irony to dwell on it.
Truly it's time the auld mither dropped her 'gallant' shawl, her 'akimbo

defiance', and substituted there for the only other attitude she knows, that with the 'tear in her e'e'. In either, one readily grants Mr Morrison, she is not a classic figure. 'The tongues of men and of angels cannot describe her,' he says. And for a moment one wonders what might happen if a lower order of being had a shot at it—though for that matter there is always the kailyaird. Meantime neighbour England, even with the tongues of men, has put up a pretty fair show—Chaucer, Spencer, Shakespeare, Milton, Wordsworth, Shelley, Keats ... down the long splendid line to the Hardys and Eliots of to-day. Yet, for old fact is stranger than new fiction, there was a time, while Scotland was still a nation with her own court and her own poets, when she figured as by no means the least important national entity in European affairs, and certainly as one of the major contributors to European culture— and that, too, at a period when by comparison England was culturally quiescent. When, therefore, Mr Morrison has his gibe at the Scottish Renaissance movement, at Mr C M Grieve's 'Not Burns, Dunbar', he is misunderstanding, presumably deliberately (for in *Albyn* Mr Grieve has put matter and intention clearly enough; and from his article it appears that Mr Morrison has at least seen this companion issue to *Caledonia*) not merely what Scotland did accomplish in her pre-Union history, but what a band of Scotsmen are attempting to do for his 'auld mither' to-day.

But before dealing with this, the most significant, aspect of the attempt to tackle the Scottish problem, let us endeavour to visualise what sort of figure it is that Mr Morrison sees in the Scot whom he is defending. While granting that it is certainly interesting to see ourselves as others sees us, yet we are not in a last resort what others see us (or would like to see us), or indeed in any significant sense anything but what we see ourselves. We are what we are—but what that distinctive essence of us may be Mr Morrison, as a Scot, makes no attempt to discover, either by deliberate personal psycho-analysis or by reference to the cultural history of Scotland, to the supreme utterance of her true artists, to the characteristic actions of her warriors and law-givers, to her varying attitudes under changing religious faiths. Instead, 'there is no doubt that the Scot of tradition possesses the following character-istics. He is "dour" and "canny", in spite of Mr Thomson and those who resent the imputation with all the violence of an inferiority complex.' (A curiously phrased statement implying that Mr Morrison himself subscribes to the 'dour' and 'canny' legend, quite apart from tradition.) After piling up the epithets 'thrifty ... parsimony ... whisky ... sentiment ... energetic in affairs ... patriotic ... fighter ... Burns ... Shorter Catechism' (the haggis and the bagpipes and the other 'half-comic insignia' having been already introduced), he says that these are the points of difference which an Englishman picks out between himself and the Scot. So, after all, it is an Englishman's picture to which Mr Morrison and tradition subscribe? Or is it not?

This Scotch Coamic, like the stage Irishman, is admittedly in a certain tradition of things with which the more complacent type of Englishman amuses himself into a warming sense of superiority, but is he anything *in reality?* The stage-Irishman, anyhow, was very literally shot to pieces all over the bogs and townships of Ireland, as every Englishman now knows with respect, and in the Abbey Theatre, Dublin, I have too often seen, ever to be impressed by any music-hall conception of national character, what a renascent culture can do in presenting the Irish character not as others see it, but as the Irish see it themselves, and see it with such truth of vision, such certainty in delineation, excusing nothing, distorting nothing, that when their Players go to London, the greatest English critics are loud in their praise and in their hope that, by reflection, the body of purely English contemporary drama may be revivified. Though even by leaving it at the Scotch Coamic stage, one might have had some sort of image at least, but when Mr Morrison goes on to quote 'other Europeans' to whom the Scot is 'sudden and quick in quarrel' ... 'a reputation of being as fiery in debate as in war', where have the 'dour' and 'canny' characteristics gone? And he finishes the pretty sketch by suggesting that 'the Scot is a sort of caricature of the Briton'—that is, of both the Englishman and himself (at least)! I admit that, with every desire in the world to get to grips with this slippery fellow, he eludes me.

But when presently an attempt is made to place him in historical perspective, the picture becomes even more inept. As a result of the Union, 'two dangers arose. One was that of absorption into the larger unit, with the forgetting of all that makes Scottish History an epic and Scottish nationality a reality. The other was the even more ignoble fate of sinking to the status of a querulous dependency filled with self-pity and jealousy, shrinking from participation in world tasks beyond its strength and solacing its bruised soul with researches into a past when the demands upon Scotland's spirit met with a more robust response.' There Mr Morrison has stated the position fairly, even with an acumen which is all too obviously sharpened by a knowledge of Scottish affairs as they exist to-day. It is in combating these two dangers, still active, that the Scottish Renaissance movement is now concerned; that all the movements towards Scottish Home Rule are directed. All of which labour, however (including the ruthless statistical compilation of *Caledonia*), is merely a beating of non-existent air, for 'both these dangers have been surmounted', says our defender. 'With a tenacity which provokes the mirth of other nations, Scotsmen have clung to one or two national symbols as expressive of their individuality as a nation. One of these symbols is Burns.' ... and the other is 'the Shorter Catechism'!

I admit it has the air of an extensive leg-pull, yet the writer is palpably serious. One can only marvel that what provokes the mirth of other nations and draws bitter irony from Mr G M Thomson as a Scot should appeal to the educated intelligence of Mr Morrison as a satisfactory solution of the 'two dangers' which have been inhibiting the distinctive Scots mind, destroying her nationalism, her sense of being a people, and driving her economically into the black death of the slums. Burns, not, it is granted, even as a poet, like Shakespeare—for a writer knows better nowadays!—but merely as a national fetish, and the Shorter Catechism—that Judaic rosary strung in England.

More slippery than ever becomes this elusive Scot—or, to be done with it, are we dealing not with any real figure of a Scot at all, but with the warm

post-prandial haze, or, more insidiously, the everyday atmosphere of 'getting
on', wherein everything must look encouraging and inviting (and if possible
tinct of the comic) so that the mind be comforted and reality shut out? Either
that, or else Mr Thomson's uncanny probing for the fatal flaw in the Scots
character spelling ultimate national dispersal and death, is the outcome of
a true instinct or intuition. And, in spite of Mr Morrison's unconscious corroboration, I am not yet prepared to grant that.

Though I admit that in his economic analysis, Mr Thomson goes a long way
to justify his apparent belief. And just here Mr Morrison's defence, in its
failure to grasp psychological significance, is in the true kailyard tradition.
He quotes *Caledonia* to the effect that 'Scots are more likely to be found in
"scrubby and subaltern positions" than as "heids o' departments,"' whereas
the chances are that had Mr Thomson desired to make such a direct statement at all he would have had an *or* in place of that *than*. For his manifest
point is that the Scots mind finds its whole outlet in aspiring to occupy the
salaried and safe headship of a department, now and then succeeding, but
generally sitting tight as 'the invoice clerk', rather than adventuring upon the
aristocratic—Live dangerously. That the department may sometimes even be
the English Government or the English Church does not invalidate the idea,
it merely bears it out with a sort of ultimate logic. Indeed, granting—what
I think no one will deny—that the Scot has as sound a logical apparatus as
any of his neighbours, it becomes inevitable, when all his faculties are centred on this 'getting on', on this achievement of departmental security in
graded ascent, that he attains to the highest posts on occasion. If he didn't,
one would have seriously to question the quality of his brains compared with
that of his neighbours'. But to strive for such 'preferment' and salaried safety
is perfectly human, if not exactly impressive, on the part of any individual:
it is when a nation's whole mind is definitely directed that way, when her
educational system, her religious bias, her kailyard 'literature', aid and abet,
that the thing becomes a portent serious and far-reaching. That, I take it, is
roughly what *Caledonia* has expressed, though with what inherent truth or
falsity Mr Morrison at any rate has not helped to make clear. And immediately one looks around at politico-economic Scotland, all the evidence does
insinuate corroboration of Mr Thomson's conception. What is the use of saying, with regard to the admitted horror of our slums, that 'the present
poverty of the industrial region of Scotland is due more to the strength than
to the weakness of Scottish character'? With every desire in the world to be
comforted by Mr Morrison, I can only find such a statement something
worse than illogical, almost as bad as his blaming Adam Smith for depopulat-
ing the Highlands! If the Scots character was strong enough to make its
industrial area boom, why has it not kept it booming; or, when the trade
cycle brought depression, why did it not according to its superior strength
superiorly keep alive? Where were its 'dourness' and 'canniness', its 'logic
and energy when it comes to affairs of government and business'?

But England has had the financial supremacy of London behind her!
Therefore Mr Morrison cannot understand why anyone should be disturbed
now by the prospect of Scotland's financial centre being shifted to London

(there being no Sir Walter Scott with his claymore these days!), or her railways, or presumably the controlling power of any other business: in other words, the complete provincialisation of Scotland is hopefully contemplated, even though it requires no expert knowledge of finance to demonstrate that the belief in any material benefit accruing from the loss of national ownership of capital is an obvious fallacy. It is, in fact, this very process of provincialisation which has brought Scotland to her present desperate economic position.

Her housing, her slums, her unemployment, her mortality, her sickness, stand in black contrast to neighbour England, not to mention other European countries. And it is not a question of the industrial belt alone. Take the opposite extreme—the Highlands. Does Mr Morrison attempt to refute the charge as to the canned meat kings, and such, lording it over a few native gillies and gamekeepers, with the stricken crofter emanating that atmosphere of decay and death, smelt by Cunninghame Graham? Of the boat-loads of Western Gaels shipped abroad like live stock? And as a Scot, a Gael, what action has he taken, or does he intend to take, about it? Does he know the facts, the blue book facts, as to the quantity of land available for cultivation, grazing, afforestation? The Smallholders 1911 Act, with its 20,000 applications and 4,000 grants? That the cost of the last battleship would be about sufficient to buy out on the basis of a twenty years' purchase all the deer forests, grouse moors, and salmon fishings in Scotland? In other words, an annual rental of under half a million would secure the whole lot for the Scots nation. He must know the miserable tale, for the facts are in *Caledonia*, which he presumes to attack.

But as in Mr Morrison's unreal picture of the Scot, with the Comic grinning through, and as in his treatment of the economic position with his only constructive suggestion pointing to the removal of financial and trade centres to London with the unquestionable effect of completing her provincialisation and abnegation of nationhood, so in his reading of her history is he untrustworthy. The Englishman, he says, 'is a unit in a civilisation of longer standing'. What sort of civilisation? And in what way in point of antiquity or culture comparable, say, to the Gaelic?—or Pictish? 'The Scots have never had the impress of any such unifying power, and it is this which renders futile the appeal to Scotland's pre-Union past which is so often on the lips of modern prophets of Scottish nationality.' Has Mr Morrison never read, for example, Mr Evan M Barron's *Scottish War of Independence*, wherein it is shown beyond all doubt that the long struggle culminating in Bannockburn was not a struggle of Anglo-Saxons (Lothians) over Anglo-Saxons as Scottish historians, such as Lang, had hitherto asserted, but a successful war, guided in its beginnings by Andrew De Moray in the North and Wallace (*not* one of the great territorial magnates) in the South, and waged by the common people, the Celtic population of Scotland, against the *national* enemy, England? And as for his statement, 'Behind the Highland Line lay unguessable potentialities of commotion and rapine', it is unpardonable, not merely as historical misstatement by innuendo but as a 'potential' insult to a brave and cultured race in a world as it then existed. The popular belief in continuous inter-tribal warfare is based on myth. That there was such warfare or feuds is true; but then we have wars and feuds to this very day, where commotion and rapine on a vast scale are not unknown; but, as in most civilised countries to-day, there were long periods of peace when literature and music and the arts flourished creatively and at least with a national distinction they have since the Union most sadly lacked.

But if the Scot, his present-day economics, and his history, appear too much for our confused apologist, I can put down the manner in which he has dismissed the contemporary Scottish Renaissance movement only to an ignorance which, being pricked by uncertainty, makes a face of amused contempt. 'Dunbar, not Burns', means for him that we are to sing 'Scottis quhilk hes' instead of 'Scots wha hae'. The crudity of this is appalling, particularly in view of the published work in the Doric of such writers as Lewis Spence, scholarly, classical, and frequently with an inspiration direct as a sword thrust or as a flash of naked colour from one of our old ballads, or Hugh McDiarmid, whose last long poem, *A Drunk Man Looks at the Thistle*, drew from an international critic the considered statement that nothing so great had appeared in English or any dialect thereof for years. These are the beginnings, for this blight that *Caledonia* shows to be resting on everything Scottish has certainly not missed the arts. Artistically in the modern world Scotland doesn't exist. No music, no drama, no letters, of any international significance. Why is this all-round sterility so complete, so without parallel in the life of any modern nation? Should not an honest attempt be made to answer that question before attacking the movement that is trying to do so? If the attempt results in the discovery of a fatal flaw in the Scots character which must result in national disintegration, then with Mr Thomson one may say so, pile up the evidence, and be done with it. But if the attempt results in the discovery that the Scots character, the distinctive Scottish mind, has merely been denied self-expression, has been inhibited and contorted, by ascertainable factors, such as *inter alia*, the loss of government of her own affairs and the acquisition of a too rigid Calvinism and of purely English criteria, then we are up against a proposition capable at least of statement in straightforward terms. For neither does Mr Thomson nor Mr Morrison deny the distinctive Scottish mind. Manifestly, then, in going back to Dunbar, the Movement is merely attempting to get at the fundamentals of Scottish psychology or character, when that character was flourishing nationally and culturally in Europe, and before it became gradually sterile under these ascertainable historical factors. Mr Morrison says that nationality is 'nothing else but the feeling of traditional tendencies, overriding and directing the eccentricities of individual temperament'. Well, this 'feeling' is precisely what the Movement is attempting to capture in its purity and *to express* and so bring within a living culture once more. It is there in Dunbar. It is not to the same extent in Burns; and, of course, to a vanishing point in the kailyard successors he inspired. The historical factors have pushed it into a stagnant backwater. At Dunbar (ultra-modern in many respects) we join the main stream again. And once in the main stream our supreme concern must be with the most vital tendencies in modern world literature and art.

In *Caledonia*, Mr Thomson showed the progressive deterioration of the 'Scottish Nation' on all counts. The process is cumulative, and if undisturbed must in the end be complete. Mr Morrison put forward no arguments to counter it. Now the various nationalist movements consider, with a wealth of contributory argument and fact, that the process can be arrested if Scotland be given charge of her own affairs—in other words, if she gets Home Rule. Is there any other way? If so, why not produce it? If not, why the gibe? In the last analysis the basic trouble is a politico-economic one, with Scotland thirled to England and her natural media for self-expression progressively inhibited. We have too much admiration for England and her splendid cultural record to desire to imitate her in a second-rate way. The Scots mind, its distinctive metaphysical twist, its analytical acuteness, its uncompromising realism, its fantasy, its stark humour, its capacity for sheer unconditional vision (consider the ballads), has been blinded, been rendered impotent. When it wins free, as I believe it will win free (the prisoning factor being not a 'natural flaw', but the indicated inhibitions) it will once more take an important place creatively in European thought and culture. But a lot of uphill work has yet to be done by those who love in word and deed this 'auld mither' before that transpires; and meantime it is not the Irish who are the enemy, nor Catholicism, nor any other bogey, so much as those whose nationality consist of toasting Burns comically and thrilling to the Shorter Catechism; it is that curious barren defeatist figure, the Anglo-Scot.

'... AND THEN REBUILD IT

An Economist's Scotland of To-morrow

SM, 1939

IN RECENT YEARS we have had many books dealing with the economic ills and mental troubles of poor old Scotland. We know she is in a bad way; in fact, we know it so well, have scanned so many columns of figures, contrasted so many percentages, dealing with slums, unemployment, public health, housing, population, that, if not finally disheartened, at least we are wearied by so depressing a tale. Yet it would be a great pity if such a feeling were to turn us away from Dr Bowie's new book. *The Future of Scotland.* Indeed, if I had any power in such matters, I would strongly recommend this book to all social study circles for this winter.

For Dr Bowie, who is Principal of the School of Economics and Commerce in Dundee, handles statistics as the trained investigator should, and sets them forth free from all political or party bias. The word Socialism does not occur once, nor the word Toryism, and Nationalism he glances at only for a moment to state that manifestly the time is not yet. That does not mean he has not his own ideas on what requires to be done. His final section is, in fact, headed 'Summary and Proposals'. These proposals represent a planning of our economy based on ascertained facts and are in themselves, whether one agrees or not, suggestive and stimulating. His outlook is neither partial nor regional, but embraces Scotland as a whole. Far from being reassured, for example, by an increase in employment in Scotland due to armaments, Dr Bowie sees the inevitability of what is going to happen when the war is over—unless we begin the right kind of industry-building now; and he knows the right kind and suggests proved methods of setting about the business.

But before tackling any man's proposals (always debatable in our country), let us consider for a little how he treats his ascertained or statistical facts. The first section in the book is entitled, 'The Population of Scotland', and deals with census figures, 'the southward drift', emigration, sex and age distribution, birth and death rates, causes of decline in the birth-rate, the effects of a declining population; in short, it covers the whole field statistically and with clear regard to cause and effect. In the ten years to 1931 the population of Scotland declined by almost 40,000, while the population of England and Wales increased by over 2,000,000. The three factors governing population are births, deaths, and emigration. Now the birth-rate is higher than the death-rate in Scotland, though both are declining; and actually the excess of births over deaths in the given period was 352,000. Accordingly there must have been an emigration of 392,000 before a decline of 40,000 in the total could be recorded. The loss to Scotland by emigration over the ten years was 8 per cent of her population, while to England the loss by emigration was only 0.5 per cent. Board of Trade Returns show that the great mass went abroad, but 63,000 must have gone to Europe and England, and, we may conclude, mostly to England; some of them would be returning English, for there was a decline in the number of English in Scotland at the end of the ten years (though those of English birth in Scotland remain much more numerous than those of Irish and Welsh birth combined). Dr Bowie gives his reasons for this excessive emigration, and remarks, 'So emigration tends to take the young, the healthy, the enterprising, the courageous and the adaptable, precisely those people of whom Scotland to-day stands most in need. There is no scientific evidence that Scotland is over-populated, and still less evidence that emigration will cure her persistent unemployment.'

At this point the amateur investigator usually stops, but Dr Bowie goes on to a clear analysis of sex and age distribution, and fact follows fact until one sees that 'as the dwindling number of children grow up each successive age-group reveals a numerical decline, with the result that Scotland is gradually becoming a land of older people'. What is going to be the outcome over, say, the next hundred years? Here one can only give 'the logical conclusions to which existing trends point'. Dr Bowie quotes one eminent authority to this effect, '... if no new social agencies intervene to check declining fertility' then 'a period of rapid decline would set in after about thirty years. In this estimate the population would be 81 per cent of its present size fifty years from now, and only 19 per cent of its present size a hundred years from now'. True, that *if* is a small but potent word, yet it can be countered only by the intervention of 'new social agencies'. We cannot get past the fact that the decline in the birth-rate has reduced this generation's potential mothers. After 1931 emigration, for various reasons, almost ceased. 'But if there is even a modest recovery in overseas emigration and if the present migration to England continues, it is probable that Scotland's decline will be expedited'.

Let us glance for a moment at the Highlands. In 1801 they contained about one-fifth of Scotland's population; to-day, about one-twentieth. All the time emigration has been draining away the best stock at a tremendous rate. Since 1931 deaths exceed births. The population is ageing. The number of potential mothers falling. 'Unless heroic measures are taken, there is every indication that the Highlands will become the Sahara of Scotland'.

Does that sound alarmist? Well, how are we going to counter the facts? Dr Bowie does not go into the economic conditions of the Highlands to-day, but to those of us who have, who are aware, for example, of the enormous amount of state aid pumped into the Hebrides every week by way of pension and dole, his figures certainly give us furiously to think. After all, St Kilda *was* evacuated. If there is not a livelihood in crofting-fishing for the average Hebridean head of a family under the existing economic dispensation— what's to be done about it? And if nothing is done?

But here I have merely been trying too compactly, to indicate the searching nature of Dr Bowie's inquiry into our population statistics. He does not leave the matter there but goes on to consider 'The quality of our people', and deals with school children, sickness, housing, nutrition, poverty, and our health services, producing facts as he goes along of a striking and often uncomfortable kind, with penetrating comment. When he comes to discuss Scotland's economic life the large issues of industry and unemployment are succinctly considered. This for many will be the vital section, because it concerns directly the future of our country.

Where fact and deduction are multiform and closely knit, it is presumptuous to try to give in a short space an adequate resumé. But here again two points may be singled out as illustration. Following the industrial revolution, Scotland specialised to an unparalleled degree in textiles and the heavy industries—coal, iron, steel and engineering. In recent years these industries have been permanently 'dethroned from their pre-eminent position, and our disproportionate dependence on them has been the root cause of our economic malaise'. Meantime, the new light industries—radio, motor car, aircraft, electrical engineering, synthetic products, and so on—'have become of fundamental importance in the modern world and offer the greatest possibilities of growth and development'; and it is just these industries that have failed to appear in any compensating measure in Scotland. Around London factories for these products have grown and are growing to an almost incredible extent, together with the necessary administrative services, 'including central and local government and commercial employment, and the satellite skilled services of banking, finance, insurance, accounting, scientific research, education, health, travel, and the defence services'.

Now we begin to get an understanding of Scotland's desperate record of unemployment, and we ask ourselves: But how could this have happened? Why should the London area have gone ahead in this way and the Glasgow area have failed? Dr Bowie discusses the matter, though here I feel he fails to isolate sufficiently the two unique factors: that London is the seat of government and the centre of finance. That London represents in itself a great market is only a comparative factor. Sweden, for example, with a population much less than London's has made enormous progress in the light electrical industries. And, after all, the Glasgow area, if we take it at a fourth or fifth of the London area, is in itself a great market, and if the light industries had developed there to a fourth or fifth of the extent they have developed around London, Scotland would have been relatively flourishing. Whether the Scots are inferior to the English in research, business method and workmanship may be debatable. That Scotland has neither a seat of government nor an integrated centre of finance is not debatable. Following on that are many supremely important psychological factors, for if nothing succeeds like success, nothing depresses like depression.

The second point I should like to mention is Dr Bowie's treatment of the Special Areas and the value of such trading estates as the one at North Hillington. To many readers this will be new matter, and Dr Bowie's inclusive view is constructive. Again the difference between Scotland and England is made clear. 'Thus in Scotland, as in no other equivalent area in England, the Special Area legislation has pooled industrial development in a small area in the West, and has doubled the difficulties under which other and now more depressed areas suffer.'

But from analysis we must pass with Dr Bowie to his constructive proposals, and here space precludes my even attempting a fair summary. But roughly Dr Bowie's idea is that we should go in for what has been called Planning, a Planned Economy. What has been attempted at North Hillington should be attempted all over. For this purpose we should not only have the necessary research and other bodies working things out, but over all a Commission with powers to apply the findings. Every issue as it arose, even to the transference of a community from a permanently derelict area, would be realistically and sympathetically dealt with.

And just here the argument starts! Not that the argument would be against Planning as such—therein lies the intrinsic value of Dr Bowie's research—for Planning has become essential to socialist and capitalist alike, while for the nationalist (who may be either) the need for building up his country is the motive power of his creed.

The trouble is that in Scotland we have historic reason to smile at the idea of any London-appointed Commission doing anything of real constructive value. We have been disillusioned too often. Granted that a perfectly constituted Commission, permanently in session, with adequate finance, could accomplish much; but your Commission in that case would be tantamount to a government, though of rather an autocratic type, because it would not be directly responsible to the people of the country in which it would be operating. Let it be responsible to the people concerned through the usual democratic channels and you have government. Without going outside our democratic conception of a state, it is difficult to see the matter in any other light. Dr Bowie seems to think it would be easier to get such a Commission than to get a Government. I wonder! After all, there is a profound psychological impulse behind the desire to govern your life in your own way; there is none in the idea of getting a Commission to do it for you. Would it be going too far to suggest that most of the individual work that has been done in recent years in examining Scottish conditions (of which the present book is an excellent example) has been a direct result of the re-awakened interest in self-government? Again, where special commissions have studied and worked and produced recommendations, what has usually happened? Little or nothing. Take one of the most fruitful—the recent inquiry into the Highlands. Dr Bowie has not dealt with the economic conditions of the Highlands, with the great industry of the sea-fisheries and the peculiar conditions of the crofting areas (how would his large 'factory' farm apply here?). But I would merely suggest that the annual grant of £65,000 for five years *spread over all the purposes stated* is just absurd. The gillie's tip on a larger scale. If even the government had said, 'We will plan the lobster fisheries, from lobster pond to transport and marketing', one would at least have seen something constructive being attempted. But that is just the sort of thing that never happens. Or take, again, the Scottish National Development Council, which in its minor way is not unlike a permanent Commission. What's happening to it now? What is it likely to do with regard to planning and bringing into being new industries for Scotland now and in the critical future? The last I heard of it was that its quarterly magazine, *Scotland*, which was devoted in some measure to that very research into economic conditions which Dr Bowie deems so fundamental, has ceased publication. In a desire to avoid controversy, we are liable to plan logical structures on a wishful basis. And the London Treasury doesn't mind—until we beg for cash to build somewhere other than in the air.

There is one direct criticism I should like to make because I think it is fundamental. It has become a commonplace to condemn the Scot for being an individualist, unable to combine in co-operative effort. Dr Bowie refers to this strongly more than once. Many go the length of saying that Scotland's present desperate condition is due almost entirely to this destructive flaw in our characters, and, as it is innate, we need not look for any material improvement in our condition.

I discussed this matter at some length in a recent issue of this magazine. Here let me conclude with a few observations upon it. Dr Bowie mentions the Scots who go south and become 'heids o' depairtments'. But a man who satisfies his ambition by departmental work, requiring for perfect functioning a high degree of co-ordination and co-operation, is manifestly not the incorrigible individualist. If the departments were available in his own country, presumably he would function in them with the same skill. The machinery for initiating and co-ordinating constructive effort in Scotland, backed by the necessary finance, does not exist. It would have to be a national machinery, directly answerable to the Scottish taxpayer whose money it would use. Any other kind of machinery would be in the nature of an insecure makeshift, that would be suspended whenever a 'state of emergency' arose—that is, at the very time (the present moment, for example) when it would be supremely important that it should be working and planning full time over against the inevitable depression that would swamp our heavy industries when 'the emergency' had passed.

One final word. A study of the Scottish scene from the early clan days of highly-developed communal effort to the institutions Scotland has tended to produce in the course of her history as a nation shows clearly that the democratic co-operative structure was natural to her from an early age. It has been said more than once that the Scottish Church system of government, with its kirk sessions and assemblies, may have given more than a few hints to the founders of the USSR! However that may be, I have the odd conviction that if a Government, based on democracy and co-operation, had been functioning in Scotland in recent decades Dr Bowie would now probably himself be the head of a department concerned with research necessary to the launching of what would be to us the usual Quinquennial Plan.

BELIEF IN OURSELVES

SM, 1945

UNLESS YOU COULD get a lift from someone with petrol coupons, a permit to show to soldiers at a barrier, the assurance of a resting-place that was officially blameless, travelling in some of the most attractive areas of the Highlands was forbidden even to those of us who had homes in the Highlands.

Now that we can freely breathe the mountain air again, and look at places, and even ask friendly questions about what's going on without raising the worst kind of suspicion, we are prepared to leave definitions of the blessed word freedom to the pundits. If we are wise, we even decide on the kind of society and its ordering that we are *not* going to have. Truly there are certain things that no good man gives up but with his life. Freedom is a noble thing, said the old poet, and we salute him across the whole landscape and history of Scotland. In our beginning was the word.

So the Highlands burst once more upon the astonished eyes. The idea that tourist traffic must be *encouraged* seems a colossal joke. Given a society with the necessities of life reasonably provided, a pocket full of holidays and pay, and we need have no fantastic worry about the places that like to be visited. They'll be visited all right.

But there remains that worry about the decent ordering of a basic economic life in the Highlands: and what I should like to do here is mention one aspect of it. It is the simplest matter in the world to set down on paper a full scheme for Highland regeneration. We all know the ingredients by this time as we know the words of an old song: crofting, hill sheep-farming, sea fisheries, hydro-electric development, afforestation, appropriate light industries, transport, and so on. But there is one thing that is always missing, one all-important matter which the paper economists forget, and that is the general lack of belief among the Highland people themselves in the future of their own land as a place where life could be lived interestingly and well.

Let me put it like this. Assuming you met a hundred Highland lads newly demobilised from the distinguished 51st Division, and said to them: 'We have word from Canada that there are excellent jobs awaiting you all over there', would they believe you? You know they would, to a man. They might or might not want to go to Canada, but they would believe you. Assuming, however, you said to them that the place was the Highlands, would there be the same response, the same automatic belief? There wouldn't. Instead you would see a sarcastic glimmer in their eye, a wonder what the leg-pull was about. First-class jobs in the Highlands! A few, who really love the Highlands, might not in the circumstances consider the joke as in the best taste. Seriously, and before committing themselves, they would then ask about the Canadian jobs, for one hopes to live with reasonable security outside the fighting line.

Now it would be no good going on to point out to these lads the real and potential wealth of the Highlands. It would be just talk. They knew what they knew, and that would be that. For what would be fundamentally lacking would be not fact, but belief. They could go to Canada, take land, blast the trees off it and make it fertile, build dams and factories, pioneer and create, as their folk had done before them (and in a way that was never better done), but to be asked to use the same creative energy at home with the certainty of at least as good a result or livelihood—no, impossible. No one did that sort of thing or believed it ever could be done in the old decaying homeland. The place is finished. It's no use making the effort. The very thought of it makes a fellow tired.

Let me look at it another way. Some time ago I had occasion to criticise a certain official report on our herring industry. I cannot go into the matter here, but roughly let it be said that, whereas the English herring fleets are run by shore syndicates, the Scottish boats are owned on the whole by the fishermen themselves and run on a co-partnership or share basis. Now, as we know, the small individually-owned business is carrying on a losing fight against the multiple concern. Before the war the Scottish boats were badly in debt, and their future looked very black. The individual hasn't the resources of the syndicate when it comes to tiding over a difficult time. The syndicate can hang on until the individual is sunk—and then take over his business or his boat.

But, it seemed to me, it would not be a very difficult bit of organising for all the individually-owned Scottish boats to group themselves into a League or Co-operative, with central resources from levies that would enable them to meet the English syndicates on their own level, and in fact beat them at their own game, for they would then have a greater concentration of shore capital and resources (they have more boats), and also could divide the profit on capital among themselves in any form they liked.

I am told that what I wrote was considered by our fishermen in one or two places. But they shook their heads. They just did not believe the thing could be done. Impossible.

But it has been done in other countries. And sea-fishing will not forever know the artificial restrictions of war-time, the reduced fleets, the certain market, the high prices. Yet there is little use pointing out these facts and drawing inevitable conclusions. Belief is lacking. The thing cannot be done in Scotland. In Norway, South Africa, the Soviet Union—yes, but that's different!

Let me consider a refreshing instance of where on a small scale a co-operative effort among a group of crofters has been successful. After the last war, the Board of Agriculture helped ex-servicemen who were crofters to combine in the possession of hill sheep-farms. Prices for sheep were very high at the time, and unfortunately the many sheep clubs thus formed had to take over from the Board at what in too many instances—especially on the West Coast—proved a crippling figure. I need not go into all that here, nor applaud the fine intentions of the Board (as the Department of Agriculture still continues to be called in our remoter places). This particular club which I visited in Caithness last week had not only weathered the storm of ever-declining prices in the inter-war years, but had at last successfully cleared off their capital indebtedness to the Board of several thousand pounds. There are twenty-six crofters in the club, and they now are the sole owners of a sheep stock of some 1500 head, managed by three shepherds. Their profit last year, after expenses of every kind were paid, amounted to £1040. In short, each crofter received £40 as his share. And, over and above, he has behind him his capital share of the stock which at current prices is a tidy sum. However you look at it, not a discouraging result for communal or co-operative effort!

I was at the sheep-clipping where all the club members turn out to give a hand. It was a pleasant gathering, with talk going strong on politics, land reclamation, and all the topics of the day, while small boys were tripping over the fleeces they bore away to those who rolled and packed them. It was a scene reminiscent of an older Highland economy, when neighbours assisted one another not only at clipping, but at peat-cutting and harvest, and indeed on any occasion when necessity called for a helping hand. The Highlands were not unused to a common or co-operative effort, out of which, in fact, the warmth of life came, with the songs, the jokes and the ceilidhs. They had belief in life in those days, and in what they could do for themselves.

To see the shepherds organising and carrying through the clipping, their ability and friendliness with everyone, to partake of their wives' hospitality, to note the fiddle hanging on the wall and to know of the bagpipes in their box, was to be assured of what yet may be accomplished on a wider scale and in many ways. I had only to remember the time when there was no club farm here. Had anyone said then that crofters' sheep would one day have the run of grouse moor and deer forest, organised on a club basis and managed by three shepherds, who would have believed him?

It took a Government Department to set it going. Well, why not? What is a Department for if not to assist enterprise which will increase the wealth of the country? The Department gave them the start, helped men who had fought for their country to do something in peace time for themselves. And so helped, the men went ahead, paid back the Department, and are now reaping the reward of their belief in what could be done in their own glen, on their own moors.

And so much more requires to be done even on these moors. Bracken has invaded the green river flats—the fertile land that could grow grass for silage and winter feed. Wintering the hoggs last year cost a pound per head. The hill drains need opening. And beyond sheep there are the new—and very old—thoughts about breeds of hardy cattle. In the old days it was an economy of cattle and sheep. A tremendous amount of research has been—and is being—done into all this. We have recently had a Report on hill sheep-farming by an independent committee. We are beginning to see what could be accomplished; and what undoubtedly will be, if only among ourselves we believed in it and went at it as we undoubtedly would—in Canada.

In all this there is one thing that particularly interests me, and that is that I should like to see the new energy and impetus provided by Highlanders themselves, by those who derive from the old traditions, the old race, so that what was distinctive and fine in our culture, our ways of life and behaviour, might continue. But vital statistics show that this will have to be done soon or it will be too late. Emigration is a remorseless way of getting rid of the best. And a dwindling population adds ever new ruins to the old ruins in the glens.

SCOTLAND MOVES

SM, 1943

IN THE YEARS before the war, I used to get an occasional letter from students in Continental universities asking questions about Scotland, which they wished to make the subject of a thesis for some diploma or other. Was there a distinct Scottish spirit, a true national ethos, and if so where could its best expression to-day be found? Was there a real difference between Highland and Lowland? And so on. Some of the questions were surprisingly searching, and I was hard put to it to give a reasonably clear answer.

To-day I have a letter from an old friend whose countrymen are not directly involved in this war, asking me if Scotland publishes a magazine which is concerned with real poetry, and whether extracts from a long poem, written by one of his friends and just published in America, might appeal to the editor of such a magazine and be printed in the usual way at the usual rates. The subject matter of the poem has an historic connection with Scotland.

Or, again, here is a professional crowd doing a 'short' for the films; the subject matter has a Scottish background, and the singing of a Gaelic chorus and of a psalm has already been recorded. Incidental music has now to be written for the film, and its idiom must clearly be Scottish in order to achieve a harmonious total effect. Could the name of a Scottish composer, who might successfully undertake the task, be given?

But most of us are aware of this interest in Scottish life on its political or economic side. As a people we are not greatly concerned about the arts. An artist or writer has still to go to London in order that he may be near what is called 'the centre of things', in other words that he may get sufficient bread and butter to keep him alive while finding an outlet for his talent or genius. Yet even here one or two careless spirits have stuck to their native heath and appear to be going on as well as could be expected. It may be a far cry to an Edinburgh of brilliance and creative force, to such an Edinburgh as in some measure the world did once upon a time know, but in quite recent days I have heard a poached salmon being wagered against a jug of beer that Edinburgh will yet attain her truly golden age—even though time may compel the wager to be paid in another place.

However, on the practical side we are all happily aware not only of the interest that has been aroused in Scottish affairs but of the sheer amount of hard work that has already been done. To anyone who has not been closely following these developments, it might be difficult to give in a word or two a fair summary of the position. For there is more in it than just what has been done either in actual accomplishment or in planning, in the sense that the whole mental approach has altered. For example, before the war, the Government recognised that something had to be done for the Highlands or they would revert to an uninhabited wilderness. So, taking their courage in their hands, those in London who control our destinies decided that nothing less than £65,000 a year for five years would meet the dreadful necessity.

Just then the war broke out, so the Government at once withdrew their munificent offer. The country could not afford so huge a sum in constructive work now that a devastating war was upon us.

Yet in recent months, we have all been following the smooth passage of the Secretary of State's Hydro-Electric Bill, wherein an expenditure of £3,000,000 is contemplated on one single aspect of Highland reconstruction, namely, the harnessing of water power.

But the change is even greater than the figures might indicate, for the Government's approach is not based on charity or dole but on what we call a real business proposition. In other words, the hydro-electric scheme is going to pay for itself. This tapping of Highland water power is not merely a something that will benefit the Highlands but a constructive act that will enrich the whole country.

This change in the mental weather is what the Highlands have needed for generations. Nothing in the long run is so deadly to a people as charity or the dole, far more deadly than to an individual who can at any moment break his fetters and clear out.

And that this new approach was just what was needed can be proved fairly simply by considering the fate of Highlanders, over the distressful generations, who were burned out of their homes and shipped to Canada, or who in despair or the name of fortune voluntarily emigrated. Names like Fraser or Mackenzie wander as mighty rivers across a continent. The defeatism bred of a paralysing history is forgotten, and an energy and resource are released that astonish the critics, and that in fact still contrive to astonish the world in the deeds of the Highland Division.

This is not said in boastfulness—that dubious form of self-expression which can more usefully be left to the psychoanalysts. Its immense importance to us lies in just this—that it should help us to assess the true potential of any new constructive measures at home. It should let us see the kind of constructive effort that is needed. By it we can recognise that the approach to the problem of harnessing Highland hydro-electric power is sound, simply because it presents the opportunity for the exercise of energy and resource at home.

There are critics who say that there are flaws in the plan, even dangers, that everything in the electric garden is not lovely. No doubt. But I have never yet had anything to do with a garden but it required a fair amount of work to keep it even presentable. But, given the garden, surely it's a poor spirit that complains before the work is started.

I have mentioned the hydro-electric scheme simply because it is perhaps the first evidence of the coming fruit. But a great deal of exploratory work is also being accomplished in other realms of Scottish life, from herring fishing to hill sheep-farming, from hospitals and rehabilitation to the inauguration of planning on a regional scale. We have had the report by the Forestry Commission, for example, duly debated in Parliament. But the majority of Scots want a separate Forestry authority for Scotland. And those who have been most vocal or active in this demand are not Nationalist or Socialists, but Tories of the House of Lords. In other words, the need for such a separate authority has become so obvious that it has cut across all party lines. It is seen to be absurd that a Forestry Commission, overwhelmingly English and with headquarters in London, should be governing the destinies of sheep farmers and forestry concerns in the Highlands. If we have a separate Department of Agriculture in St Andrew's House surely it is but commonsense that a Forestry department should also be there, so that both could combine in a long term policy which would ensure the minimum of hardship and the maximum of gain for the country as a whole. The point becomes still more obvious when we realise that the greater part of the planted acreage administered by the Forestry Commission is already in Scotland.

But having thus indicated the kind of concentration that is now taking place by Scotsmen on Scottish affairs, perhaps we need not go on giving instances. As the reports of the Secretary of State's Committees continue to appear we shall have plenty to think about—and no doubt to quarrel over. Out of all this ferment, two points may call for special attention.

First, there is the feeling—though not now so strong as it was some time ago—that all this concern with post-war conditions is in some degree unreal and in some degree dangerous because it may distract us from our main purpose of winning the war. Moreover, how can those of us who are too old to fight be trusted with the work of recreating an economy for the lads who are fighting and who are necessarily denied any criticism of our labours? For it is they who will have to work the schemes and ensure the future generations.

Let it be clear that this feeling is expressed not by the soldiers themselves, but by those of us at home who prefer to remain armchair critics of the conduct of the war and who must not be distracted from this high task by doing a spot of useful constructive labour. Take, as an instance, the Beveridge Report. Now we do know that this Report had an enormous interest for the soldiers in Libya. It aroused such enthusiasm that apparently some kind of political action had to be taken. Anyway, I think it can be safely said that the soldier felt that Sir William Beveridge was putting up a real fight for him on the home front. The value of that Report as world propaganda for our country must have been immense. If Britain can think like this, at such a time, then plainly she is not the devitalised country some nations thought she was!

Or take our Highland hydro-electric scheme. The constructional period will give work to 10,000 men for ten years. Well, we know what happened after the last war. Is there any soldier in the Highland Division who will feel less happy because a Secretary of State for Scotland is trying *now* to make fairly certain that there will be a job for him when he comes home?

If no work of this kind were being done by those of us who can fight in no other way, would not the soldier indeed have reason to condemn us as betrayers of what he has left in our charge? That is the real question which we have to answer.

The second point is this, and we have got to contemplate it with as little prejudice as possible. Such research and constructional work, through advisory councils and committees, through direct measures by our Secretary of State, and in other ways, is being done by Scotsmen in Scotland. For the first time in centuries the feeling is growing upon us that we can do things for ourselves. More than that, we are beginning to realise that we cannot expect others to do them for us; and perhaps this is the greater gain, because it holds more hope for Scotland's future.

THE GAEL WILL COME AGAIN

SM, 1931

The previous month's *Scots Magazine* had carried an article, 'Celt and Norseman: A Contrast', by Alexander Urquhart. The latter 'extolled the industry, adaptability, and hard-headed tenacity of the Norseman in his profitable development of lonely island settlements to the belittlement of the Celt, with particular reference to the [then] recent St Kilda evacuation.' The following was a reply to Urquhart, 'a defence of Celtic tradition, and a declaration of the present-day potentialities of that tradition.'

THAT MR ALEXANDER URQUHART in his article on 'Celt and Norseman' has unjustly overstated his case against the Highland Gael does not, as he may feel it would—or even should—rouse that picturesque figure of his fancy to immediate fiery wrath.

The dignity, 'frequently indistinguishable from the silliest form of vanity', may, when it exists (and where doesn't it?), be affected. That is about all. Why? Just because of that element of truth underlying the trenchancies of Mr Urquhart's charge, an element seen by the true Gael himself more than by any other. This is not a matter for sweeping comparisons and violent accusations. One may be down at heel and yet not a fool. In the world of affairs it is a commonplace that the predatory instinct triumphs over the spirit. Nor need we slip on platitudes. For what has long happened to the north-west of Scotland is now perceived as happening to Scotland as a whole. There has been an insidious process of decline, throwing up the usual symptoms, which Mr Urquhart observes in the case of the dreamer with his 'humbug', but may miss in the case of the Scot with his haggis. It might be interesting to diagnose these symptoms, but it would probably land us in the wide region of national life and affairs, where the external simplicities of Mr Urquhart's observations would neither explain nor reveal very much.

His comparisons with the Norse may be, for example, entirely misleading. It is possible that on one of his islands a thousand miles north of the Hebrides a colony of Gaels might thrive (and so repeat history), and that on St Kilda, because of those very contacts with 'civilisation', a colony of the hardiest

Norsemen might in a generation or two ask a beneficent government to help them 'to conquer fortune' (a fine phrase!) by removing them to the mainland. Any Saxon business man whom I have met would indeed consider such a move for such a purpose a natural and wise one. So that when Mr Urquhart is being ashamed over the St Kildan exodus, I feel that his shame is really not so much for Celt or Norseman as for human nature. And we all have our share of that.

Perhaps that is why Mr Urquhart cannot find the cause of the 'lethargy and slackness' of the west, though he is satisfied that it lies not in race but in the language, nurture, and tradition of the people. That is about as vague a statement as even a dreamer could make! It is, more unfortunately, an illogical one. For as Mr Urquhart asserts, at one time St Kilda carried a population of 200, who throve on the results of their own labour. I make no doubt they throve as well as did any contemporary Norse settlement similarly placed. They were also, according to travellers, given to the social arts of singing and dancing. And of that self-supporting colony, a remnant of 86 was evacuated recently and the island abandoned. Yet it was the same language, an unbroken tradition; and, in the same environment, there were presumably the same potentialities for nurture. The 'slackness and lethargy' cannot therefore be implicit in these three factors. The cause must be searched for elsewhere.

Nor is St Kilda the solitary example. The mainland was also in time past inhabited by a self-supporting people, who gave a good account of themselves not only in social life and the creative arts of poetry and music, but also in the matter of personal daring and courage. They not only fought with distinction in the wars of Europe, but took a hand in making history at home—and if they had then developed, in place of their marked individuality, this new art, which Mr Urquhart observes, of 'leaning' on each other, it is possible that that hand would have been a decisive one. But in those days there was, alas! less 'leaning' amongst them than amongst their enemies, the Saxons, who also, of course, had numberless more shoulders for the purpose.

The language, tradition, and nurture of the Gael sufficed in those days, and would have sufficed in these, if they had not been interfered with from outside. I am not now referring to tourists' tips nor charity's tinned meats, though these may be all that trouble the facile minds of travellers to-day. The root-cause is deeper and more desperate. It struck at language, at honour, at livelihood, at tradition, at their arts and amusements, in a way that for stark brutality is without parallel in modern Christendom (Ireland not excepted, that other home of the Gael). There is no space here for the petty details, though their tone might be given by quoting from the oath which a Highlander had to take after the '45. It refers to the charming matter of the pattern of the tweed he wore. This is what the Sheriff asked him to repeat:

> ... and never use tartan, plaid, or any part of the Highland garb; and if I do, may I be cursed in my undertaking, family, and property—may I never see my wife

and children, father, mother, relations—may I be killed in battle as a coward, and be without Christian burial in a strange land, far from the graves of my forebears and kindred; and may this come across me if I break my oath.

The people were not only 'cleared' out of the glens, hunted and dragooned, or shipped abroad like cattle, but those who remained, after being cowed into a mood of utter subjection, were by the most subtle and insidious means, religious and educational, made to despise their language and tradition (nurture now barely arising).

From such a gruelling onset, pursued in various guises through generations, a people does not recover all at once. It takes time. 'Lethargy and slackness' are not perhaps unnatural. Even 'dirt and squalor' might be expected. Tinned jellies are acceptable, and a little Celtic-twilight is imported for sleep.

I would pray Mr Urquhart not be intolerant and, before the Gael has quite come to himself, threaten him once more with a Norse invasion.

Also I would ask him, when he finds so certainly that the Gael's 'affinity to poetry and beauty' is 'all humbug', to inquire into the matter beyond the personal chance encounter. He would not, I presume, call the glorious record of English literature 'all humbug'—after spending a day in Clapham.

Gaelic poetry and music are no myths. There were dialectal differences all over Gaeldom, but scholar's Gaelic was common currency in Scotland and Ireland until the seventeenth century. Gaelic literature was in its flower centuries before the beginnings of English literature. Dr Johnson was revealingly ignorant when he said that there was no Gaelic MS over 100 years old. There is indeed such a wealth of Gaelic MSS in existence that one savant suggests it will take 200 years for Gaelic scholarship to deal with them. And as a Gaelic poet of to-day says of this literature as a whole: 'Its poetry is sun-bred; twilight for it is just the tremulous smoke of one day's fire. Not with dreams but with fire in the mind ...'

There might well be then the 'lethargy and slackness', but what there has been is passing before the slow but sure uprising of a new confidence. As for Sir Archibald Geikie's 'squalor, dirt, and laziness', I can but suggest that the learned geologist was singularly unfortunate in his encounters, just as any foreign visitor would be unfortunate who got his idea of the Lowlands from the Cowgate or the Cowcaddens. But Gaelic history is proverbially the comment of the outsider. Lecky found conditions a thousand times worse in the Ireland of his day—even if, incidentally, he failed to find at the same time the existence of the 'Courts of Poetry'. The Gael under the pale was certainly at his social lowest. He had lost heart, and was living in conditions utterly appalling. But he lived through that infamous time, and to-day is running his own affairs in a Free State that is financially about the only one in Europe approaching complete solvency.

In my experience of the west I may have been more fortunate in missing the 'squalor, dirt, and laziness', and finding instead hundreds of homes, humble enough materially, but at least with the graces of hospitality and a natural courtesy. The exception occurs everywhere—and here need hardly be a concern for our scorn in the face of history.

Finally, Mr Urquhart's preoccupation with his Saxon ideal of the go-getter is interesting as a personal expression but not conclusive as a way of life. It has hardly, for example, landed the world in a golden age completely devoid of poverty and squalor. In the midst of plenty (called over-production), we suffer the grisly spectacle of famine. Against the tyranny of the machine and the predatory instincts of the go-getter, new conceptions of life and work are needed. The Gael in Scotland may have had 'inferiority' drummed into him, but he will come again—only, in his own way, which may not be the way, however admirable, of the 'humdrum Saxon', nor, perhaps, will the world lose by the distinction.

A VISITOR FROM DENMARK

SM, 1937

ARNE STRÖM, the Danish writer, called on me the other day. He had worn out a pair of shoes tramping Skye. He had talked to fishermen and crofters wherever he had gone. 'Here and there a black-faced sheep!' and his gesture conveyed, with a dry smile, our agricultural condition. 'You hard-boiled individualists!' When he wished to convey irony, he generally indulged in American expressions. For he had left Denmark to go farming in a big way in America. He had been through the period of depression there, when farmers at the end of desperation had shot their stock and sometimes themselves. But his specialist knowledge of poultry had helped him through, and finally had procured him a commission from the Soviet Government to be foreign adviser or expert on one of their huge poultry farms (1932–33). The story of these experiences he has told, I believe, in one of his books. He is not only a man of wide experience, but of the shrewdest practical under-standing, caring far more for describing precisely what he has done and seen than for theorising about national politics.

I mention all this about him because of the conclusion he had come to after tramping our Highlands. 'Had I known this lovely country, had I seen it when I was twenty, I would not have gone to America. Never. I would have come here. I would have taken one hundred Danes with me. We would have set up a colony. We would have worked in co-operation. We would have done well. Not any men, but the Danes, who know how to work. And their women. For, on a farm, the woman is everything. She makes it.'

But he was too old for that now; he was forty, and a correspondent on a leading Copenhagen newspaper that had sent him to Scotland to report on our economic conditions. Did Scottish newspapers pay correspondents to go to Denmark to report what was being done there in the way of co-operative farming? Could I tell him the name of a book giving a complete and impartial survey of crofting and sea-fishing in the Highlands? Could I——? But to all his questions I could give little more than a confused negative. There were odds and ends, pamphlets, day-to-day journalism about things, I suggested haltingly. He smiled. 'This Caledonian Power Scheme?' and he eyed me, politely not wishing to commit himself until he saw to which side I belonged, for he had already tumbled to our partiality for wordy fights rather than for constructive work, for opposition rather than for co-operation. To him all the talk seemed so sterile a waste when—here and there a black-faced sheep!

His English was good, but clearly he would have liked now and then to have let himself go in his native tongue.

Perhaps, however, the restraint was even more impressive. He could hardly, he suggested, with smiling irony, explain to them in Denmark. He dare not. To explain what could be done here—if we worked—if we understood how to work—ah! that might be so successful that we might threaten the Danish market in this country. Certainly. It would not do. And I realised that he would in fact be discreet.

We walked, and I drew from him pictures of Denmark. The Denmark of a couple of generations ago, newly conquered by Prussia, Slesvig-Holstein taken from her, her farming going down before the great grain-bearing lands of America. A Denmark defeated and in despair. Then the power of the idealists, who taught them two things: their history and new ways of farming; the nationalists who said, we need faith in ourselves, in order that we may work for our own and the common good. These pioneers of the 'School of Life' inspired the simple farm labourers with stories of their country's past. They met and talked in farm kitchens, somewhat after the fashion of the Highland *ceilidh*, yet different from the *ceilidh* in this, that the tales of the past were matter of inspiration for the present and the future. They were mocked. But they persevered. They increased in numbers. Farmers met these new co-operators with pitchforks. But the ideal was strong, for it was not only based on faith but on knowledge; it was prepared not only with words but with deeds.

And out of these simple beginnings came the co-operative system of Danish farming that has commanded the admiration of the world; and, in a sense, the even more remarkable development of the kitchen *ceilidh* into the Folk High Schools. We pride ourselves on our education in Scotland. Make the most cursory examination of what Denmark has done for her working young men and women in her Folk Schools and then proceed to comparison. At this moment a student from Scotland may take the international classes in the school in Elsinore for the three months, April-July, at a total charge, including board and lodging, of £14.

Denmark is little more than half the size of Scotland and carries a population of some three and a half millions. A fifth of the country is peat moor or sand. It is flat and without metallic ores, coal, or water power. Yet these Danes, inspired by love of their own land and carrying the ideal of brotherhood in labour into the severely practical business of co-operation, have made of their country one of the most fruitful in the world. The nationalism out of which this magic has been wrought cared nothing for armies and navies and Empire. It concerned itself with the creative work of men's hands; it satisfied the aspirations of individualism while directing these aspirations towards the common good; and when personal needs were thus ordered, it continued organising these adult schools through which the mind may attempt to realise its spiritual potentialities.

I began to understand, as Arne Ström went on talking, the background to his thought, and to apprehend, if dimly, how the Highlands must appear to him. He had been picking up facts about unemployment: 25 per cent in Inverness-shire; 40 per cent in Ross. Were these figures true? Were the Highlands indeed classifiable as a distressed area? And our sea-fishing: it seemed to be in a bad way, too?

I knew most of the relevant facts. It was not easy talking. I did not care about repeating what I wrote here in the March issue on pauper lunacy. The picture seemed dark enough without referring to an unnecessary emigration, to a declining population, to an increasing dependence on dole and State money. As we walked out of Inverness, I thought of the crofting lands in front of us towards Beauly and of schools there where half the children are Glasgow orphans boarded out by the Poor Law. Where was the old virile life of this particular area, once the most fertile in the North? What had happened? What was wrong?

I turned to Ström and asked him how he could be sure, if he did bring his Danes here, that they would in fact work hard and in co-operation. I suppose I wanted to challenge him. But, after a first glance of astonishment, he laughed. It was merely inevitable that they would work in co-operation; just as no doubt it was inevitable that in a town like Inverness there should be a common water supply. It was the best way and it worked. The Danes *knew*.

But I saw that it went deeper than that. Here was an assurance, an optimism, that sprang from some root we had lost. And so real was it that it would never think of expressing itself in terms of brotherhood or idealism, but simply in terms of commonsense. The practical note was uppermost always.

It was difficult for me to put up any sort of case for the existing condition of the Highlands. It seemed futile to try to explain it by a reference to history; to suggest that the 'Forty-five and its barbarous aftermath may have started a process of breaking the spirit of the Highlander that the Clearances completed; to show the sheep farm succeeded by the deer forest, tragedy succeeded by apathy. One is reluctant to explain this to a foreigner, not merely out of pride but out of the hopelessness of making it sound reasonable. For the Danes also had had their dark period, but they had come out of it triumphantly. When America and Russia had made grain-growing uneconomic, they swung round to dairying and pig-rearing; they changed the whole nature of their agricultural policy.

But had the common folk done this spontaneously, or had they been inspired by leaders? And the all-important answer was that they had been inspired by leaders. Behind this extremely practical issue of farming and real education, we find the idealists, the men who wrote and spoke of their country because they loved it, who ousted the fashionable German and Latin tongues by the Danish speech of the people, who created and directed the new ways of life, out of which in due course a considerable literature and a more considerable science were born.

Did our trouble lie in this, then—that we had never produced our own leaders? Leaders in all ways of activity and thought the Highlands had produced, but never to express themselves at home. For action, they had gone to London or the Colonies. Administrators, governor-generals, explorers, pioneer farmers, down to political careerists and heids o' departments. Surely out of the long roll the Highlands could have retained one or two for creative organisation in the glens and on the sea—men with vision and patience and belief, who recognised the value of their old culture and ways of life, and who, like these Danes, might have inspired the people to their own economic and educational salvation? For by so doing, they would not only have *created* something for themselves but also in the process have added to the riches and knowledge of the world, as Denmark has done in her example of co-operative small-farming and Folk Schools. Of what value to the Highlands have Scottish Secretaries of State been, or to the world, or to anything positive at all that we can think of?

The best always being drawn away to London or the Colonies. None remaining to organise or inspire. Festive Highlanders boast of the great men they have exported. I ask myself: (1) Has this greatness ever achieved the *creative* record of the Danes who stayed at home; (2) does farming in Alberta or place-hunting in Whitehall make up for a derelict Highlands? If the Danes had aspired, let us say, to departmental seats in Berlin or a 'place in the sun' abroad, would Denmark have the importance she has for herself and for us to-day?

These questions may sound rhetorical. They demand an answer for all that.

My friend returned to the Caledonian Power Scheme again, because he had seen our local press full of it. Did our press also deal with the far greater problems of agriculture and fishing? Did all these local papers use the same heat, fill the same number of columns, over the condition of crofting and unemployment in the Highlands? I was compelled to admit, I am afraid, that they did not. I could not recall any heat or controversy over the desperate position of the fishermen in the Moray Firth ports or indeed anywhere on our Highland shores. Not only was this by far our greatest industry (apart from the land), not only was it hopelessly in debt and steadily declining, but the very basis of its polity—the brave old tradition of skipper-ownership— was in this moment passing away. While nothing was being done, and little said. True, there were Government offers of loans, but on terms so impossible to the defeated men that the irony would be laughable were it not so tragic.

Even the Caledonian Power Scheme—a trumpery affair economically compared with land and sea—could not be investigated on its merits on the spot, so that men of Inverness and men of the Highlands could see exactly what it would mean to them. No. Deputations, after working up antagonisms to each other, must proceed to London in order to carry out, whether they liked it or not, a lobbying of members of the House of Commons on a scale and with an intensity that made of the realities of the situation a farce and must have been to those concerned a deep indignity. And finally the English members who knew nothing about the Scheme, and Welsh members who wanted it for Wales, combined to throw it out.

There is no leadership, there are no men of vision and knowledge. The heat and the controversy are over local jealousies. How could I explain to the Dane that there are folk who do not want industries, who never trouble over the state of crofting and sea-fishing, who are comfortable themselves and therefore wish nothing to be disturbed, who talk of the salvation of the Highlands through tourists impressed by the beauty of empty glens—an attitude by no means confined to Tory reactionaries?

We proceed in our motor cars to these glens and sniff their ozone and express our pride. Yes, this is our country. Lovely, isn't it? We do not disturb ourselves by reflecting that the motor car is a product of a complicated industrialism. We must not let the thought of industrialism taint our delicate Highland nostrils. Oxy-acetylene may be useful for shipbuilding and Highlanders may have proved themselves amongst the finest seamen in the world, but that we should have a factory for its production here—what a polluting thought!

How explain all this to a Dane, looking with covetous eyes at our water power?

And when it comes to the cultural side, how could I tell him that against his Folk High Schools and Agricultural Schools (these are additional, of course, to the ordinary school-university system) we had—the Mod? The Mod as a creative factor in the flowering of our Gaelic heritage! But despair here is too deep even for irony. Meantime Norwegian scholars are fitting out an expedition to find what is left of Gaelic before it dies. Though, as I write this, a newspaper states that Gaelic is not nearly so dead as all that, because our greatest Gaelic lexicographer—a Russian—is just reported to have said that it may last a couple of generations.

Ah! the romantic Highlands, the aesthetic appeal of the glens, the bens and the heroes, the blue waves rolling by Barra and all the haunted Isles; ah! Tir nan Og, och-nan-och, and the songs of the seals! Is it too much to hope that some day this sort of thing may stick in our gullets, that we shall be roused to make it an indictable offence? This parodying of great beauty by the sentimentalists who think factory work ungenteel should fill us, not with laughter, but with shame.

Though what can be said of the jeering opponents of the twilight sleepers, the hard-boiled fellows who allege that the Highlanders are not dreamers but, on the contrary, extremely practical folk who know on which side their bread is buttered? Triumphantly they point to a 100 per cent grant from London for some section of a road as evidence not merely of the quality of Highland leadership in local affairs but of the thereby proven need for retaining the existing régime and its connection with London. After all, we were perhaps a trifle hard on the song of the seal.

Denmark, with her increasing population, could spare a few of her adventurous spirits, just as a healthy Highlands could—and did in time past. But, as things are, it was difficult for me to point to the Highlands and then suggest to Arne Ström that there was something rotten in the state of Denmark! There was, however, one regret that we shared in common—and that was that Ström and his hundred Danes had not in fact come to settle in the Highlands.

A FOOTNOTE ON CO-OPERATION

Anarchy, 1968

IN THIS AGE WE GET SO BEDEVILLED by slogans, labels, and schemes in the head, that we forget the realities underneath. Herring Boards or any other kind of Boards imposed from above will do no earthly good unless the producers themselves combine in some sort of union or co-operative. So combined they will then be in a position to take advantage of the Boards or of anything else that comes their way. If they are not combined, spoon-feeding by a Board will keep them going for a time, but in the end, when the spoon-feeding is withdrawn, they will collapse before those who have united whether on a private capitalist basis or otherwise.

That's the simple truth, and the economic history of the Highlands in recent times proves it. Facts about the decline in sea-fisheries, crofting, hill-sheep farming, and so on are known. Equally known is the success of certain northern European countries where co-operation among the producers was the basic order and help from governmental sources the natural result.

But when one mentions co-operation, folk here shake their heads. They either think it can't be done in sea-fishing and crofting or else they get tied up in hot arguments about the SCWS and the private trader.

Never mind all that. Co-operation simply means that small independent producers, threatened by syndicates or great combines, will ultimately be done down unless they come together in a combine of their own. I am not discussing the ethics of this. I am merely stating what inevitably happens.

Now by coming together in a league or co-operative, they can not only hold their own on the economic front, but they can also retain in large measure the ways of life and freedom which tradition and environment have made precious to them. If they don't want to be 'wage slaves', they needn't be. But they have got to come together. Co-operation is a coming together in their own interests.

My friend, Peter F Anson, has recently been in Eire studying fishing conditions round the coast. He has a wide knowledge of the sea-fisheries of Europe, and has surprised me (and possibly himself) by finding an Irish Sea Fisheries Association which arranges for the provision of boats and gear, co-operative marketing, and other enterprises. In the *Fishing News* he writes:

'All fishermen members are required to enter into a Co-operative Marketing Contract under which they share in the general scheme of the Association for the sale of catches. In some districts it has been found possible to guarantee members, on a seasonal basis, fixed prices at the port of landing for their catches of white fish, plus, when conditions are good, a bonus on their earnings.' The Association maintains a boat-building yard and motor repair shops, and in fact does every constructive thing it can in the general interests of the sea-fishing industry.

I knew pre-war Eire fairly well, and all I can say is that if the Irish can do that sort of thing at home, a co-operative association is no dream for Scottish fisheries. I regard self-government for Scotland as co-operation on the national level.

It was the Eire Government that set up the Irish Sea Fisheries Association. Would that Association have been in being were Irish affairs still run from London?

But I do not wish to raise any argumentative issue here. The simple point I want to make is that individual producers on sea and land will have to combine if they are going to win through. The debt on our fishermen-owned Scottish drifters before the war was as real as was the ever-increasing power of the English drifters owned and run by shore syndicates. History will repeat itself, unless we undertake to mould it nearer to our interests and desires. We can do so; but it means *doing*, action, on a basis of association or co-operation.

There is no other way that I know.

NATIONALISM AND INTERNATIONALISM

SM, 1931

THE OTHER DAY I happened to meet a Scottish painter and etcher who was kind enough to invite me to a private view of some of his recent work. It was distinguished work, full of vision, and aware of all the ways of the moderns, but by no means the least interesting part of my visit was the artist's own ideas and experiences elicited by, let me hope, natural questions. For example, a couple of his canvasses were concerned with ploughed fields. The serpentine furrow was the motif in a bare Scottish landscape. Not, possibly, what would popularly be called a 'picture'. Yet the artist had been intimately attracted by the subject, and, though believing that the attraction was peculiar and personal, had nonetheless had it included in a group of subjects from different parts of the world for a one-man show. Consider his surprise when the bare furrows caught the particular attention of the metropolitan dealers. It was almost enough to make him conclude that trips to North Africa may be fascinating, but not necessarily essential for the production of masterpieces! And if this theme provided a nearly endless one for speculation at least the one fact had emerged, namely, that by the artist's doing what he knew intimately, and what had appealed to him deeply in his own country, he had attracted the closest attention of art lovers in other countries.

I mention this experience because it happens to be the most recent of many that have, from time to time, seemed to explain to me the relationship of nationalism to internationalism. Nationalism creates that which internationalism enjoys. The more varied and multiple your nationalism, the richer and profounder your internationalism. Conversely, where the nation would disappear and the world become a single body governed by the same machinery of laws and ideas, the common stock of culture would tend to become uniform and static. For cosmopolitanism does not readily breed the intense vision or rebellion of the native or individual spirit. On the contrary, its natural attitude is to deplore it as being unnecessary, often wasteful, and nearly always in bad form. Cosmopolitanism working through this man-of-the-world conception might out of an ultimate logic create its own ideal, but it would be the deathly or neutral idea of the perfection of the beehive.

Now the question arises here:—Why, then, is there in the world of affairs to-day the idea of antagonism between nationalism and internationalism? If internationalism is nationality's flower, why war? And it is precisely in this awful region of war that so many of us lose our bearings. For nationalism breeds patriotism; patriotism, it is asserted, breeds antagonism; and antagonism needs the mailed fist.

But patriotism, as a true emotion, is full of life; it has kinship with poetry and music and none with destruction and death. From the earliest times it has been the world's singing subject. In the history of each nation it has been a unifying and precious possession. Each nation has been prepared to fight for it, when it would not quite have been prepared to fight for its music and poetry, or, indeed, for any other of the mind's preoccupations except religion. Patriotism, indeed, fed such arts as poetry and music. Possibly no other single emotion is more responsible for the creation of the world's culture.

But that sort of patriotism has as little to do with jingoism as music has with a factory siren. And it would be almost as reasonable to suggest that we could get rid of the unwelcome noise of our machine age by first of all abolishing musical scales and musical instruments as it would be to suggest that we could get rid of jingoism by first of all abolishing patriotism. There is no philosophic basis here, and the reasoning is of the kind that has been prolific of so much action, or rather restriction, in recent world legislation. What interferes with our natural love of country to-day may regulate our drink to-morrow, our clothes the day after, and our conjugal relations next year. Patriotism may yet keep us from being slaves—if only of the Wellsian aseptic city-honeycombs.

Patriotism (even already the word is beginning to have a false note) is founded in tradition, and we can no more get away from tradition than from ourselves. Indeed, immediately we get away from tradition we do get away from ourselves. A nation's traditions are the natural inspirations of its people. How much the child is the product of heredity and how much of environment may be a debatable point, but that he is the product of both is unquestionable. Out of his environment, acted upon by a traditional or national unity, he creates most profoundly. And to create is to cause or give delight. In the pure conception of patriotism there is pure pleasure just as there is in any true function of the arts. And it is only when a man is moved by the traditions and music and poetry of his own land that he is in a position to comprehend those of any other land, for already he has the eyes of sympathy and the ears of understanding.

How then has patriotism in idea got debauched by war? Simply because in time of war patriotism is so strongly roused to protect its frontiers that it has been confounded with the cause of war. Nations are the natural units in the war game, just as the family is the natural unit in the nation. But it would be as ridiculous to destroy our natural unities in the hope of destroying the war game as it would be to remove our teeth in the hope of getting rid of a pain caused by our stomachs. For, as has been said, patriotism is never a cause of war, but is merely used by war, just as other emotions are, only more profoundly. For even when nations group into compact empires or into scattered commonwealths, when they lose their nationhood and traditions, war can still use them. War can use them without patriotism. War can enjoy the spectacle of patriots of the same nation fighting each other. War is insatiable, and in the last resort cares nothing for nations. It cares only for destruction, and the earth laid waste would be its final triumph.

Why then blame this creative emotion of love of country as causing war, when we have at long last been forced to learn that war is caused by emotions quite other in origin and aim? We know something now of the appallingly defective system of producing and distributing the goods of life that obtains in the world to-day. Men of goodwill and of all political faiths are being staggered at the dreadful paradox of unemployment, hunger, disease, slums—as a result of over-production. Because we have produced more than we need, we are in danger of starvation! At least the spate of war books has made one thing clear (and particularly the German books), that the peoples themselves had no desire for war, that they feared and hated it as it continued, and that in the largest countries in Europe they smashed their own governing machines in the hope of getting some sanity, some food, and a little peace in their time.

Internationalism carried to its logical conclusion of a single centralisation of all power—arms, finance, law-making—could result in the greatest tyranny the mind of man is capable of conceiving. While the nation is still the unit (and history has shown the small unit to be singularly important—consider Greece and Palestine) the individual factor comes into play, and in a myriad personal contacts the finer elements of humanism are retained and tyranny suffered briefly, if at all. But when the governing machine becomes single in control, remote in place, and absolute in power, then hope of reform or progress—which generally means the breaking of an existing mould—would not have the heart to become articulate. Standardisation would be the keyword not only in the material things of life, but also in the spiritual. And whenever conditions got too desperate it would mean revolution, or world war on a basis of class hatred.

The small nation has always been humanity's last bulwark for the individual against that machine, for personal expression against impersonal tyranny, for the quick freedom of the spirit against the flattening steam-roller of mass. It is concerned for the intangible things called its heritage, its beliefs and arts, its distinctive institutions, for everything, in fact, that expresses it. And expression finally implies spirit in an act of creation, which is to say, culture.

Culture thus emerges in the nation, is the nation's flower. Each nation cultivates its own natural flower. The more varieties, the more surprise and pleasure for all. For nationalism in the only sense that matters is not jealous, any more than music is jealous. On the contrary, if we are gardeners or musicians we are anxious to meet gardeners or musicians of other lands and rejoice when their blooms are exquisitely different from our own. In this way life becomes enriched, and contrast is set up as a delight and an inspiration. To have no longer these means for discrimination, to lose the charm that unending variety gives, to miss the spur in the shadow of difference, 'is, on this short day of frost and sun, to sleep before evening'.

EIRE

How Dublin Received the New Constitution

SM, 1938

'TO-DAY IS CONSTITUTION DAY in Dublin.' Thus began the leading article in one of our great British daily newspapers. Mr de Valera, we were informed, would attend a Votive Mass in the Pro-Cathedral and the Chief-Justice take the oath before the Government to uphold the Constitution. In his Christmas message to his people Mr de Valera said that 1937 would stand for ever as 'the year in which our people enacted and first gave to themselves a free Constitution'. And the substance of this freedom was reflected in the change of name from the Irish Free State to Eire or Ireland.

On this side of the Irish Sea, we might have been forgiven for imagining a day of pageantry and rejoicing in Dublin. How London would have celebrated any such major historical event in her country's history—or Berlin, or Moscow! With what drama they celebrate comparatively minor events, like anniversaries, or royal or presidential successions and departures! And here for the vast majority of the Irish people, after centuries of heroic struggle, through defeats and martyrdoms that became their terrible inspiration, the undefeatable spirit at last proclaims its victory, says I am Eire, Ireland, and makes for its internal governance a Constitution from which the name of the British King is omitted.

Yet in Dublin there was not even a general holiday, and as for pageantry, I saw no sign of it! Civil servants got a holiday—when their absence from duty would not interfere with the normal flow of public business. It was like one of those bank holidays in Scotland that affect the toiling masses not at all. Constitution Day followed immediately upon the Christmas holiday and traders said they could not afford to close down for another day. The Government might perhaps like them to, but really they could not afford it, and the workers themselves had apparently no grievance in the matter. And that, from a public or spectacular point of view, was about all there was to it!

What a superb anti-climax—or how Irish! the casual visitor might think. Clearly this lack of public observance or acclamation was not deliberate. And equally clearly the Government made no effort towards a resounding show by clever propaganda or hidden dragooning or edict or lavish display, such as all of us who are good Europeans have become accustomed to. The whole thing, so to speak, was allowed to happen, and from a public point of view it hardly happened at all.

The casual visitor might even be forgiven for concluding that the Irish considered the whole affair a 'bit of a cod'. And there is a certain sense in which he might not be so very far wrong. 'Like Queen Victoria, we are not impressed', said one Irishman to me, and laughed heartily. But his position happens to be a very difficult one. He was against de Valera and 'would not go across the street to vote for him'. He was proceeding to tell me why, when another member of our party interrupted him powerfully; but refusing to be sidetracked, I shouted: 'Would you vote for Cosgrave, then?' In the silence, he looked at me and said: 'God forbid!' Tapping the mahogany with a finger nail, he proceeded: 'I am waiting for a decent Labour candidate, and whenever he appears in my constituency, he gets my vote—not that I believe in Socialism particularly.' We were a lively crowd before we had arrived at no very clear conclusions. When you ask for a half-a-pint of stout in Dublin, you get Guinness in a pewter pot, and if there is a better drink of its particular kind, the secret must be well guarded.

'In short, the days of struggle and fighting are over. We are merely all politicians now,' as it was summed up for my benefit, with a quizzical smile. The Constitution—what is it but a gathering together of odds and ends from this Treaty and that Act or Declaration of *what had already been won*? No need to make a song about it, even if it was put together by a very clever and able man (for de Valera's prestige is very high). If any fellow had aspired to solemn eulogy 'of this auspicious occasion', he would have had his leg pulled right from under him.

This absence of concern or pother implied, of course, that the Constitution is a fairly healthy piece of work to the Irish mind. Nothing to make a fuss about; good enough; it will do—because deep in them the Irish know where they stand and what they have won. No framing of constitutions can ever take the place of the living spirit, and instinctively they are aware of that and base their conduct on it. The man who said he would not cross the street to vote for de Valera has the de Valera spirit in him right to the backbone. Not that that will stop him from voting Labour and spoiling Fianna Fail in his own constituency! For he has theories now of trade and commerce and thinks it high time that 'all that old history stuff was given a rest' (history, in clearest detail, being his strong suit). So he attacks the President on the cattle embargo or other point and damns him with such heat that you would say the old friendship between him and his fellow disputant was severed for ever, whereas it will probably be strengthened. And after we leave the mahogany counter (how intelligent and friendly, the Irish barmen!) we go on talking on the street at the top of our voices, and stop now and then to drive home the thousandth 'real point'.

'But look here—all the economic nationalism—aren't you at least carrying that a bit too far? I mean——.'

'Too far, is it? By giving employment to people? What do you take us for? Here was Ireland with no industries at all. Take Humphrey there. He imported clothes—with the English cut!—and sold them to poor bloody people who couldn't afford to buy them. With one or two of a staff he did the whole thing and walked about like a gentleman. The Government stopped that. The clothes must be made here. So he had to have a factory, and now he employs hundreds and hundreds of hands. He doesn't like it, of course. Why? Because he has to work now!'

'You shut up,' said Humphrey, 'when you know nothing about anything, and listen to me. Now, you just listen——.

'If we have to listen to you, can't we go and sit down somewhere?'

At an advanced hour I gather that the Constitution is based on the family; that Ireland, having been economically destroyed under the Ascendancy, had no industries; that the only possible way—during a transition period in any case—to give her a chance to get industries going was by prohibiting altogether certain essential goods from entering the country.

To each challenge, the answer was prompt and figures were given. Industry was being created, goods were being made, and if prices were high—so were wages. Things might be done more cheaply if all industry was concentrated round Dublin—'as it is round London, for example'; but that was not the Government's policy, whose key-word in organisation is decentralisation. Therefore, factories in the country, deliberately placed here and there. No more city slums—'as in your British industrial areas'—if that can be avoided. 'It is making it more difficult for us, because of problems like transport and so on, but we know what we are heading for, and though we get the ditch now and then, begod we're doing fine. Another "gold label" all round, is it?'

And when the leading Dublin newspaper (anti-Government) brought out its free annual Supplement (a larger document than anything of its kind produced in Scotland, or, as far as I know, in England) I found that the official figures backed up all that my friends had said. Nor was it our usual 'Trade Supplement' only: it covered the whole of Irish activities, reviewing the year's radio and literature and drama as well as industry, shipping, and banks. As I write this, I find (by way of confirmation) the January issue of Lloyd's Bank Monthly Review declaring that Eire (the old Free State) probably ranks as the largest creditor nation in the world on a *per capita* international comparison, if the estimate for external investments is correct. Banking and currency problems, the scourge of so many countries, have been entirely unknown in Eire. Assessing the present economic and financial position of this small land, the authoritative writer in the Review concludes that its credit stands as high as that of any country in the world.

Or if I single out an item like drama, I have to record that trying to book a few days in advance at the Abbey Theatre for a first night of a first play by an Irish writer, I could not get a ticket. The house was sold out. The morning press reported some hissing and booing at the end of the play, as the author had apparently attempted to satirise the limitations of small-town social life in Ireland. Later in the week, I saw the play and failed to discover what there was in it either to boo or to hiss. There was a conflict of sorts between the church and a troop of ballet dancers whom the enterprising (if foreign) wife of the church organist had got to visit the town. But in pith it was a comedy of manners or cross-purposes rather than a social satire.

Yet there had been these apparent reflections on the Church, the digs at narrow vision and hypocrisy in worldly affairs that we are so used to in Scotland. The night I was there, the comedy was appreciated, and applauded at the end. It was carefully explained to me, by my enlightened friends, that the booing on the first night had come from a small clique—the usual provincially-minded type—and signified nothing.

'Alas,' I said regretfully, thinking of the new books by Scotsmen that savage Scotland weekly, 'though the satire in that play was distilled ten times, it would produce neither a boo nor a hiss in my country.'

Here was this theatre (the Mother of Repertory in Europe, as I have seen it named), backed by the State, its first night quite a social occasion, playing to packed houses a study of small-town Irish life by an Irish author. I saw the long list of new plays produced in Dublin last year—and thought of the Scots dramatist with nowhere to go! Nor is the Abbey the only theatre of its kind. The Gate was equally busy and takes its plays from all the world and produces them with distinction.

But I am not going on in this strain, lest some Irishmen with whom I have argued might think I was beginning to praise them! Eire, like every other country, has her share of troubles in front of her. If Scotsmen don't read much, Irishmen, I should say, read less. The Irish can be as provincially minded as any Scots at the back of Benachee. There is, in fact, a certain resemblance between the two countries that it is often difficult to get away from. I have run into it at far too many points. And we have a great many natural advantages over them. But there is one consideration in which the Irish have got us thoroughly beaten: they are alive, consciously and nationally. They may appear to ignore their Constitution, but if any outside Power had attempted to interfere with its coming into force, then would the casual visitor have seen what Eire means to the normal Irish body and soul.

PRESIDENT OF EIRE

The True Value of Tradition

SM, 1938

ALL SCOTTISH GAELS interested in their language who have met Dr Douglas Hyde at Celtic Congresses or known him for his scholarship in Celtic studies and Irish history would be delighted with the news that both Government and Opposition in the Eireann Parliament agreed to nominate him for the Presidency of Eire and that Dr Hyde accepted the nomination. It is the highest honour in the power of the State to bestow, and in this case the more interesting because it is the first appointment of a President under the régime that has restored its old Gaelic name to an old country. Scots Gaels will congratulate Dr Hyde—and, I hope, Dail Eireann! A certain reflection of glory will come upon themselves and perhaps a certain vague feeling of hope. For here—what the Scots Gaelic scholar and rhetorician loves—is dignity conferred in a dignified way; here is Gaelic scholarship given an honour that will be known throughout the world.

For not only in Celtic circles will this appointment be noticed. I can hardly conceive of an intelligent newspaper reader in any country, whatever its system of government, who will not feel vaguely reassured by it. For this is fundamentally a deliberate vote by a people for what we call civilisation. It is outside the game of party politics, is untouched by graft or wire-pulling or ballyhoo, and needs no family title or other social privilege as barb-wire about its elevation.

In the world as it is to-day, this is surely a fine gesture to the forces that, though submerged, still believe the true destiny of man is to be realised neither through war nor material aggrandizement but in the realm of social and spiritual achievement. That Eire is a small country does not detract from the significance of the gesture; on the contrary, it may heighten it, for history is there to record, from the early river-valley civilisations, through Greece, Palestine, Venice up to the present day, how much our inheritance of culture and high ideals of freedom owes to the small community or nation. Indeed, the very conception of democracy, of which we hear so much nowadays, was probably first consciously formulated in Scotland half a millenium ago when her poet cried that freedom is a noble thing.

Already, too, we see the fruits of this conception of freedom in the Agreement just concluded between this country and Eire. So long as Eire was denied her freedom, there was mistrust and bloodshed, and the readiness on the part of Eire to strike a blow at Britain whenever opportunity offered. Immediately the last vestiges of conquest were removed, we had the unique spectacle of the Irish leader, that implacable and irreconcilable and bitter enemy of 'English ascendency', standing up in his own Parliament and offering friendship to Britain, complimenting her ministers, and explaining how unthinkable it would be for Eire ever to be used as a base of attack against her. And as if this great reconciliation immediately affected the more bitter party elements within Eire herself, there followed by common consent the appointment of a man of learning and wisdom as the first fitting President, as though there still lingered amongst them the ancient tradition of 'an isle of saints and scholars'.

For, after all, it is tradition here that counts. Ireland fought for her freedom in order that she might grow naturally, as a plant grows, out of her own soil and accumulated tradition towards her own flowering. When that tradition is destroyed or inhibited, there is nothing of a similar fructifying nature to take its place. When T S Eliot, writing of James Joyce, calls him 'the most ethically orthodox of the more eminent writers of my time', he is aware of Joyce as the product of his Irish environment. Indeed, tradition and orthodoxy are complementary to Eliot. 'I hold ... that a *tradition* is rather a way of feeling and acting which characterises a group throughout generations; and that it must largely be, or that many of the elements in it must be, unconscious; whereas the maintenance of *orthodoxy* is a matter which calls for the exercise of all our conscious intelligence. The two will, therefore, considerably complement each other ... Tradition may be conceived as a by-product of right living, not to be aimed at directly. It is of the blood, so to speak, rather than of the brain; it is the means by which the vitality of the past enriches the life of the present. In the co-operation of both is the reconciliation of thought and feeling.'

Tradition is not a static thing; it is a living growth. And I have mentioned these two writers, who have probably had a greater influence on modern letters than any other two one could readily think of in the world to-day, because they are popularly held to be revolutionary and unorthodox.

Thus we see the true value of tradition as that vitality in the blood out of which we create for the present and ensure growth in the future. It is not entirely fortuitous that writers out of that Ireland which has fought so strenuously in recent times for the right to continue its own traditions should hold such a commanding position in letters to-day. Take four Irish writers representing amongst them poetry, prose and drama—W B Yeats, James Joyce, George Bernard Shaw and Sean O'Casey. Is there any name in the whole realm of English literature to-day that one could prefer before them? It is a thought to meditate upon.

So we may come to understand that the election of Dr Douglas Hyde as the first President of Eire was not a fortuitous happening, 'a bright idea', 'a lucky thought', but, on the contrary, a natural manifestation of a living tradition. As such, it augurs well for the future of his country, and will touch a responsive chord in the minds of thoughtful people the world over.

Now I began this article by mentioning Scottish Gaels, for I had it in my mind to make and apply certain comparisons. But I find it very difficult to go on. No writer who loves his country cares to appear to run her down, to condemn her by comparison or in any other fashion. And when he is compelled to do it, he frequently goes to excess—out of anger that he should have to do it at all. I may let myself off by suggesting that between Scotland and Ireland there is no useful comparison to be made in such major issues as I have been trying to discuss here. We look in vain for that Scottish tradition continuing in a Scottish State that could honour creative scholarship in the way that Eire has done. Is it too much to say that we not only deny our tradition but publicly cast ridicule on it in order to destroy or at least to inhibit it? With every reluctance, let me instance the 'Highland Notes' contributed to the last issue of this Magazine, where the writer ridicules 'the Celtic youth of Edinburgh University' who wholeheartedly and publicly condemned the Member of Parliament for Inverness for his strictures against the use of Gaelic. 'Reading the comprehensive commination issued against him by the Celtic Union, one wonders just what psychological process of arrested development is reserved in perpetuity for undergraduates that it should keep them ever at the mental level of Kipling's boys of Prout's House ...' And on that 'mental level'—think of Dr Hyde (in religion a Protestant) and the Gaelic League, of T S Eliot trying to define the genius of James Joyce, and you get some idea of the normal plane of our Scottish debate. Or read in the same 'Notes' the writer's relief over the defeat of the Caledonian Power Scheme and then think for a moment of what Eire has done with her Shannon Scheme. It seems to boil down to this—hitherto Scotland, denying her own tradition, has looked to London for all things. Now that part of her concerned with the continuance of a living Gaelic spirit will have to look to Dublin.

'AS DRUNK AS A BAVARIAN'

SM, 1939

The preamble to this essay on its first publication read:

'Popular imagination to-day sees Germany largely if not entirely as a nation given over to Nazi oppression, blatant militarism and economic deprivation. It is too much to believe that that is the whole of the picture. Here another side is presented by one of Scotland's leading novelists, who has just returned from a visit to Bavaria.'

I DO NOT KNOW where I first came across the phrase 'as drunk as a Bavarian', and now at the end of my journey I wonder if, after all, it merely indicates memory's faulty but revealing tricks, as the rhythm is peculiarly Chestertonian, and I find that Chesterton's actual lines run:

> You will find me drinking rum,
> Like a sailor in a slum,
> You will find me drinking beer like a Bavarian.

For obviously it was not in that genial poet's philosophy to think of a man becoming just dead drunk—though it might well be in the Scot's!

Bavaria may be a far cry with which to test any sort of theory on drinking, even where it is charged (as mine happily was) with the conception of a gargantuan wassailer, and I am not prepared to say that the journey was undertaken entirely for that purpose—though I have heard of reasons for travel far less compelling. To clear up all misunderstanding, let me say at once that though I spent some idle pleasant weeks last summer travelling about that lovely country, I never found a Bavarian drunk in the Scots sense. Truth compels me to state that I did observe two men one morning being helped suddenly out of the Hofbrauhaus in Munich by the massive attendants of that stupendous beerhouse, but then they were not drunk: they were just suddenly overcome. For which no one could really blame them, inasmuch as it was not quantity that had surprised them—for I never saw a Bavarian defeated by quantity yet—so much as quality. It came about in this way.

With a friend, I had gone out very early in the morning to see the great annual Roman Catholic procession through the town. In the old days it had been headed by the Kings of Bavaria, and I was told that it was now nothing to what it had been. Well, after watching men and women and boys and girls of that religious faith file past, some four deep, for hours on end, with bands and trumpets and banners and religious insignia of all kinds, I came to the conclusion that it must have been an incredible magnitude once upon a time! We took our final stance in the square of the cathedral whose twin domes are the city's symbol. And here the procession found its goal, as the river finds the sea.

But we never saw the end of the procession—because it was now ten o'clock, and by eleven, I was assured by my friend, the special brew of beer with which the Hofbrauhaus so nobly celebrates this religious festival would be exhausted. It had been brewed some months ago specially for this morning and was of a deep and concentrated and distinguished potency. I understood. 'They would brew only a small quantity,' I said. 'Yes,' he answered solemnly, 'only two hundred barrels.'

So he led me quickly by unobstructed side streets down to the Platzl and so into the Hofbrauhaus. As I entered by the swing doors and breasted that ocean of humanity, my breath was stopped. I hung on to him, however, in his search for a vacant seat or corner. There was none. Out again and upstairs—to a staggering cruise through a second ocean. This time he was not to be beaten and we squeezed ourselves into a table already congested behind doors that kept flapping like sails in a squall.

How the flushed waitresses of responsible age managed to serve everyone with beer and sausages and other eatables and keep an account in their heads of their innumerable transactions I do not profess to understand, and assume that long custom permitted them to trust the honesty of their clients when it came to the reckoning. Besides, on this scale, what were a few pints more or less?

Not that the beer was served in pints. So small a measure as a pint cannot be got in this house. It's the large stone mug with the blue crown on it or nothing. I brought this noble mug home with me and have ascertained that a full whisky bottle comes far short of filling it.

What the gravity of that beer was I do not know, but judging by taste and density it seemed not unlike the potent stuff sometimes sold in our pubs in very small bottles as 'barley wine' or 'number one——'. It had the same mild softness to the palate, the same deceptive innocence; but it had a flavour all its own. My friend was good enough to warn me in time, and, with further consideration, ordered those white perishable sausages with the delicate skins that, touched in the piquant sauce with which they were served, made so adequate and perfect an accompaniment to the beer, even in the morning—or, at least, on that morning. When we saw the two men with pale drooping faces being helped out, we decided that, in pardonable eagerness for liquid refreshment after their long fast, they had contrived to forget to order their sausages. Not a high percentage of casualties surely in a morning's service of two hundred barrels of so generous a drink.

The largest beer garden in the world is in Munich (not the Hofbrauhaus, which is merely an immense place). And why wouldn't it be, for where else in the world is the beer so good and—particularly—of so consistent and perfect a temperature? I know of English connoisseurs in this matter who stake their reputations on a glass of English ale. And I am prepared to back a glass of the best Edinburgh against anything that England can produce. Glasses, yes. But in Munich—why in Munich folk *drink* beer. Yet though I travelled by road, resting under the shady vines of many a wayside garden, until I finally landed in Austria, I failed to encounter my drunken Bavarian. Sometimes—for a litre is a considerable measure—I was forced to conclude that the Bavarian is himself so good-natured and pleasant a fellow that his beer, however generous, could not, as it were, outdo him.

Ah, but this was nothing, I was informed. To test my theory, I must come back, they said, at carnival time in January and February. A carnival that runs for two months? I asked. No, they answered, only for seven weeks. And I was so taken by this outsize in social measurement, that I there and then rashly promised to appear in February.

And now the landscape was white. The vine grounds were frozen. The dark trunks of the orchard trees had branches in exquisite white traceries of frost. And almost with an equal suggestion of delicacy the church steeple of small town or village rose at some little distance through the morning mist. Fairy-like the scene looked often, yet with that mediaeval body in it that is so characteristic of much of this southern Germany. Parts of Munich carry over this atmosphere of the Middle Ages so tangibly that you feel it like something thick. No wonder Chesterton drew his happy Bavarian in timeless outlines! The coffee was good and the butter and honey plentiful. But I had no German money, and to pay in English money was to pay more than twice. The dining-car attendant perfectly understood. When I cashed my traveller's cheque in Munich, I could then no doubt pay for my breakfast. I had great difficulty in finding the place to pay, but I did find it, for, other considerations apart, one would not willingly like to be outdone in courtesy by a stranger.

And here was dear old Munich once more. It is a town that grows on you. And if it weren't for the need of hunting out that drunken Bavarian, I might try to hunt out the reason for this attraction, not only through art galleries, museums, the theatre, the new architecture and the old, but, more elusively, through its living presence. The centuries meet naturally here; just as hill folk and city folk meet in the innumerable cafes; just as the old Bavarian yodelling and country farce and broad innuendo of the Platzl can live a few streets away from the Opera House where I heard Beethoven's 'Fidelio' produced so magnificently.

But this was Fasching (carnival) time and hardly the moment for serious interpretations. There seemed to be about a score of fancy dress balls on each night. I thought I had better have a look at one and was taken to the Regina (where Mr Chamberlain had stayed—as everyone told me). But at the inner doorway I was halted. Fancy dress was *de rigueur*. In the basement of that hotel I interviewed chef and waiter and was turned out in a tall-capped whiteness that noticeably met the needs of the occasion. It was a good night, but I had seen bottles of wine in ice before, and beer mugs were not allowed until nearly two in the morning. All very bourgeois or cosmopolitan or what you will.

But then Munich took hold of me herself.

We started by eating at seven in the evening and we left at six in the morning while the gaiety was still going strong. I think perhaps it was the most perfectly care-free, good-natured, and pleasant night of its kind I have ever seen—that night in the Schwabing or artists' district of Munich. Fasching has its conventions, and one of them appears to be the natural irresponsibility of the healthily happy human being. Dancing was on at least three different floors, with three bands, brilliant colour effects and decently subdued lighting. If a man felt like laughing in the middle of the floor, he laughed; and if he felt like saluting his partner, he saluted her; and if he encountered friends with whom he desired to join forces in a temporary jing-a-ring, he did that, too.

The fancy dresses were a riot, and a slim enough riot often on the feminine side. And wine flowed and casks gushed forth. Yet there was never at any time the slightest sign either of ill-temper or of drunkenness.

So we took to the hills, to the Tirol. We drank in Goethe's old dark-panelled inn—the Golden Eagle—in Innsbruck. How memorable a town that is, with its arcades that suggest the sunny south and its main street from which you look straight up at the snow-crowned Alps. And in a small aerial cabin we were borne to the highest peak over pine forests whose cones looked like tiny catkins.

In the Marien-Platz in Munich there is an old lady who sells British newspapers like *The Times* and the *Daily Mail*. Once I bought a paper, but not again. Why should a man's peace on a short holiday be disturbed? There will be war-talk and ideologies enow presently.

Back to my first and last hope, the Hofbrauhaus. And there he materialised. He had broad shoulders, a grey beard, and a great head of grey hair. Under every sign of heavy weather, he got up and made for the door, tacking carefully. Then the brass band which had wandered from the outer world into some far corner of the great beer hall started in on the Blue Danube. At the door he paused and, extending his hands lightly, began to execute a *pas seul* that lost nothing in distinction by its deliberate care. Having revolved back to where his old friend the taxi-driver was applauding him, he ordered two more litres. He danced again. But in the long run he did actually reach the door and went through it. We were still drying our eyes—for the whole indescribable scene had made delicious comedy—when the flapping doors swung inward once more—to admit him gravely yet adventurously to our midst. Only then did I recognise that he was drunk as a Bavarian.

The sleeping-car came on at Wurtzburg and, as I was from Munich, the attendant asked me if I had been to Fasching. I pleaded guilty, saying that it would appear those Bavarians know how to enjoy themselves. He shook his head with a sceptical smile. 'Munich? If you want real Fasching, you must come to Cologne.'

And I think I was at the stage where I was prepared to believe anything—except just that.

HOW THE GERMAN SEES THE SCOT

SMT Mag, 1940

AS I HAD BEEN IN Germany for some weeks about a month before the September 1938 crisis and again in the spring of last year, I am inevitably asked various questions about conditions in that country, and reply, like any other visitor, as best I can. But a query which has a more pointed interest, and which might be worth looking at for a little in an unbiased way, is: What does the German think of Scotland, or does he in fact think of it as a separate country at all?

Broadly speaking, the answer here is pretty much the same as it would be in the case of other European lands, namely, that Scotland is not thought of as a separate country, though it may be known as the regional district of a geographical whole, which is England. Just as to us a Breton is a Frenchman and a Bavarian a German, so to the Continental peoples a Scotsman is an Englishman. In my experience they never use the term Britisher or Briton for an inhabitant of Great Britain. He is always an Englishman, pure and simple. 'You English—' 'Pardon me,' you may interrupt, 'I am a Scotsman.' You see the eyes sparkle with interest and humour. Ah, the intelligent ones are going to get some information now! They ask about this Scotland. You live in Scotland? How interesting! You wonder if they think you live in the middle ages, and by the time you have tried to explain what Scotland is or means— and possibly most of us may try it once—you are left with the slightly uncomfortable feeling that perhaps after all 'Scotland and the Scots' does have a rather mediaeval connotation. It may be a subject for curious talk, but as a reality of any significance in this modern world—well, one does not wish to be rude, but is it? No?

Unless you are very fluent and likely to be understood, what is there for you to do but smile? You cannot expect foreigners to be interested in nice distinctions with no power behind them, when already they have the all-inclusive substance in the word England. And in any case, how can you blame them, when in our own Parliament members of the Government regularly annoy patriotic Scots, if we may judge from the correspondence columns of our Press, by their use of English and England when referring not only to this island but also to the Empire?

I was once the cause of an amusing verbal passage between two Germans in a southern town. As it happened, they were the two principal directors of a large firm, one a quiet old Bavarian and the other a fair-haired, blue-eyed Prussian. They were asking me about Scotland in the usual polite way, but in particular about the Highlands. I described the Highlands as well as I could, and likened its scenery to the Bavarian Alps, and even found a certain correspondence in the easy-going attitude of the respective inhabitants to so fundamental a matter as the importance of time, but, I concluded, in the Highlands we had the sea coming right into the mountains. 'Ah,' said the Bavarian without the flicker of a smile, 'I wish we had the sea coming to the foot of our Alps.' This hope for the submergence of northern Germany was received by the Prussian with the merriest laughter. I had heard such passages between Scot and Englishman.

Another instance, this time from a more learned source, may illustrate the conception of Scottish local affairs. A year or more ago I received a letter from an official of the town of Ohlau, near Breslau, asking me if I could supply him with any genealogical details about a Colonel John von Gunn, who had built the old Wall of Ohlau, had been a very important personage there, and had died in 1640 (photograph of grave enclosed). Some months ago (he wrote in fluent English) he had addressed a letter on this subject, without, he regretted to say, having received any reply, to 'The Mayor of Golspie'.

The said John Gunn was a soldier of fortune from up Kildonan way. And if his 'ancestral hall' may not have been so large as learned Continental gentlemen assume, still I have no doubt John was able to state that the blood of the chief of a great clan ran in his veins. Possibly he is even my 'distinguished ancestor'. In the lack of any evidence to the contrary, it would surely be ungracious of me to deny it absolutely. However that may be, here we are dealing with an area in East Prussia where the story of Scotland lingers on in many a (slightly changed) Scottish name. I am told that the Scottish tradition, right from the days of Gustavus Adolphus, is still fairly strong. The Scots were traders here, too, and in my own day the export of cured herring from the Moray Firth to the German-speaking towns of the Baltic was considerable.

But, broadly speaking, as I have said, the position seems to be that Scotland to the Continental mind is a lost province, of some historic interest perhaps to the student, but otherwise of no interest at all—except in one popular respect: in Germany, exactly as in England, Scotland or Scotsman is a synonym for meanness. Though that is not quite right, because there is always the air of a joke about it—just as in England. It is really remarkable how universal this music-hall conception of the Scotsman's meanness has become. I have seen a foreigner, who had no English, laugh and mime the act of counting money into his palm. Yes? It is even becoming a bit boring in Dublin.

That is roughly the picture from my experience, and it is possible that in the long run little would have been left of us but the legend of our meanness (for other peoples will naturally want to have an eternal scapegoat for their own meanness), were it not for that odd manifestation some years ago in our midst called the Scottish Renaissance. This may seem a somewhat bold assertion, particularly as some of us know the sarcastic things that folk at home have levelled at this alleged rebirth of Scottish letters since the last war. There is, of course, the modern Scots tendency to belittle any serious efforts in the arts by the native makar, particularly if he is foolish enough to stay at home; and then again stuff like genuine poetry isn't very fruitful as a music-hall gag. On the other hand, it may be that the foreigner in such matters is a simple fellow. I can only tell of what I happened to encounter, and it does seem as if literary people abroad are or were interested in what may have been done or attempted here in Scotland.

Let me try to illustrate, in this way. In the year or so prior to the outbreak of war I have had letters from three students in Germany and three in France, each of whom was dealing with a modern Scottish writer for his or her University thesis or *diplôme*. The questions asked me were of the most searching kind and referred not to critical estimates of the writer's ability but to the nature of the background out of which he wrote. This difference between Highland and Lowland! It was their most difficult nut to crack. For to the student, the modern Scottish background, industrial and pastoral, was supremely important. Their researches carried them into consideration of Scottish Nationalism and its present-day political movement. For everything had to be understood so that they could complete their thesis, make their case for the existence of a distinctive Scottish national culture. And if I had to do my best with six such cases, how many more must others have had to deal with.

I met a German who lectured in a country hall in Bavaria on modern Scottish letters, and enlivened his discourse with two gramophone records—one the 'Eriskay Love Lilt' and the other a roaring, ranting reel. The reel was received with great gusto.

I have heard it said at home that in Continental countries, particularly certain of them, any interest in Scottish nationalism has no more than a sinister political basis. All I can say is that I have no personal knowledge of this, never having been approached at any time in any way in any country by any one on this matter. And I have a long enough experience of political manoeuvring to see the way the wind is blowing before a conversation has gone very far. No; in Belgium, France, Germany, and other countries, the simple fact is that long before the present war came upon us, men interested in literature were making critical estimates of one or two living Scottish writers against a Scottish background and discussing a rebirth of Scottish values.

I do not wish to imply that there was much of this. On the contrary. But however little, it was there, and it was the only thing I found to indicate a conception of us as a people with a known tradition and a real background.

But why be concerned about this matter? I have been asked by a brother Scot, who is passionately concerned about the Finns.

Questions on profound, intangible matters are so easy; the replies so difficult. Here is.the simple question again, and I would ask the reader to imagine the genuine expression of a polite foreigner awaiting his answer: What is Scotland?

A mere geographical definition does not prove very satisfying; it does not seem to enlighten the foreigner who wants to know in what way you are unique or different from other peoples, what it is that makes you want to call yourself a Scotsman. Very troublesome, almost irritating, that one should get bogged in so simple a matter. The foreigner's polite smile at embarrassing you is not very helpful!

And so we come back to our first question as to what the foreigner thinks of Scotland, if he knows of it as a separate country at all, and find the question being addressed, not to the foreigner, but to ourselves.

As I have dealt only with my own experiences, perhaps I had better conclude by suggesting my own answer to the question; or rather that small part of the answer which happens to meet, in my opinion, the condition of the world to-day.

At least we, as Scots, are all supposed to know about Bannockburn and Bruce. After the glory of Bannockburn, if ever there was a man who had won to the blessed state of dictator, surely that man was the idolised Bruce. Yet a few years after the battle we find the community of Scotland addressing a letter to the Pope in which they state that if ever Bruce, to whom they now adhered, should interfere with their freedom by showing 'any inclinations' to subject them to another people, they would at once expel him as their enemy and take a new leader in his place; for, said they (in 1320), 'it is not for glory, riches, and honours we fight, but only for liberty, which no good man loseth but with his life'.

Nothing very mean about that declaration, made over 600 years ago. A people who could consciously rise to such heights were unique in their time, had already formulated that democratic ideal to which in so stumbling and often so questionable a fashion we attempt to give expression to-day.

SECTION IV

LIGHT

ON BACKGROUNDS

SM, 1941

I HAVE BEEN READING some long-short stories by Somerset Maugham with renewed admiration for his technique, his wit, and his detached and some-times profound understanding of human motive. But what has struck me more than ever before is how essentially English this writer is. His theme more often than not is cast in the ends of the earth, in Samoa, in Borneo, on the Siberian railway. Down a side street in Singapore, he will introduce us to a house where the daughters of joy are all Japanese, or all Chinese, with the perfect discretion, the tolerant human sympathy of the man of the world, but always the man of the world who is also the civilised Englishman. The painted faces of the Chinese girls 'were like masks. They looked at the stranger with black derisive eyes. They were strangely inhuman.' For the purpose of this story nothing could be more complete than that swift, sure note.

Across eastern seas, in strange estuaries, with the lonely white man or two white men of the outpost, in virgin forest—everywhere the eyes look and see and pass on, with that same penetration and that same calm restlessness. For it is not an obvious restlessness of the spirit seeking satisfaction, never a disturbing intrusion of the ego or soul seeking fulfilment, but always a continuous curiosity that observes in passing because, after all, there is little more to be done, and certainly nothing more by the artist. To expect any-thing other than the chance happening, the momentary drama, and the evanescent pattern that happening and drama describe, is to ask of life what detached observation is unable to find in it. In any case, here are the find-ings, here are the stories, and if you are interested in the didactic processes of judgement, well, that is your personal affair. You may permit yourself the naive pleasure of imagining on the part of the author a faint shrug, a sardonic expression this side of a smile, but no more, or you would become talkative and ingenuous, while if you took a few steps beyond, you would be—Mr Maugham often uses the word—flamboyant. Indeed you might then be on the verge of becoming interesting. But still, you would be flamboyant. And things often happen to the flamboyant of a dreadful nature. You might find yourself half in and half out the water on a South Sea beach with your throat cut, or lost in a primeval jungle whose green descends like a merciful curtain to hide the horrors of your unimaginable death.

But to appreciate how extremely well-bred is this art, you have to read Mr Maugham when he is dealing with English upper-class life, with someone's place in the country or with that attractive mixture of social privilege and highbrow unconventionality that appears to be London's special distinction. Now he is at home, where he belongs, and to point contrast, he introduces his cosmopolitan element, say his Jew. We see the Jew of the third generation of ownership of a large, perfectly run English estate trying to be the English gentleman. Here Mr Maugham's insight is infallible and its expression flawless. Irony supervenes, but it is an irony of understanding, especially understanding of the Jew who, in the third generation, by the occult impulse of blood or race, prefers piano-playing to a title and an English estate, who would ultimately rather be a Jew of the ghetto than an English gentleman. In the climax the Jew does not even blow out his brains; he puts his sporting gun to his breast and blows out his heart. So far as Mr Maugham's irony may ever be considered partial, it may here be seen directed against the conception of the English gentleman, a conception static in its behaviour pattern, repressive of impulse, of art, lest its supreme ruling power be endangered. Almost, indeed, it seems that this repressive power is too much for so sensitive an artist and thus sets him wandering about the ends of the earth.

But however that may be—and no man can know all the factors behind his simplest motive—at least here we see an effort at the creation of a cosmopolitan understanding, a cosmopolitan art. Nothing could be further removed from the provincial in subject matter and style than Mr Maugham's writings. Yet no writing with which I am acquainted is so surely English in manner and essence. It may even be the English of a certain social class, the expression of its particular culture, but it is palpably there, and nowhere does one become more conscious of it than down, say, a side street in Singapore.

There is no intention here to assess the value of this well-known writer's work. In these pages now and again I have tried to estimate the value and meaning of tradition. I think it is important that in Scotland, whose traditions have been weakening over a long period, we should get some sort of notion of what tradition means, particularly as we hear so much these days of universal brotherhood and the evils of nationalism, for nothing is so destructive of any kind of standards, whether of behaviour or of art, than just such vague hearsay or uplift.

Now, it may appear that I have been concerned to show that here we have a highly cultured writer who is a product of his background, who cannot get away from this background, and who to that extent is handicapped in his effort to achieve a universal art. Than this conclusion nothing could be further from the truth. It is his background, its very limitations, its discipline, that has helped him to achieve what he has achieved. All art is a matter of selection, and selection means limitations and discipline. You cannot draw without a pencil, nor write without a pen, nor type without the irreducible mechanism of a typewriter. You are limited by the size of your canvas, by the conventions of your medium in paint or word. Mind and instinct have been conditioned and shaped by background (which includes tradition), have been given by it standards of judgement, often unconscious, subtle, and exhibited in reaction as well as action. We rely on such standards at critical moments. They are our strength, not our weakness. Their limitation is something we can grip and lean against or use like a tool or a weapon. They are in any case the only real things at hand. One cannot lean against vague uplift. At the critical moment it isn't there, and a man lands on his back to perceive, with some dismay, his heels where his head should be.

How great the individual achievement may be is another matter—is, in fact, an individual affair. Unless a man be potentially great in himself he cannot achieve greatness. But what concerns us here is that a living tradition is an aid to achievement, and the lack of it a deterrent. So simple a statement may admit of some qualification, but essentially it is true. One may say, for example, with his publishers, that Maugham is distinguished by 'his almost surgical dissection of human nature'. Many certainly find him lacking in warmth, and some are conscious not merely of a penetrating sardonic intelligence that is not greatly impressed by the spectacle of life but also of a pervasive something that affects them like the thought of cruelty. But if we revert to the conception of the English gentleman, with its static behaviour pattern, its innate desire for continued dominance, and therefore its necessary antipathy to art (which is forever working a revolution in mental attitude), we can at least imagine, in Mr Maugham's case, his need for dealing with it in no less drastic a manner than by a surgical dissection. If we go the length of saying that the static conception has frustrated the artist, then even a pervasive air of something approaching the thought of cruelty in his reaction, however unconscious, is not inconceivable. In any case, all such qualification or discussion does not take the writer away from his background; on the contrary, it draws him ever nearer to its core.

But it is impossible to deal here with this matter at any length, although a 'surgical dissection' along the lines suggested might produce some interesting results, particularly when we got the length of the ultimate English Empire ruler over against the ultimate English artist. There may be something more significant in all this than is usually contemplated by the normal processes of literary criticism. Perhaps that is why it is so difficult for his contemporaries, even for the artist himself, to realise wherein his unique significance lies.

Meantime, however, our concern in these pages is not with the English tradition but with our own. If we can illustrate our subject from outside, that is all to the good. One may now be struck by that note on the Chinese girls and wonder, with not unpleasant speculation, what was the nature of the derision in the 'derisive eyes' and why, being delightfully human, they were yet 'strangely inhuman'.

Not a long time ago, I tuned in to one of those ceilidh broadcasts from a certain Highland locality and could readily imagine the impression created on musical ears listening in alien detachment. The voices were poor, the singing of doubtful merit, and the whole affair might well seem artificial, trumped up, and altogether a rather miserable show. It was so easy to imagine, in contrast, the slickness of an English comedy production, or the perfect unison of Welsh singing, its force and finish. Why should that be so? What has happened to tradition here? And, in particular, what does really take place inside the ceilidh, and how is a certain curious quality of folk intimacy affected by translation into a public performance?

All this is more than a problem in literary values. It is finally a problem in life values. We get the greatest satisfaction out of life when our background is peopled by those to whom we are akin and who enjoy a tradition that is alive and dynamic. A distinguished anthropologist, touching on the 'gregarious impulse', quotes with approval from McDougal's *Introduction to Social Psychology*: 'In any human being the instinct operates most powerfully in relation to, and receives the highest degree of satisfaction from the presence of, the human beings who most closely resemble that individual, those who behave in like manner and respond to the same situations with similar emotions.'

In recent years the field anthropologist has done a lot to help us realise how much we are the children of our background, of our own particular culture pattern, however fondly we may have believed that ours was the only 'right' and therefore universally applicable one.

ON TRADITION

SM, 1940

AT THE MERE MENTION of the word 'tradition' some of us grow impatient, feeling that we have had too much of the stuff, that the world at the moment is all too literally and painfully sick of its effects, and that until we sweep its encumbering mess into limbo we shall have no new brave world.

There is something invigorating and hopeful in the thought of a clean sweep and a fresh start. Privilege, religious persecution, old school ties, economic injustice, systematic brutality, social taboos, misunderstood sex— let us put a depth charge under the lot and leave the wreckage to the black bottom of the Atlantic. Nor is this always a vague attitude—as we soon find out if we make even a cursory study of what is called advanced thought in specific fields of human endeavour, such as, say, politics and literature. In politics we talk of the revolutionary principle. Not gradualism, not a slow evolutionary process, but revolution, the clean sweep and a quite new beginning. In one very advanced literary periodical, formerly published in Paris, certain words, such as beauty, were taboo. I remember a poem in it to the effect that if a person mentioned the word 'beauty', the poet would reply with a very rude word indeed, and if the person persisted in mentioning the word 'beauty', the poet would leave the room on the principle that sexual advances were being made to him.

Now all this is interesting and significant, and if the clean sweep could be made and we could start off fresh and healthy, amid social equality and with new conceptions of (not to mention the thrill of a new word for) beauty, then surely all of us would plump for the depth charge. But alas! this whole attitude would appear to arise from wishful thinking. Not that one need object to wishful thinking, for at least it can be less harmful than some other kinds of thinking, but it does tend to forget basic facts, and the trouble with basic facts is just that they will not be ignored indefinitely. That may be a pity because their irruption can be a nuisance, and sometimes a calamity, and often, in truth, we feel we could get on very well without being reminded of them at all.

Even my newspaper, however, persists in reminding me of them. Here is a paragraph explaining how some of our gallant airmen who have crashed are being successfully treated for shock. Now the treatment does not consist in dealing with the fear, the noise, the shock of the actual terrifying experience itself. It consists in going back into the childhood of the airman and finding an incident there which he has completely forgotten and which, indeed, requires some considerable effort on the part of his doctor to bring up into his conscious mind. When this long-forgotten experience, this little basic fact lurking in the black deeps, is brought to the surface and looked at and understood, then at last the victim of shock finds relief and goes onward again.

In short, it seems that we cannot get entirely away from our past, that we cannot blow up tradition, for our roots are there, however deep and however dark. But the psychologist has shown us this singular fact, namely, that to attempt to cover up or sink deep some ill or evil in our past may be worse than futile. What, in the hour of our trial, we have got to do, on the contrary, is to fish it up, to examine it, to understand it, and, in understanding, to be freed from its hidden compulsion. If this is true for medical science in the case of the individual, the chances are that it is true for political science in the case of nations, which are aggregates of individuals. Accordingly, if war is in fact an evil that resides in nationality, we can hardly hope to get rid of this evil by the revolutionary process of denying nationality and aspiring to a nationless world. As we have seen, we can deny basic facts only at our peril, and nations are at the moment very basic facts indeed. Only when each nation sees the war evil within itself, sees it, understands it, and overcomes it, will the next step towards international harmony inevitably rise.

Unfortunately this business of analysis is often difficult and irksome. Even the person who gives himself up to be psycho-analysed for his own good, can become so appalled at the nature of what lies hidden in him that he may resort to all sorts of dodges to hang on to his old respectable image of himself. And such an individual is not blatant, in the way a nation almost invariably is.

The whole problem of war would in truth be incredibly difficult of solution, were it not for one supreme fact, namely, that before a modern war breaks out the vast majority of all nations, all peoples—say, 99 per cent of them—fear and hate the very thought of it. When the psychologist first suggests to the airman that his quick terrors and trembling flesh are a result not so much of the gruelling experience he has come through as of some long-buried incident of childhood, the airman may be forgiven for feeling sceptical if not insulted. By evoking an unresolved ancestral memory, one man can lead ninety-nine against their normal desires upon what may prove the bloodiest courses. The long-buried, the unresolved thing may at any moment rise up and have us by the throat. To weaken its grip, to destroy its power, we have got to look at it, to know it for what exactly it is, to understand it. There is no other way of overcoming it.

So that if we thus regard tradition—and each country has its own tradition—in its worst aspect, upon its dark evil side, we are forced to conclude that the only way of getting rid of the evil is not by bombing it or running away from it, but by an analysis that leads to its clear understanding. Only through understanding do we achieve freedom.

Fortunately the study of tradition is not an unrelieved study of evil. On the contrary, it is largely a study of our highest good. Only inside his own tradition can a man realise his greatest potentiality; just as, quite literally, he can find words for his profoundest emotion only in his own native speech or language. This admits of no doubt, and literature, which is accepted as man's deepest expression of himself, is there to prove it.

Tradition would thus, on all counts, appear to be a very important thing indeed, for within it we realise our greatest potentialities for good and evil. Interfere with that tradition, try to supplant it by another tradition, and at once the creative potential is adversely affected. History shows that this admits of no exception.

Perhaps it is along some such line of thought that certain recent and somewhat sporadic movements in our own country may be finally understood. Let us see. I know, for example, that at the mere mention of such words as Scottish Renaissance or Scottish Nationalism there are at once aroused all sorts of mixed feelings, including wariness and much suspicion. I am not going to give myself away to the chance psycho-analyst. No fear. If he probes too far I am going to laugh and dodge. Yet in a calmer moment, if I have any intellectual curiosity left, I am bound to ask myself why these particular Scottish manifestations (or eruptions, or rashes, or as you will) should appear. They are symptoms—of what?

Let us try to examine them with the interested detachment of a psycho-analyst dealing with a case of shock. For the chances are that they do represent a state of illness, indeed almost precisely a state of shock inasmuch as the actuating irritant is buried so deep that it cannot be clearly discerned.

But first of all let us be sure that we have a fairly clear grasp of what we understand by tradition, or at least aspects of it upon which we can agree. What tradition means to each one of us in our blood is difficult to define. But how tradition has expressed itself outwardly we can at least see. And the two main ways of expression are through language and social institution. As the saying goes, we can tell a people by their literature and social institutions; for, given these, we know their tradition, the inmost feelings and impulses and aspirations by which they live and move and have their being. Now psychology has shown that you cannot supplant or destroy what is vital; you merely drive it into the dark deeps. This is the very important new knowledge that science has given us. A man can drive underground a vital experience of his past; a people can drive underground the vital part of their tradition; but the time comes when that which was driven under must come to the surface if life and health are to continue. A man can die. A people can die. But so long as a people, whose tradition has been driven underground, are not yet dead, they will in moments of crisis, of sickness, want to liberate their traditions so that they may have life abundantly again. And the two main symptoms of this condition will inevitably take the form of a desire for expression in language and in social institution, for a literary renaissance and a political nationalism. This does not merely apply to Scotland. It has applied to every country in Europe at one time or another.

Of course it may be unfortunate that all this should be the case, and some of us may find that the best way of getting over the trouble is by refusing to believe it. We proceed to have other ideas; in fact, we have other ideals. We fly off at a tangent with our ideals, those pale, abstracted, rootless, and therefore deadly things. There is a wise old Gaelic proverb which says: 'Whoever burns his bottom must himself sit on it.' But with our ideals we have persuaded ourselves that the basic fact, being politely unmentionable, need not be sat upon; or we can get an inferior people to sit upon it; or we can all stand; or, by much millennial aspiration, sprout wings and fly. Meantime, however, the poor fellow with the burn has to sit down. It's hard luck on him.

ON BELIEF

SM, 1940

I HAVE JUST BEEN READING a book called *I Believe*, containing 'the personal philosophies of twenty-three eminent men and women of our time'. As I turned over the last few pages, where the work of some of these men and women is advertised, I was struck by a success in sales which must surely throw a reflection on belief in general. Usually a remark about a best-seller is taken as referring to a novelist or one of his books. That need no longer be the case. Here are books by so eminent a mathematician and social thinker as Bertrand Russell running into their seventh, eight, and tenth impressions. H J Laski's *Grammar of Politics* is in the seventh impression of its fourth edition. Lancelot Hogben's *Mathematics for the Million* is in its '150th thousand in English'. And so on. In comparison with such figures, the works of many of our most eminent literary men may be considered still-born. For example, of one of the contributors to this volume, an editorial note says: 'E M Forster, since the death of D H Lawrence, would probably by many critics be ranked as the foremost living English novelist. He has attained his eminence by the production of few books and these have generally reached only a small audience.' The truth would seem to be that literature has gone out of fashion and popularisation of science and political ideologies have taken its place.

It is with all the more interest, then, that we turn to the 'personal philosophies' of these eminent men and women. And, looking for eminence, the eye inevitably pauses first before that great name, Albert Einstein. 'The ideals,' says Einstein, 'which have always shone before me and filled me with the joy of living are goodness, beauty, and truth.'

And there, in words that have haunted the poet from the beginning of time, is summed up the path of what the others in varying ways—through religion to political materialism—strive to assert. That is what remains, after personal immortality is saluted or discredited, after God is seen to be a lingering tribal myth or the divine power that still animates the universe. It is in the light of that old conception of the meaning and worth of human life that totalitarian power, brutality, capitalism, cruelty, destitution, and, above all, war, are condemned. Here Professor J B S Haldane says: 'My philosophy is the philosophy of Marx and Engels, of Lenin and Stalin.' He analyses the social condition of the world, goes through the Marxist creed, and optimistically hopes that we shall avoid the final disaster of Fascism on the one hand and a prolonged and bloody civil war, as in Russia, on the other, and, with the help of reason, carry the 'old culture into a new economic system'. To Bertrand Russell, 'Fascism and Communism, when analysed psychologically, are seen to be extraordinarily similar. They are both creeds by which ambitious politicians seek to concentrate in their own persons the power that has hitherto been divided between politicians and capitalists. Of course they have their differing ideologies. But an ideology is merely the politician's weapon; it is to him what the rifle is to the soldier.' For 'it is not by violence, cruelty and despotism that the happiness of mankind is secured'. And he brings history to witness.

So we have strophe and antistrophe, but always so that the profound human values, which it has been the business of literature to apprehend and vitalise in all lands, among all peoples, may come to flower in a stable society. Indeed, E M Forster, surrounded by 'militant creeds—in a world rent by racial and religious persecution—where ignorance rules, and science, who ought to have ruled, plays the subservient pimp' does not even believe in belief. 'I have, however, to live in an Age of Faith—the sort of thing I used to hear praised and recommended when I was a boy. It is damned unpleasant, really. It is bloody in every sense of the word. And I have to keep my end up in it. Where do I start?' He starts with personal relationships, the only comparatively solid thing left, and they require 'tolerance, good temper and sympathy'. 'Personal relations are despised to-day. They are regarded as bourgeois luxuries, as products of a time of fair weather which has now passed, and we are urged to get rid of them, and to dedicate ourselves to some movement or cause instead. I hate the idea of dying for a cause, and if I had to choose between betraying my country and betraying my friend, I hope I should have the guts to betray my country.'

But every essay has its moment of personal revelation. W H Auden, the young poet, starts the alphabetic series. He lists himself as a schoolmaster, and his paragraphs, tidily numbered and subdivided, set forth his beliefs on matters economic, educational, legislative, individual and social. It is a fair summary of what many believe to-day. We seem to have been reading it these last few years in some form or other almost everywhere. But of it all the opening sentence is what may remain in the mind; 'Goodness is easier to recognise than to define; only the greatest novelists can portray good people.'

And if we next take the word truth, there is nothing in this volume that touches the issue so closely as the article by Sir Arthur Keith, world famous for his researches in the antiquity of man, beginning: 'Deep in my heart I find a strange reluctance to set down here my innermost beliefs concerning God, man, and the universe.' These innermost beliefs are in themselves not unusual because they spring from scientific convictions and are held by perhaps the majority of scientists, but what is unusual is his sensitive concern for their expression where they might give offence or cause pain in the world of personal relationships. 'Allowances are made for me. The vicar of the parish, a man of my own age, is my nearest neighbour. We are on good terms—— Church and chapel decorate our village. Life to be enjoyed has to be decorated. Bare subsistence is not enough.' He would be distressed were he to return a thousand years hence to find churches and churchmen swept from the face of Kent. 'This attitude of mine toward the church and to all forms of religion is a bone of contention between me and many of my fellow rationalists of England. Many of them are militant. "Is it not the duty of everyone," they demand, "to fight for the truth and to destroy error—in season and out of season?" On such occasions I am pacifist. I hold that truth has to make its way in its own right without browbeating. A forced truth, like a forced peace, has no enduring value.'

Tolerance, good temper, sympathy. Perhaps their clearest expression may be found in the contribution by the Chinese writer, Lin Yutang. 'A thing may be so logical you are convinced it must be wrong—— The more complacent, self-satisfied and foolishly logical systems, like Hegel's philosophy of history and Calvin's doctrine of total depravity, arouse in me only a smile. On a still lower level, the political ideologies, like Fascism and Communism as they are usually represented to-day, seem to be but caricatures of thought—both are products of Western intellectualism and show to me a curious lack of self-restraint.' He quotes Confucius: 'There is no one who does not eat and drink, but few there are who really know flavour.' And Mencius: 'He who attends to his greater self becomes a great man, and he who attends to his smaller self becomes a small man.' In the chiefs of 'some of the Fascist nations' he sees 'images of beasts filled with greed and cunning and egotism.' Yet he refuses to admit that in the most warlike nations 'more than 1 per cent of the people, down in their hearts, welcome another war.'—an assertion that is worth pondering, and one which I, from experience, believe. When we all tend towards despair or cynicism, that conviction about the 1 per cent—surely within near reach of certainty—provides a solid anchor-hold for optimism. 'Science is but a sense of curiosity about life, religion is a sense of reverence for life, literature is a sense of wonder at life, art is a taste for life, while philosophy is an attitude towards life——'.

How assertive, almost shrill, sounds H G Wells against that background! Here we are at system-building and world-building again. But I have never been able to follow Mr Wells into his higher social-speculative regions. Most of us must seem to him like bees who refuse to run our hive with the efficiency of real bees, though he demonstrates, complete with flower-seed packets, the only way to do it (even if his demonstrations change with the years). Jettisonning the immortal soul of the individual, he, however, believes in 'the immortal soul of the race'. 'Naturally my ideas of politics is an open conspiracy to hurry these tiresome, wasteful, evil things—nationality and war—out of existence.' He does not define the evil that resides in nationality. Is it implied that nationality is the sole cause of war? But later on he says: 'All war is not nationalist.' In fact in another moment he finds the war danger arising from 'a great release of human energy and a rapid dissolution of social classes, through the ever-increasing efficiency of economic organisation and the utilisation of mechanical power'. The terrific internal war in Russia was not nationalist, and if wholesome progressive countries like Norway and Denmark and Holland had had their wish they would have had less than nothing to do with this war. 'This world and its future is not for feeble folk any more than it is for selfish folk. It is not for the multitude but for the best,' says Mr Wells. Who, among the present belligerents, proclaim themselves to be the best, the chosen people, fighting for the immortal soul of the race? I can feel this vague emotion of uplift toward finer things, but I still have to start from the actual ground under my feet. My nationality, as my particular background and heredity, is still very real to me. Just as its music—say, Gaelic music—is real to me. If someone said to me that Gaelic music, in its particularism, should be abolished as an evil in favour of some still-to-be-developed synthetic-symphonic form, I should simply feel bogged. To cut what is known and loved from under my feet and in the same breath to tell me to march is to require of a poor fellow, who knows himself as one of the multitude, an excessive nimbleness. If I had to choose between betraying my friend and betraying the immortal soul of the race, it would not require a great drain upon guts for me to plump for my friend. In short, I feel that Mr Wells is playing a high earnest game with his head, and loves moving the pieces about on the board. But somehow I don't find a deep spiritual concern for these pieces, not a great deal of that 'elemental sense of piety or reverence for life', in Lin Yutang's phrase.

However, let us leave all strident crying about ideologies and systems, and, for refreshment, consider an altogether new kind of thought about this warring world. For Jules Romains there is always 'some aspect of the mind for reality to uncover, some aspect it has not discerned before, or which it has sized up badly. On the other hand, reality itself is changing more or less quickly. When the mind therefore is impeded by a system or a credo, it is really reduced to losing contact with reality'. And then: 'I believe that experience always has the last word—— I shall never admit that reason should refuse to consider a fact of experience merely because it is improbable and contrary to the postulates of science to date. All the worse for science to date. Taking into account the new fact, it must simply begin anew its exposition of the nature of things. For example: perhaps some day two or three experiments only, but conducted under absolutely rigorous critical control, will demonstrate that certain persons in a particular psychic state are able to foresee and describe a future event in a way that excludes all possibility of explanation through coincidence, logical foresight, the realisation of some unconscious desire, or suggestion. When this happens, I hold that human reason will have to discard very nearly all its current ideas about time, space, causality, the determinism or indeterminism of phenomena, human free will, the nature of the soul and the cosmos. This would be the greatest revolution conceivable.'

In the Highlands we have long been used to this notion, as exemplified in second sight. In the Highlands, too, there has remained over from an old culture much of that elemental sense of piety or reverence for life. The spirit still has an instinctive urge to dodge restrictive mechanisms. It might even be an interesting and revealing exercise to attempt a psychological analysis of the peculiar native reaction to unemployment insurance stamps!

For it would seem clear that a system or ideology of the highest intention may in practice result in the most barbarous cruelty; that knowledge, as knowledge, obtained from a host of best-selling books on science and politics, may lead to an increasingly destructive materialism; unless, behind system and book, there is a concern for the living spirit of man, for those qualities that shone before Einstein and which it has always been literature's dedicated task to keep vivid and alive.

ON LOOKING AT THINGS

SM, 1940

TO KEEP THE MIND focused on danger or fear does not always help it when the critical moment arrives. There is much hysterical folly written these days around the word 'escape' or 'escapism'. Indeed there are persons who think it wrong to live outside a vague welter of sensational fear, as if to do so were in some way a betrayal.

We all in a certain measure understand this mood. But it can become a tyranny and a weakening. If a man is mud-stained, he does not take a mud-bath. When his eyes are tired he shuts them. We forever need contrast if we are to be strengthened or refreshed. A man who, in a flash of vision, sees the beauty in his aeroplane, will pilot her all the better for that instant of detachment. We are strong because of our resources gathered in moments other than the moment of conflict. And like the petrol tank our resources need constant refuelling.

All of which may seem like an apology for introducing so inconsequential a subject as the art of looking at a thing, the more so as I have no particular proficiency in the art myself. But at least I have got to that stage where I recognise it is an art, that is, something which has to be learned. Even with the artist, it is not enough for him to have an aptitude for seeing directly and vividly: the eye has to be trained for years, indeed all through his life, and its powers of exquisite observation seem inexhaustible. It is the same, of course, with the ear of the musician. Indeed those of us who are not musicians but merely like music know how long it can take for the ear to get even a moderate understanding of the musical import of a master.

But our concern here is neither with artist nor musician, but with the act, which is within everyman's compass, of looking consciously at a thing instead of glancing at it half-consciously. This may seem a very simple act, but as it requires a direct effort of the will, it can prove tedious. For at the back of it is the thought: why bother? Where's the point if one is not a professional artist? Besides, there are so many things to look at, most of them seen over and over again and therefore commonplace. In short, why cumber the already harassed mind with futile detail about the shape of a tree or the colour of a primrose or the flight of a blackbird? The whole affair is so trumpery that it is irritating, like the chatter of gossipy women when they meet or of sparrows. Besides, there is a lot of make-believe about it all, and in its high falutin form not a little of that artistic *blah* which seems pretty anaemic to a man who has a spot of real work to do.

This reaction of the busy man is understandable but quite wrong. Why? Because he is deliberately throwing away something which costs him nothing. By simply not training his eye to look at a thing, he is denying himself a whole realm of amusement and delight. For it is never a question here of educating the mind or improving the morals or becoming a better citizen or anything 'good' like that: it is purely an affair of pleasure, like the pleasure one gets from sound drink in contradistinction to bad drink *when one knows the difference.*

Of course, in a matter like drink, a man will pretend he knows the difference, simply because he would be ashamed to deny the quality of his palate and the immediate pleasure that comes from its use. Here he apprehends the point immediately and will stick, say, to his own brand of Scotch with conviction. I have seen a man do this who yet had no real knowledge of whisky from its various single malts to its innumerable blends. But I have heard another man question the barman in such fashion that I immediately recognised the trained palate. The first could be cheated by any wily barman, but not the second.

When it comes to wine, a man must, of course, be able to show discrimination almost as a matter of form; be able to use simple terms like full-bodied, thin, smooth, dry, with some conviction. I can remember a time when I modestly believed I could do some distinguishing in the matter of claret—until I was referred to a gentleman who, blindfold, could tell vintage and year.

In this matter of palate, then, we see the point of educating the sense of taste. We admit the extra and higher pleasures achieved by the connoisseur in drink, and we generally think of him as a man of taste and refinement. And very properly, because he would be the last to abuse the instrument of his pleasure. Restraint and judgement are inherent in its exercise. He is not going to kill the palate that presents him with his golden moments. He has grown wise.

But claret and whisky—especially whisky in these sad days—present one great difficulty in this matter of educating a sense, and that is their cost in cash. For most of us, it is insuperable. There is one sense, however—and probably the greatest of the five—whose exercise costs nothing, infringes no trade-union rules, is shared equally by capitalist and communist, animal, bird, and reptile. It is the one with which we are concerned.

Is there some special way, then, of looking at a thing?

A year or so ago I happened to be with a distinguished Scottish artist in a wooded burn in the wilds beneath Ben Nevis. It was a hot day and the chequer of shadows on the cool rock beneath the trees beside the clear running stream was very pleasant. The green leaves dimmed the light and gave a richness to the ferns. The water was crystal clear and in the course of ages had hollowed great basins out of the living rock into which it now swirled in clearly defined eddies of sheer surprise and of mathematical beauty. The greeny-blue rock had been worn to a remarkable smoothness and seemed to communicate its colouring to the water in the basins, so that they set a smile hovering over the thought of antique baths and woodland nymphs. Let us say that it was one of those places to which anyone might give a second glance.

I remarked that often a scene would come vividly back into my mind to which I was conscious of having given no particular attention at the moment of seeing it and that it might not be necessary consciously to impress a scene on the mind. But the artist said that I was quite wrong and that it was necessary to impress a scene on the mind if one desired really to possess it permanently. He instanced the scene we were looking at. 'You have not only to see it now in all its features, but you have deliberately to look at it in your mind tomorrow to make sure that it is still there, and again the day after.' Not until you had gone through this process could you be said to possess the scene in the sense that you possess a deposit in a bank.

He was, of course, quite right, as anyone may find by making the experiment. And it does not require a great deal of effort to make the experiment once. But it requires effort. We have to *use* our eyes.

Well, supposing this is done, what then? In what consists the pleasure of having the scene firmly implanted in the mind? The answer to this is very difficult, because the nature of delight is insusceptible of precise definition. To a man who had never tasted a strawberry, we should find it difficult to communicate the flavour of the berry. Many of us may have experienced the boredom of being led round his vegetable garden by an enthusiastic amateur cultivator. But perhaps a time came when with a house of our own we were compelled to do something about growing vegetables for a home-made salad. The ground is laboriously dug, the straight rows made, the seeds covered in—and from that final moment our attitude to vegetable growing is completely changed. We soon begin a daily visit to see if the seeds are coming through. Any indications of cat-scrapes or sparrow-baths arouse strong indignation, accompanied not infrequently by murderous intentions. And at last—lo! the delicate green shoots appear. If a poet said that this was a miracle, the gardener would be justly incensed at so impersonal an assertion. It is a miracle certainly, but one for which the gardener feels more than a little responsible.

So now with this scene that one has deliberately made a personal possession. But as a scene in the mind is much more intangible than a solid lettuce in the garden, one must expect similar differentiation in the nature of the pleasure. And so it is. But the pleasure is there, in however slight a degree—to begin with.

Assuming, for example, one is a clerk in a city (to take a simple case). A day comes inevitably when one is bored. The same eternal round of desks and ledgers, of making entries, of totting up figures. Life is drab and dry as dust. There is no help now—except from one's own mind. But from this mind one can take out a pleasant cool scene of ferns and greeny-blue rock-basins where nymphs bathe. One glances up and out through the window at the sky. And if one cannot see the sky because of a nearby canyon wall, there is at least light on the wall, the sun's light—even though the sun itself be hidden. Does that help at all? Probably not, for it rouses only a deeper dissatisfaction with the office boredom. So delectable appears the remembered scene that its coolness and atmosphere of freedom do little more than irritate now.

Practising scales is not a happy business, and often enough one could smash the violin. But a time comes when the fingers fall correctly without effort, and the melody emerges.

As the eye becomes expert at looking at a thing, the laboriousness in registering the effect almost entirely disappears. In the hour of boredom, not one but a multitude of scenes are available for inspection. Though actually the affair is much more subtle than one of number. In our present world, a man with a large bank balance can (or could) walk along the street feeling fairly secure. He does not have to think of its extent; it is enough that it is there.

Now bank balances are perishable, like lettuces. Indeed one may look forward to growing a new lettuce but not always a new bank balance. The scenes, however, that are stored away in the mind are imperishable. You don't require to take them out and count them, unless you happen to feel in the mood for so specific and pleasant an exercise, because they have become part of you.

That seems a simple statement but in reality it is rather a tremendous one. The most notable thing about a man who makes a 300 break at billiards is the consummate ease with which he does it. The balls run to his bidding with a smooth obedience as if they were enchanted. So with the scenes, with the multitudinous forms and colours and substances of the world around, once they have really become part of the mind, of one's personality.

The mind now can, almost in any situation, achieve a certain detachment. It has fallen into the habit of seeing things with clear eyes. So out of his learning and habit of thought does the true scholar achieve detachment. With this detachment comes a singular feeling of confidence, of pleasure, and, too, of perpetual wonder. With this as a background, one can face up to the desperations of the world with some measure of steadiness and assurance, and perhaps with that quiet solitary sense of humour that is primordial and good.

ON MAGIC

SM, 1940

THE TROUBLE ABOUT MAGIC, as about all old customs and superstitions, is our difficulty in appreciating the emotions of those who came under its influence. Where sympathy is lacking, understanding is not only incomplete but is also inclined to be critically destructive and even contemptuous. Many write of what they call the old superstitions as of a particularly horrible kind of ignorance from which an enlightened scientific age has mercifully freed us. There is, of course, some point and value in this attitude in so far as it is based on an innate desire, or instinct, for freedom. Where all is governed by necessity, absolute freedom must remain a notion or a myth; nevertheless, it is a notion whose fulfilment we grope after. And when stark logic, in front of what modern systems of thought call 'economic necessity', has to admit that absolute freedom is a myth, it tackles the conception of freedom itself from another angle, and considers that in the very act of recognising necessity we rise superior to it and so attain the only and the true freedom.

This is very nice, but not, for some mysterious reason, completely satisfying. For it is remarkable how the least prejudiced among us will often, in the face of clear logic, maintain an attitude of doubt. This new (and also very old) conception of freedom, arising out of the dialectical process, appears to have in it a certain casuistry, a certain hankering after a notion which yet, by definition, it expels. And this notion is, without doubt, the old magical content in our apprehension of that strange condition which man persists in calling freedom, *tout court*.

For the real trouble about logic is that it is inclined to repel or expel the purely emotional condition surrounding or interpenetrating that which it is about to examine. The logician is not concerned with the *feeling* that we may have here; indeed, experience has told him to mistrust this feeling, as a contorting influence, at the outset.

Which is all very fine, and all very sound, when the business on hand is a scientific investigation of matter. The mathematician would certainly confuse the issue if he allowed any private feeling that one and one make three to interfere with his equations. In analysing the grey matter of the brain the physicist neither looks for nor expects to find our sense of beauty.

The physicist and the chemist have a certain clear function to perform and they perform it with remarkable skill; but it is directed towards the physical side of our universe.

There remains the mental side, and here the scientific investigator works with materials and under conditions quite different from those of physicist and chemist. Here it is the feeling that is important, not the grey matter. In the act of drinking a glass of wine, we are content to be completely ignorant of its chemical composition—and no doubt some curious fellow has broken it up and analysed it. In fact, if such a curious fellow presented us with a glass of ruby liquid and said that it contained all the elements of a true port, what is the first thing we should do? We should, of course, sniff the wine, and if we found that the characteristic bouquet was lacking, we should shake our heads and decline the potion, saying: 'This may contain all the elements of a true port, but it is not port.'

So with any metaphysical concept or emotion: we may analyse them into what may be their factors, their elements, but if in so doing we lose their characteristic bouquet—the intangible something, the state of mind, out of which they were precipitated in the first instance—then we remain dissatis-fied. It may be true that as creatures living in conditions of 'economic necessity' we cannot attain a state of individual freedom. It may be true that therefore the only proper concept of freedom is that which in the very act of recognising necessity becomes as it were freed from it (much as we become freed from the fear of lightning once we have understood its nature and set up a lightning conductor). It may be true, but we do not quite believe it, because it does not altogether tally with our feelings, because at times we have feelings of pure freedom and at other times feelings of pure necessity. We must eat: that is necessary. But we are not always eating.

Very well, says the economic determinist; let us so arrange our affairs that we have to devote the minimum of time to economic necessity and the maximum amount of time to what you call freedom; let us introduce a new social order with these aims in view.

What could be more desirable? But—the poor irrational fellow, cluttered about with his feelings, cocks an eye at the economic determinist. Can he trust him and his new social order? What about the fellows who are setting up new social orders all over Europe, with much shouting about freedom and the common good? They don't seem to him to be good enough. But if we could get right at the back of his mind, I fancy what we should find there is a suspicion that in any of the new orders he would feel trapped, that he would lose this curious, imponderable thing which he calls personal free-dom, and which lies beyond reason, in the region of the irrational attitude, the magical thrill.

This may be extremely crass of him and superstitious. But he doesn't care about that. However difficult his 'economic necessity' at the moment, at least he feels that he has not got his head in a poke. His head is free—and that's something. The rest of the body will struggle out somehow.

Moreover, in the course of his varied history he has had a considerable experience of fellows with systems. In the simplicity of his heart he is enjoying, let us say, his reactions to Nature. Nature contains many remarkable and mysterious things and manifestations, and in his reactions to them he has had curiosity and wonder, fears and thrills. Along comes the witch-doctor who, for reasons best known to himself—and not unconnected with human power, gathers all the elements and reactions into a system of worship, and slowly turns the primordially hopeful and good into the fearful and bad, and, by propitiatory need, into at last the dark and bloody deed. The magical relation of man to his background, the white magic that is still the essence of art or lyric in its purest form, suffers a land change into dark superstition, into black magic.

All of which is not something that merely happened long ago. It is happening now, in one form or another, everywhere, from power politics to sex. The black magic of sex is perversion.

Turning up the pages of *Carmina Gadelica* to check a reference, I found myself some half-hour later lost in the account of what used to happen out in Uist on the eve of St Michael. It is a truly remarkable account of a festival by the common folk, given a whole meaning and cohesion by what we would call superstition. The very air seems full of magic. And the whole is steeped in a profound happiness and goodness. 'It is proper that every husbandman in the townsland should give, on the day of St Michael's Feast, a peck of meal, a quarter of struan, a quarter of lamb, a quarter of cheese, and a platter of butter to the poor and forlorn ...' They ride in procession round the graves of their fathers and then hasten to the sports field. The riders in the horse races are without bonnets and shoes, in shirts and shorts. 'Occasionally girls compete with one another and sometimes with men.' On St Michael's night a great ball is held in every townland. Gifts are exchanged between young men and women. Song and dance, mirth and merriment 'are continued all night, many curious scenes being enacted, and many curious dances being performed, some of them in character'. Altogether there is a suggestion of eager life, a wonder upon things, a freshness in the eye, a vivid delight.

The leaves turn over, and my eye falls upon what happened to a famous violin player in the island of Eigg. 'He was known for his old-style airs, which died with him. A preacher denounced him, saying: "Thou art down there behind the door, thou miserable man with the grey hair, playing thine old fiddle with the cold hand without, and the devil's fire within." His family pressed the man to burn his fiddle and never to play again. ... The voice of the old man faltered and the tear fell. He was never again seen to smile.' Presumably he thus attained freedom from his violin playing by recognising necessity under Divine Law.

So man naturally has grown a trifle wary about any denouncing of his superstitions. It so often happens to him, that what he takes delight in seems to be wrong, that he is beginning to doubt all witch-doctors, all leaders, and not a little even the conception of progress itself. For it is the fashion of the modern conception to be logical and scientific, while it is from the illogical, the irrational, that most of his fun and frolic, not to mention the profounder movements in his spirit, would seem to arise. The sea is a great mass of water of known composition from which he can get fish and in which he can drown. But in his sailing boat on a summer morning, the sea is much more to him than that. So with the wind; with trees, and mountains, and the shapes of valleys. In certain moments their contemplation moves him to extreme delight, even at times to something approaching ecstasy, so that, not caring a rap for witch-doctor and system, he will shout and dance and bubble with merriment.

Science may take from him the god of the sea, of the tree, of the mountain (though precious little, he realises at the height of his irrational moment, science knows about any sort of god, least of all the imagined one!), but when science tries to take away, or analyse away, the magical thrill, then let science either attend to its own proper business or go to the devil. And as for the witch-doctor, keep an ever more wary eye upon him. We don't hanker after any brand new system. All that most of us want is that those disabling factors (such as poverty and slums) which stand between us and our delight may be increasingly removed. We will take a long chance on 'progress' or 'improvements', if we are able to live more vividly, to experience the magic thrill of living out of which, so long ago, the one undying conception of freedom was born. In the most perfectly regulated hive, where economic necessity is the supreme law, the working bee has become a neuter.

ON DESTRUCTION

SM, 1941

WHEN I WAS A BOY we played Redskins. We were fierce and cunning warriors, and though we 'chose sides' and proceeded to consult together on major strategy, the subsequent action over wooded terrain was a highly individualist affair. We made our own laws covering the general conduct of operations and defining, in particular, when a man must account himself dead or captured. As, at a critical moment, we were all umpires, there was occasionally some difficulty in this matter of definition, and a dead man, feeling himself deeply injured, might be inclined to assert himself in a lively manner. The really important thing, however, was the achievement, by conjoint exercise of woodland craft and swift boldness, of a deed of derring-do. Our textbooks clearly exemplified the true nature of derring-do. They were often, perhaps, a little out of date, as we could never be certain of the financial resources to cover the cost of a regular 'order'. But the principles that guided both the moral conduct and the general prowess, against desperate odds, of the great hero, Buffalo Bill, never varied. When our parents referred to them as 'that trash' and refused them house-room, we accepted their ignorance and their ruling with the proper stoicism and turned a drystone dike or a byre-loft into 'a secret cache'. A bout of reading generated an idea and led to action. A book like *Tom Brown's School Days* would have bored us very much. But then we gravely suspected all books, perhaps not without reason, for we carried a few of them to school.

Something of this flashed back into my mind as the boy handed me a pistol the other evening. He had disposed two opposing armies of lead soldiers on the floor. One was guarding a fort which he had cleverly constructed out of empty cigarette boxes, and the other was deployed to capture the fort. I had to shoot his soldiers in the fort and he had to destroy my attacking troops. Shot about; and he politely handed me 'the first go'.

The deadly massacre proceeded ruthlessly, and when one side had been defeated to the last man, the troops were deployed again and a fresh battle started.

The excitement of the continuous action was heightened by graphic accounts of a recent film wherein, it appears, the Foreign Legion is exhibited in an engagement whose realism leaves nothing to fancy. The sounds of the rifle shots, and the different ways in which a man clutches at himself, reels and falls dead, were reproduced for my benefit with striking verisimilitude.

Naturally our conversation grew eager, but when I questioned a certain small military detail, he disposed of me at once, and that even without taking the poker or other convenient implement to represent a rifle. He performed his soldier's drill with an invisible rifle, and so precise were his arm movements that it required no effort of the imagination to see the rifle and hear the hand slap. Such perfection could have been achieved only after long concentration and effort, voluntarily undertaken. I am quite sure that when he is unable to perform this flawless drill in his dreams, he has nightmares.

And then I got a slight shock. I asked him, in the usual grown-up manner, what he would like to be, expecting to receive a picture of an officer leading his men against desperate odds, for he is a boy of courage and considerable resource. At football, I understand, he barges into a dangerous melee with complete enthusiasm. His physical courage and aptitude for swift decision make him a natural leader. But he replied to my question by saying that he would like to be a private soldier.

'No,' he answered a further question, 'I would not care to be an officer. An officer has great responsibilities, but a private—a private is *free*.'

Now I am quite sure that he did not acquire this point of view from anyone. It worked itself out *purely* in his boyish mind. It was a philosophic assessment of a situation known to many soldiers from experience.

To go into the point further would be to raise too many issues of deep psychological import. I would merely suggest that this apparent fear of responsibility implies neither weakness of character nor an absence of the natural ambition to excel. I found, for example, that this boy did fear 'a wrong order that would endanger the lives of others'. By 'others' he meant, of course, his 'comrades'. Already his social sense mistrusts a self-seeking destructive egotism.

But the point that first jumped to my mind was a very simple and practical one. I saw in a moment how little boys, excellent lads, shaping well for fine citizenship, could be used by a tyrant for purposes of mass destruction. Let the tyrant be represented as the Absolute One (the Father, according to Freud) and let 'the order' issuing from his responsibility be infallibly 'right', then the fight is on to the death, and all the more so should it have the 'glory' of being against 'desperate odds'. But how can the tyrant be made the Absolute One, and his orders right? The answer is: by propaganda working inclusively and subtly on the known elements of the child mind. The normal, healthy, balanced child already knows that an order of his own may be fallible, with disastrous results. He lives in a world where life and death orders are given. He therefore desires the infallible order. That alone will 'free' him from personal and social disaster.

Now add to that the fact that one of the strong elements in the child mind is an urge to destroy, an irresponsible urge, and a warlike situation becomes truly menacing. One begins to perceive that talk of wiping out a given civilisation need not be rhetorical.

This urge towards destruction that inhabits us comes out in many curious ways. I have a letter from a friend whose town has been recently fiercely bombed. He expected to be scared stiff, but actually found himself moved by 'a hellish curiosity'. One is prepared to take considerable risk to satisfy this curiosity.

When the mind wanders away by itself after such a piece of news, say, as the sinking of the *Hood*, does one come upon it indulging in an orgy of cunning counter-destruction? These phantasies of destruction, how common they must have become to us all! Phantasies of annihilating destruction! In the child mind, their proportions must occasionally be colossal.

And not only in the child mind. I have just read a novel by a distinguished writer which is devoted entirely to a period of strife—or revolution—in a remote country. The piling up of horror is so continuous that finally one is hardly moved, presumably because one is glutted. In the attitude of the writer himself, I fancy I detect a detachment that though continuously observant and curious, is spiritually weary and tainted by sadism. But I may be wrong.

Freud deals with what he supposes to be two opposite tendencies in man: the will to create and the will to destroy. The destructive instinct he finds in every living being and its object is apparently to overcome the living element and reduce it to inert matter. When this instinct cannot find satisfaction outwardly, it may turn inward, and after doing its best or worst with phantasies may set up a morbid or pathological condition. The only sure way of avoiding this morbid condition is by giving free play to the destructive impulse—or 'death instinct' as it has been called—in the outside world.

So the whole situation regarding the shooting of lead soldiers becomes extremely and ominously complicated.

But do not let us wander too readily into the realm of theory. We know what theory can do in the hands of a tyrant. We even know how man can be cursed and destroyed in the name of an ideal. When D H Lawrence mistrusts all idealisations, he may be sound. What is certain is that the practical application of an ideal to human affairs has often resulted in bloody tyranny. History records the fact. Let us hang on, quite simply, to facts and effects. In the name of communal brotherhood, it may be argued, brothers have to be slain. Argue away, but note very carefully the fact of the slaying. There is a destructive impulse somewhere in us and a creative impulse, but Freud's analysis is only an hypothesis.

Whatever the nature of, or reason for, the destructive impulse, we are quite sure that we don't want to be turned into inert matter. That is fact number one. The tyrant recognises it and tells his men that they are 'fighting for their lives'. Not even a megalomaniac would get men to fight for death. It may start as a fight for a special kind of life, a new order of existence, or what not, but in the actual struggle itself the issue is simplified to life or death, and then one fights 'for dear life'.

What I suddenly saw very clearly while knocking over the lead soldiers which were under the command of my young opponent (for ideally in this game he himself was the Absolute One) was that by a combination of elements and circumstances, such as I have here hinted at, the destructive impulse can be elevated into a predominant principle of action. Its capacity for destroying human life and creative human institutions then becomes colossal. The morbid phantasy is projected into the external world and made factual.

I am not, of course, here trying to establish a theory which most of us have already accepted. What was made clear to me was the *actual process* whereby the destructive is made dominant and becomes active on a vast scale. Until we understand and see clearly the process itself, we will never understand how to set about organising and elevating the creative impulse, which is its opposite and which is stronger than it. (Were it not stronger, we should have disappeared off this earth long ago.)

Let me go back to my old Redskins. Actually our bouts of deathly tracking and hunting were sporadic and frequently had about them an air of play-acting, especially when accompanied by blood-curdling whoops. But all through our young lives there was contact with sea and land, with fish and fur and feather, sun and rain and mud and misery and happiness. Against that large and natural background of varied living and adventure in a considerable degree of freedom, the Redskins occupied a very minor part. They were something imported, and perhaps well designed to set off the superior cunning of the hunter, of primeval man out after food.

Anyway, I am quite certain that the boy whose thoughts are occupied by drill and lead soldiers, could have them diverted to other natural and boyish pursuits with equal intensity and far greater delight. For the delight in life has always been greater than the delight in death, and the creative impulse satisfies more finely the natural organism than does the destructive.

How to set about organising the creative impulse is another matter, and one that would require not only an understanding of the psychological elements involved but also of the economic and other institutions which man has produced. But such an understanding is also required by the tyrant who organises the destructive impulse, and we see him at work both on the child mind and the economic institution. His technique is worth the closest study, and evidence of his fell work is as near as the shadow that falls across lead soldiers and the head of a little boy in a remote and quiet living-room.

THE NEW COMMUNITY OF IONA

SM, 1938

A LOT OF CONTROVERSY has arisen around the effort by Dr George F MacLeod to establish on Iona a community of students of the Church of Scotland. 'The immediate hope,' he wrote in the Press in the spring of this year, 'is that some twenty students every year will, on completion of their course, and after licence, pledge themselves for two years to a community whose summer centre will be a log hut settlement within the Abbey grounds of Iona. They will study the peculiar modern task that faces us and the best approach to meet it; and half the day will be spent in manual labour. The very stones of the Abbey cry out to be rebuilded to form the permanent home of the new alignment. But each October the members will lay down pick and trowel and go off, two by two, to work in the housing schemes under the complete direction of their parish ministers. At the end of the two years' contact they will normally apply for a parish in the usual way.'

In short, the aim seemed to be a deliberate effort to revive in a small way the old Columban idea of fellowship, communal labour and ministry, together with a realisation of what we call 'modern conditions', and of the urgent need within the Church of Scotland itself for a revivifying impulse.

As a non-churchman, I offer my own opinions on this project with the utmost diffidence; yet as a Scotsman, aware in some measure of the influences and forces that made our country, I am perhaps entitled to offer some criticism of any attempt to interfere with historic evidence, even if such evidence be no more than a ruin, a tomb, a standing stone. The spiritual heritage of a people is the most real thing about them, and all the institutions they have formed have been instruments for its expression, in church or law or social custom. It is their tradition. It is that which distinguishes them from another people. Through it and it only can they express themselves to the full; can they draw from life its profoundest savour, its deepest meanings. To interfere with this heritage in a harmful or destructive way is to limit the full expression of each individual. Whereupon the whole people suffer, and that which they created of spiritual value tends to decay, and the common stock of humanity—its civilisation, its culture, call it what you will—is diminished at least to the degree in which the contribution of that people was unique. You have only to study the history of Scotland in the last century or two to appreciate in how precise a way this is true. The very fact that Dr MacLeod should find it necessary, in his special province of the Church, to attempt so seemingly romantic or extravagant a revival of fellowship and faith amidst his own brethren and amidst the Scottish people is surely in itself illuminating.

Accordingly, he was bound to meet both with opposition and with complete indifference. Indifference we may ignore here, for, by the very nature of the given circumstances, it is inevitable. Opposition tends to take three forms.

First of all, there are those who object to any interference with so important a ruin as the Abbey of Iona. They call it sacrilege and see in Dr MacLeod a man who wants publicity at any price. For, they argue, if this man desires an immortal name for himself let him go and organise his fellowship in the distressed areas of our land, let him gird up his loins and sally forth, through dangers and tribulations, as his inspired master. Columba, did fourteen hundred years ago. This battening on an established tradition of pilgrimage to the Holy Isle is too easy. And, further, it will destroy the inspirational force of these old stone ruins that time, under the hand of God, has weathered to a deeper, more universal purpose than they served even in their architectural prime. Twenty thousand pilgrims a year must deplore this attempt at sacrilege by an individual too obviously anxious to gain some personal notoriety.

I have here been trying to summarise some of the objections I have come upon in the Press. I do not know Dr MacLeod and can testify neither to a personal romanticism nor a desire for publicity. And I feel I can appreciate in some degree the spirit that informs this particular sort of criticism. For I know Iona well, have come under its spell of light and of history, and have the haunting feeling that I should like to go·back to it at any time and find once again its incomparable peace and quiet.

Yet that feeling and those objections, I realise quite clearly, partake of the death instinct. We do not need to read Freud to understand this. Why, let us ask ourselves, has Scottish scholarship got such a deep antiquarian bias? Study its endless quarrels over historical minutiae. Whole societies can be roused to bitter personalities over whether it is proper or not to wear a certain sort of tie—or is it a waistcoat?—with a dress kilt. We are in love with our past because we are not conscious of a creative present. It is the death instinct at work in our heritage, calling defeatism by soft names, hanging on to some lovely thing—or thing our nostalgia has made lovely—to the point of rather seeing it perish than having it touched by any hand, least of all the creator's.

For consider how groundless these objections are even historically. Columba's settlement of wattle-and-daub huts and wooden church have completely disappeared. These ruined walls were the work of builders many centuries later. Their monastic function was not that conceived by Columba. The history of Saxon Margaret's influence in this island is worth investigating over against the organisation of that early Celtic Church. But however that may be, these ruins are not Columba's. They represent buildings used to carry on Columba's chief message. If Dr MacLeod thinks he can reconstruct them for the same purpose, he is at least fulfilling their traditional function.

Secondly, the notion of Columba as a missionary sallying forth into the unknown and settling by pure chance on a little island off our barbarian shores sounds very adventurous and heroic, but I doubt if that was the way it actually happened. In 1560 the Synod of Argyll destroyed 360 sculptured stones of Iona on the plea that they were 'monuments of idolatrie'. That Columba and his brethren of the wattle-and-daub huts, or their successors, erected these 'standing stones' is extremely unlikely. From some knowledge of early history or pre-history, we may confidently assume that they belonged to a vastly older age, Druidic and pre-Druidic. In a word, Iona was probably a religious centre of some importance at least a millennium before Columba landed on it. In view of the existence of Dalriada, he was bound to have known this and to have made use of it, with all the persuasive wisdom these early Christians showed towards the tolerant pagans they came amongst. If Dr MacLeod is trying to take advantage of a given religious atmosphere in Iona to assist his new missionary enterprise, he is merely following the general strategy of the far-seeing Columcille.

The second objection is concerned with what is deemed the artificiality and futility (not to mention heresy) of setting up a Christian brotherhood on Iona at this time of day, as if 'cowled monks chanting again in solitude; a community withdrawn from the snares of the world' were contemplated. But manifestly this is not what is contemplated. On the contrary, the scheme would appear to follow, in however small a way, the authentic Columban inspiration. Young men will meet here in brotherhood, will toil with their hands and have the communion of fellowship before setting out to bring what understanding and selfless devotion they may have learned to their brothers in the derelict areas of our civilisation. There is nothing unreal or heretical about this. Even in the matter of secular education the Danes have a parallel in their folk schools, where men and women of over eighteen meet and learn, and wash up their dishes and make their beds. It is the very ancient ideal of brotherhood and service, and the world would be none the worse of a lesson in its potency from whatever source, religious, educational, or political.

The third objection is raised by those who feel that as the religion of the churches is played out anyway, such an effort as Dr MacLeod's should merely be scorned. The 'progressive thinker' need have no fear of its 'reactionary tendencies'. It is the staging of a costume-piece and about as far removed from the realities of life as a millionaire is from the effects of the dole.

Now this objection is the only real one of the three, not in its direct criticism of the Church so much as in what is implied by its attitude. It is the attitude of those who feel they have not only something to say but something very positive to do. Dr MacLeod has referred to the 'lesser creeds' of Communism and Fascism. Let him consider for a moment what moves in the heart of the ardent young Communist or Socialist in our own country to-day. Never mind for the moment whether he is right or wrong; the important thing—as no churchman needs to be told—is what he believes. And his belief is the ancient one of brotherhood and justice between men. He sees that the ideal of brotherhood and justice has been betrayed. He can state the extent of the betrayal not merely in an impassioned logic but in a display of statistics where horror and degradation are worked out to an incontrovertible decimal point. And he accuses the Church of having allowed the betrayal to continue: nay, of having, by complacency, indirect action, and its own desire to retain power, assisted in the betrayal.

Those who accuse Dr MacLeod of envisaging something soft and easy when contrasted with the rigorous life of the Columban brotherhood can have hardly worked out the realities of the situation. It was probably softer and easier for the ancient missionary to preach amongst the groves of the pagan Picts than for his modern descendant to hope to move effectively amongst the slag heaps of our age. Assuming always, of course, that the modern is prepared to do it with the same zeal and self-denial and charity and faith.

Why should a non-churchman, like myself, be concerned about this one way or another? It is difficult to answer in a few words. But I think it might be said briefly that he is aware of an ever-decreasing amount of spirituality in the modern world. The increasing mechanisation of life, the loss of individual freedom under political tyrannies, the suppression of original thought and the manufacture by the Press of a public opinion—everywhere massed force, under a lust of power or a psychosis of fear, is robbing man of his dignity and life of its ecstasy, its profoundest delight. It is not inconceivable to forecast a rigid condition of affairs when little colonies of persons, secretly, will once more, in the old phrase, go out into the desert, to save man's spiritual life from extinction. And by spiritual life I mean the striving towards the achievement of harmony in the mind, that condition of synthesis, of fulfilment, which all the religious leaders and mystics and poets have striven for throughout the human history of our planet; which the scientist searches for in the constitution of matter; and which Columba knew so profoundly as a state of light.

Iona is the island of light.

From Iona this light, this vision without which the people perish, might in some measure be made manifest again. That Scotsmen should attempt the effort is logically sound, for they will start with a tradition and environment that is their heritage, physical and spiritual. But whether this particular new Iona Community will be able to rise above a narrow sectarianism, an effort to resuscitate their own particular church, with its conventional trappings and exclusiveness and conceptions of a jealous God, is another matter. Were it not for the existence of Iona itself, I should, perhaps, doubt it. But then strange miracles of light were wrought long ago on that small island in the Western Sea.

THE HERON'S LEGS

SR, 1958

SECOND SIGHT, magical charms, incantations, apparitions, other states of mind—the Highlands are as full of them as of scenery. Years ago or yesterday, a strange happening, an etched scene. What does all this odd traffic amount to? Whence—and whither? The same old questions, but with the old answers becoming less positive, the explanations less satisfying, even as the old scientist's final 'final indivisible particle of matter' becomes a spot of energy that jumps its location in an inexplicable way and leaves at least some scientists now talking of a substratum where the ultimate spot may be either material or mental, with emphasis possibly on the mental.

Superstition, I find myself involuntarily turning up the dictionary, not for a definition of the word, which I fancy I know, but for its root. And its root means to stand over or above. Which is exactly what happens at the moment of experiencing the odd happening or 'other' state of mind. One comes upon oneself standing there with a feeling of intense reality.

I am not concerned here with attempting 'final answers' to anything, for the excellent and even cheerful reason that I don't know them. And, anyway, unless the experiencing comes first, the knowing amounts to nothing. But there *is* this Highland background, so the Highland mind, being notoriously inquisitive, begins to wonder what happens beyond its own territory, within other countries, in this matter of unusual states of mind; and, to begin with, even in so elementary a thing as scenery.

A southern poet has said he could stand and stare. That's something. Vague a bit, but the stance is right. To ask what he is staring at might be like asking the point in a joke. Never mind. One asks. For here one must ask anything and everything with cheerful ruthlessness. Did the fellow see anything when he stared, inside him or outside, and if so what, more or less, was it? You don't destroy a wine by discussing its bouquet. So—was there anything beyond? After all, we know our way about this old territory. We are not going to be put off by the pretty-pretty or the vague that peters out. We know the English countryside. And so on—until Wordsworth suddenly says:

> I heard among the solitary hills
> Low breathings coming after me ...

Now the Highlander is caught, and doesn't become more comfortable when Wordsworth takes his stance:

> ... I would stand,
> Beneath some rock, listening to sounds that are
> The ghostly language of the ancient earth,
> Or make their dim abode in distant winds.

The Englishman even goes on to use the word 'audible':

> ... in all things new
> I saw one life, and felt that it was joy.
> One song they sang, and it was audible ...

But even when it comes down to specific bits of scenery, he is no less troubling. How often in the wilds of the Highlands I have filled a kettle from a burn and happening to look up and around, in that half-light which isolates, the grey light of magical suspension amid the fresh tingling earth scents ... the remote cry of a hill bird ... have seen the arch of the bridge at hand as a suddenly frozen frame for the picture. 'The lifeless arch of stones in air suspended', says Wordsworth. That glimpse of the lifeless, like the first glimpse of a 'frozen' hare.

So 'the sight' is not peculiar to the Highlands. Indeed if we went beyond Wordsworth to William Blake we would find it in full flow in the sense that human figures, invisible to others, would, as they passed by on the street, receive his salute. In fact, if I may trust my memory, he sometimes took them home to dinner and had long talks with them afterwards. And I suspect that their after-dinner speeches were not of the kind with which in the ordinary way we are familiar. But that is taking us too far ben in the Highland mental home. For the moment we are concerned only with bits of scenery, the elementary beginnings, the things we take so much for granted that we pass by without seeing them.

Let me try another country, and as Wordsworth has spoken of 'one life' that was 'joy'—an obvious unity for him, or even Unity in the full Eastern sense—let us go as far East as possible, to Japan.

As it happens, I have been in correspondence with Professor Nakamura, who deals with English in Tokyo University and is particularly interested in Scottish literature. But apart from such evidence of impeccable taste, what interested me was an early observation of his to the effect that life in the Highlands, as described in certain novels, reminded him of his own boyhood in Japan. This, I confess, astonished me, like the arch of the bridge. East is East, we had been told, and West is West, and never the twain shall meet. But here, bless us, was the bridge. Its arch was thrown over.

Not only that, for he next introduced what was an old Highland custom, one still observed on particular occasions. In brief, he assured me that in his land it was customary, on the occasion of a first special visit, to bring a gift. In due course it arrived, a recently published volume de luxe of early Japanese art.

Now I knew nothing about Japanese art, apart from those commercial prints of moons and cherry blossom, though even these had the kind of arrestment or suspension in mid air that had made me look at them more than once. But my extra difficulty with the large Japanese volume was, of course, that I could not read the letterpress, those ideograms, so fascinating to stare at. I often stared at them, noted their arrangement and order, and wondered what, in the realm of practical sense or information, they so mysteriously veiled. But then I could remember having done that with the lines that my remote ancestors had scrawled on stones. Once when I had stared at a bit of ogham script long enough I saw the primitive hand at work; and the primitive in action is a vividly potent force.

However, I had caught a glimpse, in the modern way, of what Eastern ideograms could represent, from a cosmopolitan like Ezra Pound, who had, among other things, done some translating. In particular, one Chinese poem comes to mind, and though, without the book, I could not reproduce a line of it, its impact is still fresh. Entitled 'The Exile's Letter', it evoked for me the Highland scene, with memories of two Highlanders, close friends, meeting at ceilidhs, having drinks, and parting. The texture, the feel, of the whole thing was somehow as familiar as the smell of peat smoke. In 'The Canadian Boatsong', evocative phrases like 'the lone shieling' or 'the misty island' gather potency because the rowers were exiles from their fathers' land. Uprooted. The far-wandering, the exile—half the history of any Highland clachan.

But to leave verse or words and come back to these Japanese paintings, for which I was given no words: or, even better, to real prints, not the commercial ones. Through the generosity, which is inexpressible, of my learned correspondent, I became the possessor of two coloured prints, one by Harunobu and the other by Hiroshige. In my ignorance, I wondered if these names might be mentioned in a recent issue of the Encyclopaedia Britannica, and on turning up the section dealing with Japanese painting I found not only the names but reproductions of their work. I was among the old masters of Japan. Here, anyhow, was something quite different from the Highland scene, so different that at first glance I found them attractive. Rather foreign of course, but quite attractive. Like that.

Then I began to look at Harunobu, from time to time. A pretty scene of two figures, plum blossom and a wooden fence. The figures have flowing draperies, and one is up on the fence cutting off a branch of blossom for the other. Lovers, presumably, though the ovals of their faces, with only a line or two to show they are faces, suggest neither sex nor emotion. It took me quite a time to notice the fence consciously, though actually it was more highly coloured than the rest, and when I did I began to wonder why its solid square posts, and the squares made by the two wooden horizontals, the whole running off the diagonal into the heart of the picture, did not disrupt it; for up above were flowing lines, blossom, and, containing them as it were, what looked like a meandering timeless river.

I can find no disruption. I think of an ancient monk doing an initial letter for the Book of Kells. At the odd moment when wireless reception is good in the Highlands, something from Mozart comes over clear. As a still rarer moment, I am visited by the exciting if not revolutionary notion that perfection may not be dull; even that it dwells beyond the exciting and revolutionary, like the plum blossom.

But that, again, is going beyond bits of scenery. So may I mention a third print in order to bring back the Highland scene, this time not with the troubling 'sight', but with the rarer serenity that, like the perfection of Harunobu's art, has delight at its core?

It is a picture of a heron, by Tanan (early sixteenth century). Now I have seen herons in many places of the Highlands, on pine trees or slowly, deliberately wading, but to come upon the bird in the evening, the solitary bird, almost to its knees in the water, still as a slender tree stump, fishing, its size magnified in the fading light, stops me in my stance, as if I had come upon more than the bird in that quiet place. This is the moment that is never forgotten.

Tanan has painted that bird, realistic to the fishing eye so sharply in its head. Yet when I look closely at the head the whole top half of it is one marvellous brush stroke. And the beak is another—a deadly spear. In the grey light, with a reed and a broken reed. Such economy of means, each stroke so inevitable, so final. A glance—and lonely Highland places do not have to be remembered in order to evoke the breath-taking wonder of having been there.

Can this wonder, and the serenity in which it lingers, be caught in words? Can it be set down, written, with the ultimate inspired simplicity, economy, of the single brush stroke? For me it was so caught when, unexpectedly as one comes upon the solitary heron, I came upon this poem out of the ideograms:

> With the evening breeze
> The water laps against
> The heron's legs.

THE FLASH

SR, 1958

KEEP SILENT AND STILL and watch what happens. This is a trick that has got to be learned, as the bird watcher knows when he hopes to record the new and surprising. Something of this I tried to indicate in my last article, when I came on the heron fishing a quiet stretch of a Highland river.

This experience was brought vividly back to mind, however, not by another such Highland experience on anyone's part, but by a Japanese painting of a heron. Here was something added to the 'new and surprising'. That a foreigner should see what I fancied I had seen and then fix it for good in a master's painting! In one sweep of his brush, what might be considered the local, the provincial, had vanished. It was certainly a silent comment on any small nation preoccupied with, say, its literature, to a degree that may occasionally be more than noisy, and certainly hopeless for bird watching.

But there was a shift here, a shift from the natural scene, the scene in nature, to the scene in the painting. The heron so to speak was beginning to occupy a scene behind my eyes. And in this mental scenery, as it opened out, I began to catch a glimpse of something more new and surprising than is normally observable in the realm of birds.

Now this something is very elusive, and as the rest of these articles are concerned with trying to get a glimpse of it from various angles, let me begin at the beginning with ordinary visual scenery. I had established a certain correspondence between the Highland way of looking at a heron and the Japanese way. Pictorially at least here was some accord. I had something to go on. But when I ventured into the realm of the Japanese mind, the scenery was so different from what I had been accustomed to that I found myself lost.

Normally at this point one gets back into the old familiar places as quickly as possible. But if the surprise, the shock, of finding oneself in such new and surprising scenery is great enough, there may be induced the involuntary reflection: That I should be here! I—here—amid the strange and bewildering! At such a moment, if the shock has really been astonishing enough, the 'I' has a new feel, a new taste. It is in a way as if one had never really met this 'I' before. It is suddenly isolated, new born—and the strange or bewildering element of the familiar in it makes its newness more felt. New born, or born again—as an apparition is born, magically. And coming upon an apparition is so rare an experience that it is unforgettable.

I am aware that this effort to be as precise as I know how may seem anything but, for in the ordinary way of living we imagine that 'I' is the one thing that is always with us, that we know it only too well, that we are forever being exhilarated by it, or betrayed, or bored to death.

As this is the kind of paradox I have been trying to resolve for a long time, and as I concern myself with its importance here, may I revert once more to the natural scene that included the heron, so that I may check what was written spontaneously about it. When I came upon the fishing heron I was stopped in my stance, I wrote, 'as if I had come upon more than the bird in that quiet place. This is the moment that is never forgotten'. I had been reluctant, I can now see, to say that the 'more' included, as its most surprising element, myself. And the reluctance sprang no doubt from sympathy or consideration for the reader, upon whom one can hardly unload a dubious or egoistical subjective experience. Let it be hinted at, and pass on. And don't *now* begin to go all self-conscious about it.

All of which is beside the point, almost meaningless; even this use of the word 'self-conscious' is so ironically a misuse that one can do little but, as it is said, smile. For the real point of the experience is that one comes upon oneself, the 'I', as one may never have done before, almost as though it were outside oneself, in a detachment evoked by the strangeness of the scene and the moment. In this sense it is objective, not subjective. One apprehends one's presence there as one might the presence of a stranger. And the experience is incredibly refreshing, cool as birch-scented air, and full of wonder.

If I may appear to have over-elaborated all this it is in an effort to indicate the only kind of unusual instrument I had with which to tackle certain Eastern modes of thought or states of being. So now let me forget it, while I attempt to get a practical bearing on the Eastern modes and states which finally led me to what is called the Great Doctrine.

My first difficulty in this mental country was catching a glimpse of half a bearing before it disappeared. I soon realised that the logical process, as we know it, was of little use here, for it goes on from one thing to another, as cause to effect; it seems linear, one-dimensional, continues like a straight line, adding to itself until it is stopped by a QED, and so fulfils itself.

But nothing seemed to stop in this Eastern mode of thinking. It was never a case of a thing being either correct or incorrect; not even altogether of its being both at the same time, which could be absurd and therefore amusing. Far from having an absurd air, the Eastern performer was like one of those bland jugglers who keeps any number of things—balls, plates, clubs—whirling around him, flawlessly; as in the case of those more complicated atoms which our scientists sometimes condescend to set in toylike motion in order to help our understanding. But throw a QED spanner into the scientist's whirling toy and at that moment it would not fulfil itself, it would collapse.

To make things more difficult I had to think of the juggler as a living nucleus at the centre of his sphere of whirling electronic thoughts or apprehensions; as a living organism in action. And so I began to stumble towards the notion that this Eastern way of thinking was not linear, one dimensional, logical, but somehow three dimensional and organismal.

Now this was more than a trifle disturbing, because it interfered with security, with so to speak the welfare state of the mind. When our ideas are stopped being handed to us on a plate, where are we? When our Western ways of thinking, and all the psychological analyses of them on which we can lay hands, do not meet the Eastern occasion, what next? I confess my own instinctive reaction is at once to take cover behind the outworks that our science has made so marvellously available for sniping from. Let every idea or notion from an illogical or irrational outside be shot at, picked off, by a bullet from a rifle that works logically. It is bad enough when the physical welfare state is called in question, but the mental! So let me give our all-inclusive Science a capital initial, even at the risk of making it seem our god and scientific materialism our creed. One has got to have some sort of certainty in this warfare.

Yet at once, in this secure region, the word 'certainty' evokes by association that 'uncertainty principle' which has been troubling our physicists for some time. From certainty to uncertainty about the behaviour of specific things, actual things that can be manipulated, like the infinitesimals of matter, and manipulated so potently that any day now they may blow our whole secure world to smithereens.

I gathered that the words 'uncertainty principle' were like a gift to mentalists, mystics, and those who so think or think they fundamentally understand. Clearly one has got to be particularly careful here, because a vague state of mind about 'ultimates' can induce an emotional colouring or comforting that is wonderfully satisfying—as psychoanalysis has done its best to show. So let me hang on for a minute to what I conceive to be our logical approach to this uncertainty.

To quote scientists in the context where the uncertainty principle has its innings would not be difficult, for they have done their lucid best to make it intelligible to a groping layman like myself. Let that be taken for granted, while I go on to show the difficulty I experienced over what may seem a simple enough matter to many but which, from the logical viewpoint, rather stumped me. Difficulties over position and velocity of an electron, for example, I was pleased to leave to the scientist concerned with limitations to our possible knowledge, but the nature of the electron interested me because it seemed to involve an illogicality. Under one experimental set-up it was a particle; under another it was a wave. I could throw a pebble into a pond and set up waves on the pond. In this old pictorial way of under-standing, I perceived a difference between the pebble and the waves. Clearly the pictorial method in the new context was as out of date as the billard balls or pebbles of the old mechanics. In short, I had to ask myself could one thing be two different things at the same time in this strange world of the infinitesimal electron. Then listening-in one night to a radio discussion among experts in different fields of knowledge, I was interested to hear the mathematical physicist explaining that though he appreciated the difficulty here in terms of the old classical logic, he found no difficulty in terms of mathe-matical logic which could produce an equation to cover or include such 'contrary' manifestations on the part of the electron. And the equation worked.

Now I seemed to find a distinction or difference between classical logic and mathematical logic, much as physicists to-day distinguish between classical mechanics and quantum mechanics. It is not a case of saying, if I dimly apprehend the matter, that the laws of classical mechanics are 'wrong' but of saying that they are not sufficiently inclusive of reality, as we now under-stand it, to cover whatever laws operate down among the infinitesimals of matter.

After such gropings, I decided that I could not reasonably apply my notion of western logic to Eastern ways of thought and confidently demolish such ways if they appeared to run counter to my logic. It was even more unsettling than that, for the more I pursued the matter the more I found that what were logical absolutes to me were no more than different aspects of reality to the Eastern psychologist, much as particles and waves were different aspects of an electron to our physicist. It was still more unsettling when I realised that what had long appeared to be absolutes to us were now, among the infinitesi-mals, not only 'aspects' but 'complementary'. It almost began to look as if our physicists, dealing with the ultimate reaches of matter, were beginning to set up some sort of comparison or analogy with the Eastern thinker dealing with the ultimate reaches of mind. And if I had a tremendous respect for our physicist, could I have less for the other who, after all, had been working in his realm for an extra millennium or two?

One further point here. Hunting for what ammunition I could find to deal with the East, I came across *Science and the Modern World*, by A N Whitehead. Here the distinguished mathematical logician, in searching for a new look at the ultimates of matter, decides on the evidence that the old doctrine of scientific materialism has to be abandoned in favour of 'an alternative philosophy of science in which *organism* takes the place of *matter*'. And if such a quotation may be unpardonably brief from so vast a range of thought, at least that word *organism* looked back at me from the page in a way that evoked my picture of the Eastern juggler.

But did all this elementary rooting among Western ways of thought help me any when at last I came in contact with the Great Doctrine? It did not. I simply got lost. Nor did it help when I discovered that any master of the Doctrine, Zen master, refused to talk about it on the basis that words were futile and misleading. Apparently it was no good asking how on earth one could understand without words, without reasoned expositions. To get knocked out in the ring is natural enough, but to get knocked out before one enters! So I cast around for anything that would provide some sort of insight and found a book called *The Zen Doctrine of No-Mind*, by D T Suzuki.

First, no words; next, no-mind. I began to feel like the old Highland reiver who decided he might as well be hanged for a sheep as a lamb. I even suspected that no-mind had some sort of specific, even technical meaning, denoting the state of mind that results when there is no mind in it. Which sounded Highland enough. And as for our modern semantics, didn't Confucius remark, some 600BC, 'If language is not correct, then what is said is not what is meant'?

So where was I? And where were my tentative pokings into the nature of logic when Dr Suzuki observed,'All we can state about Zen is that its uniqueness lies in its irrationality or its passing beyond our logical comprehension'? Soon I was prepared to admit this fully. So perhaps I was not completely lost because I knew I was lost. Was this a conceivable angle of approach? And Zen itself? 'There is a school of Buddhism known as Zen. It claims to transmit the quintessence of Buddhist teaching . . .' I had once tried to understand the ordinary teaching and given up. So everything was shaping well. I should soon be in the delicious middle of pure incoherency. And I was, for I got finally sunk in that ultimate experience of Zen called *satori*. Here is one of Dr Suzuki's simpler attempts to make this remarkable mental state clear to our Western minds: 'Satori makes the Unconscious articulate. And the articulated Unconscious expresses itself in terms of logic incoherently but most eloquently from the Zen point of view. This "incoherency" is Zen.' And this Unconscious, let it be plain, was far from being Freud's.

Why this began to affect me with delight I hardly knew, though I knew, too, that it was not altogether because of its 'incoherency', or, as we might say, absurdity. Nor was the delight lessened when a Zen master's aphorism reached my mental condition: 'In walking, just walk. In sitting, just sit. Above all, don't wobble.' I fancied I saw his eyes, and suddenly remembered Yeats and his lines on three Chinamen as they stare down, from the hillside they are climbing, upon 'all the tragic scene', with one asking 'for mournful melodies'. As the accomplished fingers begin to play.

> Their eyes mid many wrinkles, their eyes,
> Their ancient, glittering eyes, are gay.

And I knew that among all the poets of our modern age Yeats alone could have achieved that final 'gay'.

However, it is far from my intention or ability even to suggest the scope of Zen or what living by Zen means, with its difficult conceptions of morality, immortality, eternity. As for our unending torrents of words, our philosophical systems, our gargantuan Joycean outpourings, I caught a glimpse of a Zen master being affected by them as by a verbal diarrhoea that only silence could effectively medicate.

But perhaps I have suggested enough to indicate how one Highlander got lost in a new way of thinking that concerned the essence of being alive. Yet that may be a trifle misleading, because I fancied I followed Dr Suzuki through some of his books with reasonable intelligence, as indeed one should for he uses our Western philosophical modes of communication with a skill and an analytical subtlety that are fascinating. But though I *knew* in this fashion I also knew that I did not *understand*. At once the difference between knowing and understanding assumed crucial importance. Digging into past experiences for possible enlightenment, I remembered how more than once

I thought I knew a subject, could have passed exams in it, then someone had come along and spoken on the same subject, and in a flash I had realised that never until that moment had I *understood* it. Whereupon the comment in wonder: So *this* is what it meant!

Much of which comes into focus in these words by Dr Suzuki: 'The living by Zen makes us aware of a mysterious something which escapes intellectual grasp.'

Apparently I had not got the 'something'. Accustomed as the Highland mind may be to apparitions, second sight, 'other' states of mind, even herons' legs—

And then in a flash it came. The 'something' was of the nature of the 'I' which I have tried to isolate in the opening paragraphs of this article. It was of that kind, in that realm of experience, and was lit by the same certainty. There is never any doubt when this happens, just as there is never any doubt of a taste in the mouth, or of a garden seen through a door that opens in a wall, or of a far country seen through a gap. That I should be here—in the country where the Eastern mind has been adventuring! It does not matter whether one can as yet see 'the way' or not, this is the country through which the way runs. Here is exploration in territory which our Western psychologies have either not seen or not understood.

But I had better forsake incoherency at this point, for the flash lit up such peculiar aspects of everything from literature to psychiatry's descriptions of delusions that I must leave an attempt at getting less lost to another article.

EIGHT TIMES UP

SR, 1958

THE NEEDLE IN THE HAYSTACK has nothing on the self lost in 'incoherency', as my previous article attempted to indicate. Finding the self is as astonishing as finding the needle, and as rare. The quest in this region of the mind is comparable with the physicist's in his region of the infinitesimals, and the results as astonishing. I want to stress that this is a practical affair, where getting down to mind in one region is like getting down to earth in the other, and has to be so pursued. Only results matter. Admittedly the vague or 'mystical' will interfere however one tries to exclude them, for the quest is into the unknown or uncertain. A physicist at the extremity of his particular knowledge has been known to get a hunch. When pursuing his hunch he occasionally astonishes himself by discovering, say, X-rays. But he would not have made the discovery if he had not been, as the East has it, 'on the way'.

Long pursuit, sheer hard work, concentration, discipline, a hunch, and, with luck, an astonishment. That applies in both regions. And if an ordinary man were to indulge in the luxury of a hunch, *en passant*, it might take the mythical form of seeing both the investigators, in mind and matter, East and West, pursuing with comparable logics (psychological and mathematical) their individual ways, and finding themselves, as they went, drawing nearer and nearer to each other until finally, in a flash, their ultimate findings coalesced. That would certainly settle Duality!

Is the myth too fantastic? Yet what is a myth but a hunch? If waves and particles are 'aspects' of an electron, what are mind and matter 'aspects' of? For the one thing that has been indubitably happening in science is that old absolutes—like Newton's space, time, matter, force—are being better understood as aspects of a four-dimensional continuum or other concept of a 'higher' reality. That appears to be the way things are going, whether we like it or not. And as atoms here seem to have more unchancy and fearsome attributes than any myths or fairy stories I know, let me get back to my simple concern with finding the self, that needle in the haystack.

Simple, but rare, very rare, this coming upon the self, as in that complex of the quiet evening and the fishing heron, which subsequently gave an insight into a Japanese painting and a poem. When we use the expression 'self-aware', we are not, I find in actual talk, being aware of the self in the way I mean. We can say 'self-aware' without at that moment being aware of the self at all. The use of this intellectual counter gives no guarantee that the user has ever experienced that awareness of himself with which I am here concerned. In fact the sound of words inhibits the evocation of the awareness and thus (as I in this instant discover) gives a pointer to the meaning or purpose of the Zen master's silence.

Let me try to get over this difficulty of communication by using the familiar pictorial device. Picture the person who has come upon that quiet evening scene and is involuntarily stopped in his tracks by the fishing heron. What happens inside his mind? A complete stoppage of all words, all thoughts. Even his breathing stops as though its physical action would interfere with an alertness that sustains itself in order to catch what is beyond hearing. Not with effort, but in pure wonder. A suspension of the whole being, body and mind, in a condition of wonder that has the feel of 'something' beyond the intellect which is magical. He gets this feel of himself, there. And this feel or consciousness takes as it were the shape of himself in the involuntary apprehension: That I should be here! The 'I' is like an apparition of himself, at once strange and familiar. In this sense it is objective, detached; though, more precisely, 'objective' and 'subjective' become two aspects of, in that moment, the abiding reality of the 'I'. To become self-aware in this way is, as far as I know, rare.

Yet what a jumble that last paragraph really is, difficult as it may have been to put together! Take the words 'stoppage of all words, all thoughts'. They have practically no meaning unless one has tried to stop them at some time or other. Try three o'clock in the morning, when a nagging worry prevents sleep. Attempt to stop the ceaseless flow of thoughts and observe what happens. One may succeed for five seconds the first time, but after that one gives up, the effort is too great. There is no controlling self, no will, to stop the idiotic flow. One gets into a complete subjective mess. Irritation may mount to fury, all to no purpose. The appalling cinema show goes on, and the only attendant consciousness is a humiliating recognition of one's utter automatic futility. Then contrast that state with the other and its abiding 'I'.

Or take that word 'magical'. Its imprecision is at once suspect. Did I use it as an anthropologist would, or a psychiatrist dealing with delusional states of mind, or a poet, or a writer of fairy tales, or as some elusive essence of them all? This is where one wishes semantics well! But the trouble with definition here is that by its very rigidity, its logical pattern, it must fail to confine what is illogical or irrational, like wonder. One might as well try to define colour for a man born colour blind. Scientifically it can be defined for him with precision on the basis of different wave-lengths for different colours. And if the scientist could make him a gadget which measured the wave-lengths and recorded them in figures, the man could go about directing the gadget at things in a garden and with some assurance say 'red' of the poppies and 'green' of the cabbages, but of redness and greenness, not to mention their use in art, he would have no dimmest inkling.

Let me now try to give 'magical' its magical twist in the field of the heron (even if the field was the quiet bend of a river). For magic looks two ways; like any other emotional experience, it has its ambivalence, and this is of fundamental importance, as the psychologist knows. As whatever I say here will over-simplify, let me be as simple as possible and suggest that psycho-analytic probing into magic is concerned with the pathology of the human mind, with the mind that has lost its grip on reality and is taking refuge in retrogression to the primitive. Essentially the analysis deals with a process of mental disintegration. That is one way of looking at magic.

The other way is exactly opposed to that. Now the look is towards inte-gration and the feeling of magical wholeness (as experienced in the field of the heron). And it is this aspect of the mind's two-way traffic, of ambivalence, that I find has been almost totally neglected by researchers into the human condition.

The literature on illness is immense, psychic, somatic, and psychosomatic. But of the opposite, of the human condition of wholeness, scarcely a word. It goes deeper than that. For example, listening-in to 'The Critics' one Sunday morning, I heard a male critic refer to a book as having a certain healthy quality, and immediately the female critic chimed in: 'Healthy! Oh, if you mean hygienic! ...' And there was a laugh. To speak of the healthy, in art, really! The male critic joined in the laugh. How clearly over the air came this modern instance of taboo!

But we know all about that, all about every kind of description and analysis of misery and destruction. We have had our noses continuously rubbed in it until the skin is gone. It is time we stopped having our noses rubbed for a while, artistically or brutally, brutally artistically or artistically brutally, primitively, apprehensively, analytically, fearfully, suggestively, totali-tarianly, fantastically, monosyllabically, polysyllabically, unendingly, with dots or without, because our noses are sore. Destruction destroys. Soon there won't be a nose left to put our fingers to. When that happens, we're through. It's time we had a let-up on all this.

So back to the heron, the Godot that did at least turn up. Here was no destruction, no slightest apprehension of it. The very opposite. Not broken bits falling apart, but a calm cohering whole. Not fear but assurance. Not terror but delight. Not an internal subjective mess but an external objective scene, cool as the evening, held in a clarity that bathed the eyes and made them see as they had never seen.

This clarity is Wordsworth's light that never was on sea or land. Not any longer a vague light, but quite specifically this.

So with Keats' 'magic casements'. This is the light in which they were seen. Some time or other—perhaps by a forlorn Highland sea-loch—Keats came upon himself as he stood and stared. When that happens one sees in a memorable way; that is, quite literally, in a way that memory cannot forget. What the imaginative faculty may do with the experience afterwards, in tranquillity, is a poet's business. Here the critic can only be speculative (as with the Highland sea-loch) and obscure, for the logical faculty is not the imaginative, but Keats is neither speculative nor obscure, he is precise and clear. And if I had to ask a question here, it would be the searching one: How is it that what was so memorable to Keats has also been so memorable to so many?

But if we must give speculation an innings, let it be with a writer like D H Lawrence, because he had more than his share of the restlessness of our age. Why so restless that he had to keep shifting from place to place? What was he hunting? Did he ever find it, and, if so, precisely when? In such biographies of him as I have read I can find no clear answers to my questions. Possibly to expect an answer may seem absurd, because we all know this vague restlessness only too well, and it bites none the less for being vague, even the more. One gets bitten by gnats in places one can't scratch.

Then I began to notice that when Lawrence had left behind his gnat-bitten self in, say, England, and come upon himself whole and fresh, in new territory, like Sicily, the restlessness vanished and he wrote divinely. It was as if this kind of environmental shock were needed to destroy the gnats, to let Lawrence emerge and find himself again, whole, among his trees and wild flowers, and in this way, in this light, to see the trees and wild flowers with such clarity, so magically, that he could use blue anemones to light the way even to hell, memorably.

In Dr F R Leavis's book on Lawrence I found this quotation from *The Rainbow*: 'Self was a oneness with the infinite. To be oneself was a supreme gleaming triumph of infinity.'

Now the one thing Lawrence detested was conventional attitudes or modes that smothered the quick. That was death to him, and he warred against it, especially in sex, because here hypocrisy, social hypocrisy, seemed to him particularly virulent. But elsewhere, too, against all vague soul upliftings and such. It was from this context that the quotation stood out. Accordingly I had to assume that Lawrence in using these words was being as specific as he knew how about an actual experience; and when it comes to know-how in modern writing I cannot readily think of a better craftsman. So I had to put it to myself as impersonally as possible: when Lawrence found this 'Self' that was at one with the infinite, was it the self, the 'I', which I am concerned with here—and concerned, may I say once more, not in any 'mystical' sense but as a matter of fact in actual living!

At least for Lawrence such moments would seem to have been as rare as I believe them to be. For normally it takes an emotional shock, environmental or other, to bring them into being. But the East has long known this, as Dr Suzuki makes plain: 'An intense emotional disturbance often awakens in us a mysterious power of which we have ordinarily been unaware.'

When Proust writes of the 'identity underlying all the works of a great writer; the comparisons of critics are of no interest compared with this secret beauty'. I seem to see, from the aesthetic angle, the underlying identity as the identity of the self, the 'I'—I can think of no other underlying identity. And when I equate Proust's 'beauty' with Suzuki 'mysterious power' I am conscious of trying to be as precise in this region as the physicist in his. 'Mysterious' may look like a vague or magical word. 'Mysterious power.' But power here is the equivalent of force in the region of matter, and force to the physicist is just as mysterious as power to Suzuki. What gravitational force *is*, or electrical force, or nuclear force, the physicist does not know. He knows them by what they do, and can calculate their doings with exactitude. He knows, for example, that this force falls off inversely as the square of the distance and so with confidence sends sputniks aloft. But what this enormously powerful gravitational force is, he does not know, and in his groping to find out he is not unlike primitive man taking a glance over his shoulder to surprise what cannot be seen. There is magic in both realms, mind and matter, and here the twin exploratory attempt to discover the laws by which magic works may result in a vast extension of human knowledge and understanding. May I be forgiven the involuntary reflection; how stupid, how dull, to blow man to bits as he stands on such a threshold!

And when I hold the reflection for a minute I hear Bertrand Russell remarking that man has a fifty-fifty chance of survival. An even chance that the bombs won't go off. A shade more optimistic, I put the favourable odds at eight to seven. But then, again, I am probably being influenced by this exploratory trip East. It is said of Bodhidharma that he sat so long in meditation that his legs fell off. Whereupon the Japanese made a legless doll so weighted inside that however you knocked it down it sat up again; and then made a popular song:

> Such is life—
> Seven times down,
> Eight times up!

I hope to come up for a final round in the next article and, with help from fragments of a remarkable esoteric teaching, make a final effort to arrest and have a close look at this elusive 'I'.

REMEMBER YOURSELF

SR, 1959

OCCASIONALLY AN EXPERIENCE that seems personal and unique is discovered to be neither. The moment of this discovery is always delightful. I mentioned fragments of an esoteric teaching at the end of my last article because in them I found an effort to isolate that very 'I' which I had been concerned to arrest and make real, the 'I' that is so rare an evocation of the self that it turns even the moment's environment magical.

Now I had gone what seemed to me a considerable distance in my investigation of the nature of this experience, far enough to check it against the actual experiences of other ordinary folk who had no knowledge of mystical or esoteric religions or literatures. In at least three instances I found the intensity of their experience far beyond what I have tried to evoke or communicate in the simple incident of the heron. I cannot truthfully say that they were far beyond anything of the kind I had ever experienced myself because if they had been I should not have been able to appreciate them. Here it is almost a law that one cannot see or appreciate beyond one's own level of being and cannot communicate except to those on at least a similar level. I say 'almost' because it is not quite; despite certain Eastern teachings, not in my experience. However, that is a refinement or distinction of no particular significance at the moment. The extraordinary thing to me was that the importance of the experience did not seem to be recognised by our philosophies or psychologists, yet the more I tried to grasp its nature in a realistic way the more important it became.

Then I happened on a book called *In Search of the Miraculous* by P D Ouspensky. Its sub title runs, *Fragments of an Unknown Teaching.* The teacher of the fragments was Georges Gurdjieff whom Ouspensky met in Moscow in 1915. The book describes the meeting, and what it led to, in the interesting human way that one may encounter in a good novel. Finally a group or 'school' was formed and Ouspensky, as one of the group, recorded Gurdjieff's teaching.

Now manifestly Ouspensky was not only a brilliant linguist but also deeply versed in our Western philosophies and sciences, with a particular flair for logic and mathematics. I had not—and have not yet—read his books which have a slant, in particular, I gather, on the 'mathematicalness' of everything in the world. I can only speak out of impressions gained from reading the 'miraculous' book, and when he went East in search of this miraculous I envisaged him as I might a mathematical physicist in search of some equation that would resolve apparent opposites or contradictions, that would turn as it were old 'absolutes' into new 'aspects' of a higher or more inclusive reality. 'There is a dark inscrutable workmanship that reconciles discordant elements,' says Wordsworth with a poet's assurance. Ouspensky had obviously some such hunch, and his equipment was not only impressive but, for such as myself, reassuring.

His search for the 'esoteric schools' of the East failed, but in Gurdjieff he found enough fragments of their 'unknown' teaching to keep him busy for the rest of his life.

Gurdjieff, as seen through Ouspensky's eyes, is a much more elusive character. He has been seen through other eyes, and a considerable literature has grown up about him, and particularly about an establishment he set up and ran for a time near Fontainebleau in France. But I know little or nothing of this and I am concerned here only with one quite precise personal experience (as indicated in the heron incident) and what I am searching for now is some verification of it from outside, some external estimate of its validity and, if possible, its significance or importance.

Accordingly I make no reference to the extraordinary range of Gurdjieff's teaching; to its astonishing if not fantastic cosmology, for example. Yet for my purpose, one or two cardinal points should be made; and, first, that only a normal man can benefit from the teaching. The abnormal, the obsessed, the pathological are excluded. Why this is so is made quite clear. Secondly, the basis of the whole teaching is material, but materiality is the noun used, not materialism. Just as matter is ultimately an affair of 'vibrations' to the physicist, so is mind also to Gurdjieff, who talks of 'vibrations' (manifestations of energy) much as our scientists do. When this seemed too material by half at a first glance, I had to grope around for some handhold or other, and as vibrations suggested music, I had to realise that basically music is a matter of vibrations. Getting all the implications here was as hard work as learning to play the violin. From vibrations to the profound experience of great music—but I must leave it there, trusting that I have at least been able to indicate the context out of which one day Gurdjieff asked the members of his group what it was in his teaching that had so far impressed them, or, as he put it. 'What is the most important thing that we notice during self-observation?'

They all had a shot at answering, but Gurdjieff was dissatisfied. 'Not one of you noticed,' he said, 'that you *do not remember yourselves*. You do not feel *yourselves* ... you are not conscious of *yourselves* ... Only those results will have any value that are accompanied by self-remembering. Otherwise you yourselves do not exist in your observations. In which case what are all your observations worth?'

That flummoxed them. And, later, he rubbed it in: 'If you ask a man whether he can remember himself, he will of course answer that he can. If you tell him that he cannot remember himself, he will either be angry with you, or think you an utter fool.'

So Ouspensky really got going on this difficult exercise of self-remembering and in time became convinced that 'I was faced with an *entirely new problem which science and philosophy had not, so far, come across.*' The italics are his and conveyed to me something of the astonishment and revelation by which he was struck.

Struck myself—as I was—I might have left it there. But not so Ouspensky. Whenever Ouspensky is struck he flies to mathematics and draws a diagram. In this case he drew an arrow, a fine long arrow, with the barbed end pointing at 'the observed phenomenon', and of course away from himself. But now if he were going to remember himself at the same time as he was observing the phenomenon, he would also have to have the arrow pointing at himself. So he put a barb on the other end, the end towards himself. Now the arrow was barbed at both ends; was directed simultaneously both at the observed phenomenon and at himself. In brief, he had to be conscious both of object and subject at the same time. Somehow or other there had to be a 'self' present that was aware of this difficult operation and succeeded in observing it.

Anyone may test the difficulty for himself, but if he can for an instant catch a glimpse of this 'self', he will find that the experience has quite a different feel or taste from that which arises in the ordinary way when he uses the expression 'conscious self'. Anyway, this is what Ouspensky found; and found also that the experience is very rare and of such importance that, as we have seen, it drove him to italics.

Now all this seemed so near my heron experience, if I may so call it, that I began to feel 'warm'. But I could not be certain because of two differences: in the first place, my experience had not only been not difficult but quite involuntary, and, in the second, memory or 'remembering' had had nothing to do with it. Far from 'remembering myself', or remembering this aspect of the self (the 'I'), I had come upon it with surprise. In fact when I had described at length a similar boyhood experience in a book I had used the expression 'come upon myself'. But perhaps I have already made this distinction clear enough.

So here I was with a nice piece of detection on hand, prepared to follow Ouspensky through every twist of his hunt at trying to grasp this elusive affair. The 'involuntary' difference was soon disposed of, because Ouspensky discovered, when he thought back into his childhood, that he had had this experience quite involuntarily. Again he makes it clear that he had subsequently come upon it in a dramatic change of environment, with the involuntary comment: 'That I should be here!'

So far so good. But what of the 'remembering' element? and, after all, 'self-remembering' was Gurdjieff's term, and as his psychological analysis is to me of an unequalled clarity, I might have to give his term a technical status. Nowhere does Ouspensky in his book or Gurdjieff in his teaching specifically exclude the 'remembering' element, or at least what the word 'remembering' means to me.

Now all this may seem at first contact a small terminological wrangle about what doesn't fundamentally matter anyhow, but clearly to Ouspensky self-remembering held a profound significance which our science and philosophy had missed. I can see him laying hold of it as a physicist might some new element or particle among the infinitesimals. And as for Gurdjieff—it meant nothing less than that only at the moment of self-remembering is a man *conscious*. Now if his self-remembering was the same as my 'coming upon myself', then I could gather what he meant when he went on to say that at all other moments man is *not* conscious of himself. So he differentiates man *conscious* from man *unconscious*. *Unconscious* man is mechanical man, a piece of mechanism to which things happen. *Conscious* man is the man who has come upon his own self, the 'I', the conscious self that can take control and master mechanical happenings. This realisation is the first step on the way to levels or dimensions of being with which his teaching is concerned.

As I read, it began to dawn on me that perhaps Gurdjieff meant that what had been rare and involuntary to me and to others should not—and need not—be so. It could be cultivated. One must make an effort every now and then to isolate the self or 'I', to remember to do it, to self-remember. Self-remembering could be his expression for this conscious effort.

But to bring my attempt at detection to a finish, let me refer to a volume by Ouspensky called *The Fourth Way*, published in 1957, posthumously published, for both Gurdjieff and Ouspensky are dead. It consists mostly of 'verbatim extracts' from talks given by Ouspensky, and his answers to questions, over a number of years. Here at last is his answer to a direct question on the meaning of self-remembering: 'Self-remembering is not really connected with memory: it is simply an expression. It means self-awareness, or self-consciousness. One must be conscious of oneself. It begins with the mental process of trying to remember oneself ...'

As an assessment of the heron experience from outside, this seemed good enough to me. Whether evoked involuntarily or voluntarily, by chance or by deliberate 'remembering', the 'I' was apparently one and the same.

THE TASTE

As I look over the articles in this series now concluding I wonder if, finally, it would be possible to give a working name to the 'mysterious something' which escapes intellectual grasp, as Suzuki put it, but which the 'I' experiences. Can it be brought down from something like transcendence onto the practical level of living?

Certainly this 'something' usually remains hidden in all kinds of learned discussion or esoteric teaching, so hidden that it does not seem to be there. Consider disquisitions on ethics, theology, aesthetics, etc. Listen to the voice intoning or thundering from a pulpit. Or to the calm voice of the botanist relating the life history of a strawberry and then to the chemist's voice in a detailed analysis of the berry. Or even to my own voice on the growing of strawberries, for I grow a lot of them. At this moment I am resting a broken back from a bout on the strawberry bed. What final knowledge, then what ultimate something, do I get from my arduous cultivation of the berry? Its *taste.*

If its taste were not delightful would I pursue it through sweat to a broken back, would I remorselessly hunt the underground infiltrations of bishop-weed (how did it get that name?) or couch grass? And if a psychiatrist, who knows about couches, began to explain that such weeds led an underground life of virulent and unkillable strength and that every here and there, unpredictably, they sent up visible shoots to throttle the berry, what would I answer? I would answer, You're telling me! If the bishops and psychiatrists got into a high falutin' wrangle about all this, enough to fill tomes of surpassing subtlety, what would they forget? The *taste* of the berry.

To me this is not fanciful, it is the one thing I know. Here the 'something' is for me as real as the berry. This, as far as I am concerned, is what the berry is for. But I do not expect the berry in some 'mystical' fashion to fall into my mouth. Work and sweat and, unless I have grown cunning about it, lumbago. If there isn't the taste, the rest is sweat for nothing. Meaningless. The taste is the meaning. But surely there is some high and wonderful meaning beyond this, surely if ...? A Zen master would politely wait until you had woven your metaphysical yarn into its most distinguished pattern and then, according to Dr Suzuki, reply: 'I think it is going to rain'. Strawberries need a fair amount of rain. Then you have strawberries and cream.

Now, words convoluting in thin air may lead to an ultimate concept like Enlightenment, as the East has made plain. But does such a concept have a *taste*? Back to mind comes the Zen master and for him at least I am convinced it has. That's why his eyes, to use Yeats's word, are 'gay'. He knows the *taste* of Enlightenment as a simple gardener the taste of a berry. In the Zen region, so to speak, if strawberries are not about they are in the offing. Here the very pulse of life is spontaneous, not laboured, not solemnly 'mystical'.

When a writer imagines he clearly understands something which he would like to communicate, then for him clarity is all and obscurity the enemy. That is why, I suspect, I have been wrapping 'mystical' in inverted commas. So let me have a closer look at the word and its everyday use.

Normally it has human connotations of vagueness, obscurity, and the general reaction is to shrug it off with the expression 'poor fellow' as one might in the case of a drunk who had achieved inarticulation. Gone all mystical, poor chap!

The involuntary picture of the fellow has usually an Indian background, where the sun reduces clothing to a loincloth respectable yet small enough to permit contemplation of the navel. If the fellow lives in our climate, with topcoat and a muffler, the only decent thing a friend can do is, as delicately as possible, to direct him to a psychiatrist, who may discover retrogression to a childhood dependence on the mother, or even to the pre-natal womb-like security. From life's stormy seas, this is his unconscious method of escape. Nirvanic: back to Nirvana. West or East, topcoat or loincloth, the same thing.

Now what always bothered me here was getting a grip on any reality behind 'mystical', getting the *taste* of the mystical performance. For I had to assume to begin with that the Indian mind had been trying to cultivate its berry. For me to repeat a word like Nirvana and then think I understand all about it is too childish, especially when I know that the East can make metaphysical rings round me with the greatest ease. If a Harley Street psychiatrist, with his penetrating knowledge of mental regression, were to impute some such condition to a Zen master, the master might suggest that the psychiatrist should take up golf, and, when he could go round St Andrews in 67, come back and they might have a little talk. For many of these Zen masters are also masters of the arrow and the sword.

In the usual solemn 'mystical' regions, however, all seems to be struggle and sweat, with not a glimpse of strawberries in an offing howsoever remote. That is my difficulty with 'mystical', and manifestly the difficulty of others, too. For where does the road run from here, towards what, if any, unimaginable berries? Of an answer to that practical question not a practical word.

Not even by Gurdjieff and Ouspensky. And when it comes to orthodox Buddhism it seems worse. Not a suggestion of human delight anywhere, not a taste.

I am far from being irreverent. If my loincloth knows anything at this verbal moment, it is sweat. Words are scrub and cacti in an all but impenetrable wadi. If, for anthological relief and variety, I look up Mr Aldous Huxley's *Perennial Philosophy*, I may vaguely find myself on the 'divine Ground', but of a strawberry bed do I catch a beckoning glimpse? It cannot be altogether a deficiency in my vision that makes me think Mr Huxley is not very good at strawberries because what I do see is his beckoning on, on towards regions of the four Noble Truths and the Eightfold Path.

Very well. Once again I will dive into these Truths.

It is unnecessary for me to say now that far from being knowledgeable here I am but a lost traveller, the ordinary man who doesn't know where he is, as he gazes at what is around him. But I submit that the theologians or esoterics (or even Mr Huxley, whom I deeply respect) should not jump on me for that. If this is their territory, why haven't they put up signposts? If I saw a signpost with the inscription. 'To the Strawberry Bed—Third Wadi on the left.' I might have some notion of where I was.

So here's for the Truths and the Path as signposts! ...

After an hour I surfaced with the bewildered feeling that I had been all wrong, that I had been lost in the wilderness, crying like a child for strawberries, whereas what I should have been concerned to do in this enigmatic desert of pain and suffering, what I should have strenuously striven to do, was kill my craving for strawberries.

But of course. I should have remembered. I had been there before.

So where am I now in this hunt of mine? Back, doggedly back, to the heron's legs, hanging on by the skin of them to the intimation of a strange delight, of an 'I' that came upon itself there and knew that the created moment was good. And of a smile, too, beyond the blundering questions and the solemn words; a smile that comes on its own like a silent strawberry flower on the air.

As I write this I am surrounded by some acres of birches newly fledged, translucent in a green sunlight, and as I pause to listen critically to the singing of the birds I have to admit that they cannot go wrong. With them, I suppose, it is involuntary.

So one last effort at the voluntary, at the subdual of what Gurdjieff calls 'the negative emotions' and the Eightfold teaching calls our cravings.

But yet, and once more, for what? Where, where is the hidden berry, the *taste* that gives delight? Can it be that the ultimate berry here is some form of immortality? But what I am concerned about to the point of sweat and lumbago is the here and now, the living now. Eternity is irrelevant, and those who ask questions about it are futuristic and beside the point. However, in a last desperate sally, I return to the strenuous teachings—and discover, in a strange suspension of all thought, that when Buddha was questioned about the eternity of the universe and existence after death, he refused to answer. What did he do? According to the paintings and the statues, he smiled.

Then, as if the taste of some real berry were still in his mouth, he said: 'May every living thing be full of bliss.'

SOURCES

'Caithness and Sutherland' appeared in *Scottish Country* ed George Scott Moncrieff (Wishart Books, 1935), pp59–76; 'East to Buchan' in *Scots Magazine* 31 ((Sept 1939), pp419–24; 'Autumn in the Cuillin' in *Scots Magazine* 16 (Dec 1931), pp174–6; 'Doom in the Moray Firth' (by Dane McNeil) in *Scots Magazine* 24 (Oct 1935), pp24–7; 'One Fisher Went Sailing ...' in *Scots Magazine* 27 (Sept 1937) pp414–8; 'The Family Boat' in *Scots Magazine* 27 (June 1937), pp169–74; 'The Wonder Story of the Moray Firth' in *Anarchy* 86, 188, 4 (1968), pp122–5; 'The French Smack' in *Scots Magazine* 33 (Aug 1940), pp366–70; 'The First Salmon' in *Scots Magazine* 29 (April 1938), pp17–20; 'Black Cattle in Lochaber' in *Scots Magazine* 37 (Sept 1942), pp450–4; 'Landscape Inside' in *Saltire Review* 6, 19 (Autumn 1959), pp43–6; 'Highland Space' in *Saltire Review* 6, 23 (Winter 1961), pp45–8; 'New Golden Age for Scottish Letters' in *Daily Record and Mail*, May 28 1930; 'The Scottish Literary Renaissance Movement' in *Wick Mercantile Debating Society Journal* (April 1929), reprinted in *Scottish Literary Journal* 4, 2 (Dec 1977), pp58–61; 'The Scottish Renascence', in *Scots Magazine* 19 (June, 1933), pp201–4; 'Scottish Renaissance' in *Scottish Field* 109, 716 (Aug 1962), p34; 'Nationalism in Writing I' in *Scots Magazine* 30 (Oct 1938), pp28–35; 'Nationalism in Writing II' in *Scots Magazine* 30 (Dec 1938), pp194–8; 'Nationalism in Writing III' in *Scots Magazine* 31 (July 1939), pp275–82; 'Literature: Class or National?' in *Outlook* 1, 4 (July 1936), pp54–8; 'Muir's *Scott and Scotland*' in *Scots Magazine* 26 (Oct 1936), pp72–8; 'On Reviewing' in *Scots Magazine* 35 (Aug, 1941), pp346–7; 'The Novel at Home' in *Scots Magazine* 45 (April 1946), pp1–5—this essay, according to a preamble, 'was written originally for an American publication, *The Writer*, whose contributors deal with a writer's problems'; 'Why I Write' in *Gangrel* (1951), pp10–11; 'The Essence of Nationalism' in *Scots Magazine* 37 (June 1942), pp169–72; 'Defensio Scotorum' (by Dane McNeil) in *Scots Magazine* 9 (April 1928), pp51–8; 'And Then Rebuild It' in *Scots Magazine* 32 (Dec 1939), pp173–8; 'Belief in Ourselves' in *Scots Magazine* 43 (Sept 1945), pp424–7; 'Scotland Moves' in *Scots Magazine* 39 (Sept 1943), pp447–50; 'The Gael Will Come Again' (by Dane McNeil) in *Scots Magazine* 14 (Feb 1931), pp324–7; 'A Visitor From Denmark' in *Scots Magazine* 27 (May 1937), pp96–101; 'A Footnote on Co-operation' in *Anarchy* 86, 188, 4 (1968), pp116–7; 'Nationalism and Internationalism' in *Scots Magazine* 15 (June 1931), pp185–8; 'Eire: How Dublin Received the New Constitution' in *Scots Magazine* 28 (Feb 1938), pp340–4; 'President of Eire' (by Dane McNeil) in *Scots Magazine* 29 (June 1938), pp177–80; 'As Drunk as a Bavarian' in *Scots Magazine* 31 (April 1939), pp30–5; 'How the German Sees The Scot' in *SMT Magazine* 25, 5 (May 1940), pp21–3; 'On Backgrounds' in *Scots Magazine* 34 (March 1941), pp437–40; 'On Tradition' in *Scots Magazine* 34 (Nov 1940), pp131–4; 'On Belief' in *Scots Magazine* 34 (Oct 1940), pp51–5; 'On Looking at Things' in *Scots Magazine* 33

(June 1940), pp170–4; 'On Magic' in *Scots Magazine* 33 (Sept 1940), pp433–6; 'On Destruction' in *Scots Magazine* 35 (July 1941), pp290–4; 'The New Community of Iona' (by Dane McNeil) in *Scots Magazine* 30 (Dec 1938), pp169–74; 'The Heron's Legs' in *Saltire Review* 5, 15 (Summer 1958), pp19–22; 'The Flash' in *Saltire Review* 5, 16 (Autumn 1958), pp18–23; 'Eight Times Up' in *Saltire Review* 5, 17 (Winter 1958), pp19–23; 'Remember Yourself' in *Saltire Review* 6, 18 (Spring 1959), pp22–8.

INDEX